The English Country House

an art and a way of life

The English

with 269 plates, 22 in colour

photographs by A. F. Kersting

Country House

an art and a way of life

OLIVE COOK

THAMES AND HUDSON

Acknowledgments

The publishers are grateful to the following individuals and institutions for supplying photographs or allowing them to be reproduced.
Audley End House 97; Devonshire Collection, Chatsworth, Reproduced by Permission of the Trustees of the Chatsworth Settlement 84, 165, 166, 173, 184; the Administrator, Clandon Park (photo Hawkley Studio Associates) 164; The Clarendon Press, Oxford 230 (from Mark Girouard, *The Victorian Country House*); Copyright Country Life 25, 63, 75, 104, 146, 220, 221, 222, 223; Courtauld Institute of Art, University of London 85, 140, 162; Crown copyright, reproduced with the permission of the Controller of Her Majesty's Stationery Office 165, 173; Giraudon, by permission of the Ville de Bayeux 6; the Rt Hon. the Earl of Leicester 162, 178; Eric de Maré 244; The National Maritime Museum, London 51, 107 (after G. H. Chettle, *The Queen's House, Greenwich*, 1937); National Monuments Record, London 33, 41, 43, 50, 69, 86, 96, 105, 123, 174, 178; National Portrait Gallery, London 68, 73, 108, 144, 153, 181, 191; The National Trust 42, 218; F. H. M. FitzRoy Newdegate, Esq. 211; Penguin Books 20 (after *The Penguin Dictionary of Architecture*), 39, 52, 64, 78, 102, 107, 194, 202 (all after Sir John Summerson, *Architecture in Britain: 1530–1830*); Royal Commission on Historical Monuments (England) 102; Royal Institute of British Architects, London 93, 117, 149, 242; The Tate Gallery, London 163; Major Ralph Verney (photo Hutchinson Publishing Group) 106; Victoria and Albert Museum, London 125 (at Ham House); by courtesy of the Provost and Fellows of Worcester College, Oxford 116; Gordon Winter, from his book *A Country Camera* 232. Ill. 225 is from J. Britton, *Illustrations of Fonthill Abbey*, 1823; ills. 5 and 15 are from J. H. and J. Parker, *Some Account of Domestic Architecture in England*, 1859.

Printed in Japan

Contents

Of all the great things that the English have invented and made part of the credit of the national character, the most perfect, the most characteristic, the only one they have mastered completely in all its details so that it becomes a compendious illustration of their social genius and their manners, is the well appointed, well administered, well filled country house.

HENRY JAMES

I   THE GROWTH OF A TRADITION

the early medieval background

IT IS SURELY SIGNIFICANT as well as ironic that the decline of the English country house, like that of the parish church, has been accompanied by mounting interest. Visiting country houses is among the most popular of present pastimes; country houses have inspired a number of nostalgic autobiographical accounts by writers whose early years were spent in such places as Knole, Renishaw and Castle Cary, and have prompted a series of brilliant scholarly investigations. The attraction cannot only derive from changes in society, from the shift of power from those who lived in these houses to an impersonal centre of authority and the consequent removal of former antagonism: it must also lie in the contrast between all that the country house stood for and our own way of living, between our uprootedness and the continuity and stability of the life led in the great mansion, between our dislocation, diffusion and isolation and that image of community and intensity. This modest and necessarily limited addition to the vast stream of literature on the subject attempts to give substance to the mood of country-house visitors by relating the country house as a work of art to the changing manners and habits of mind which made its evolution possible.

The early significance of such houses in the social fabric is still plainly expressed in the landscape: despite industrial and suburban sprawl, the ancient feudal contours are still there, and everywhere the centre of the manorial pattern is the country house. The older the house, the more clearly proclaimed are its associations with this pattern. They are announced by the very components of the structure, which were originally dictated by practical needs and tradition rather than by high creative impulses.

I, II,   The first sight of a house like Ightham Mote does of course stir emotions which
     I   have nothing to do with the hard facts of history. Lying in its secluded Kentish hollow, a reflected quadrangle of irregular ragstone, brick and timber buildings of varying ages, moulded by years, weather and the preserver's hand into a single intricate pattern, exquisitely attuned to the texture of the embracing landscape, it awakens thoughts of Tennyson's 'lonely moated grange', for there are the 'marish mosses' creeping on the edge of the dark water, there is the silver-green poplar and, looking down through the latticed windows from the higher ground beyond the moat, there is the thick-moted sunbeam so loathed by Mariana slanting across a dim chamber. For this islanded dwelling is essentially romantic. It merely toys with the idea of defence, so thoroughly have the fangs of a former military theme been drawn. Enveloped in silence, which in the present age is itself a thing to wonder at, it wears the semblance of a dream, annihilating time.

Yet the very fact that defence is suggested shows that this cluster of buildings is part of a progression. That moat was not called into existence to mirror gables, tower and long, low walls: it was but the usual form of protection of early timber enclosures which later, as here, might be replaced by structures of more durable materials. A closer look at the existing buildings at Ightham shows them to be not an altogether haphazard group but a combination, varied and enriched by later accretions, of the standard components of the medieval house, components which, differently organized, form the basis also of such widely disparate houses as Great Chalfield in Wiltshire, Longthorpe Tower in Northamptonshire, or Cotehele in 12, 2 Cornwall. These components are the great hall, open to the roof, the two-storeyed cross-wing and the tower, which at Ightham is the shape assumed by the gatehouse.

The way in which this manor house evolved is typical of the home of the country squire before the days of planned symmetry. The first recorded owners were a family called Cawne who built the hall and a two-storeyed block containing the chapel. The Cawnes were succeeded by the Hauts, of whom Richard married a Woodville and shared in that family's rise to prosperity through the union of its daughter Elizabeth with Edward IV, just as at the accession of Richard III in 1483 he shared their downfall. Richard Haut was arrested, sent to Pontefract and beheaded. By then he had built the gate tower at Ightham, inserted a fine window and a wall fireplace in the hall and had raised the atmospheric battery of chimneys in the south-east angle of the courtyard.

After Haut's abrupt death Ightham passed into the hands of the wealthy Sir Richard Clement, who further altered the house by dividing the chapel horizontally into two floors and building a new chapel to overhang the moat on the north side of the court. 11 This chapel, with its painted barrel-vault, little screen and linenfold panelling, remains as Sir Richard Clement left it at the end of the fifteenth century. He sold the 'Mote' to a rich mercer, Sir John Allen, who was twice Lord Mayor of London. The Selbys, who lived at Ightham from the end of Queen Elizabeth I's reign, more than 350 years ago, until the present century, converted outbuildings to the north of the gatehouse into the Jacobean drawing-room and finally, in the eighteenth century, they inserted a Palladian window in the west gable of this range, a detail which would seem as incongruous as it is surprising, were it not that the picturesque informality of the place and its apparently inconsequent ramblings easily contain this isolated product of an alien style.

This compressed account reveals a development dictated mainly by necessity, self-importance, piety and the desire to keep abreast of fashion. It also affords a glimpse of the organization of society from which the history of the buildings cannot be separated. It suggests, for instance, a certain fluidity, for where a tradesman could rise to the position of lord of the manor there could be no hard and fast distinction between them. At the same time the long residence of the Selbys illustrates the element of stability and the sense of continuity which such long-established families gave to country society. Sir John Allen's choice of Ightham as his home rather than the capital where he was bred and where he made his fortune is also significant. It illustrates the preference for rural as opposed to town life which from the beginning characterized the English landowner, a fact which made the English country house so much more than a house in the country and distinguished it from the historic châteaux and villas of the Continent. This unique preference was as influential in the crystallization of the English country gentry as the fact that this class was constantly infiltrated from below.

Although the word 'manor' (French *manoir*, a dwelling) was first introduced into the English language by the Norman clerks of William the Conqueror, the manorial system was in existence before Domesday. Something akin to it can even be said to have flourished in Roman Britain, where the organization of agriculture was based upon the 'villa' or big country house with fields around it. The manor house was frequently associated with the village and the parish church, yet manor and village by no means always coincided. The term 'manor' came to mean the whole estate of a lord: there might well be more than one manor house in a village, just as there might also be a manor house standing remote from the village in its fields. The manor was an economic unit in which all the tenants were bound to the lord and his demesne farm, the free tenants paying rent for their land and helping the lord at busy seasons, the unfree tenants or villeins doing weekly labour service, and all of them attending their lord's court of justice, his *moot* (hence the name Ightham *Mote*) which was held fortnightly in the great hall of his house.

The moot was the great contribution of the early manor house to society. Its jurisdiction was among the most valuable of feudal rights. It was presided over by the lord's seneschal or steward, and the assessors or jurymen who stated the local customs on which the court's judgments were based were the tenants themselves. Those customs were handed down and recorded on the court rolls from the thirteenth century onwards. The moot thus focused public opinion and tradition; expressed the common experience and conscience of the neighbourhood; and helped to fit humble Englishmen for a free system of society.

The rise of the private ownership of land had taken place before the Conquest, and William tried at first to govern his new kingdom with the help of the Saxon

1 Ightham Mote, Kent, from the south: fourteenth-century masonry, an overhanging timber storey of the fifteenth century, Tudor windows and chimneys of diverse designs.

thegns. But the followers without whom his victory would have been impossible insisted on their reward: when the Domesday Book (first and foremost a directory of landowners) was compiled in 1086, only two of the King's leading tenants were Englishmen. The magnates of Domesday England scarcely numbered two hundred and they were responsible for raising an army of at least four thousand knights. Some barons maintained a force of knights in their household, others, more numerous, gave land in return for the promise of military service. The knights were not nobles at first; indeed, they were essentially retainers who came from miscellaneous backgrounds. Their status changed very slowly, its rise marked by the development of the science of heraldry – an increasingly formal and intricate system of devices on the helmets and shields of knights, to distinguish them when, fully armoured, they took part in what became a frequent, regular feature of social life, the tournament.

Thus, apart from the barons, the lords of the manors did not constitute a rigid class. Their ranks were penetrated by yet another element when men who were not knights and had no military qualifications acquired manors on the principle of scutage, the payment of money instead of the performance of service. The interests of the landowner who avoided military service by thus paying 'shield money' became more and more agricultural and peaceful. His pleasure was to improve his domain and to go on the rounds with his steward. He was in course of becoming the 'country gentleman', something vastly different from the Continental noble, for he was never a member of a closed caste. One strong reason for this was that in the centuries after the Conquest, with the adoption of the rule of primogeniture whereby the eldest son inherited all the estate, it became the custom for the younger sons of the manor to leave home to become merchants, lawyers or adventurers – often returning to the country to build houses of their own.

Where the dense forests of Saxon England had been cleared the manorial system imposed upon the landscape an arrangement of open fields, each covering a few hundred acres. In the wilder regions small fields of irregular shape were characteristic; in south-eastern England long narrow strips produced the pattern generally associated with medieval agriculture, while in country suitable for grazing, such as Kent, plots were enclosed by hedges at an early date. To these field-shapes were added the lord's private park. The word 'park' did not then bear its present meaning: it was a game preserve. But nevertheless these medieval game preserves did in many instances represent the beginnings of later country-house parks. The first mention of what is now the largest park in the north of England, Knowsley in Lancashire, occurs in 1292 when Sir Robert de Latham had a 'wood which is called a park'. The park at Ashridge in Hertfordshire is likewise first heard of in the thirteenth century.

The manor house itself existed in two distinct forms in Norman England. The commonest, the origin of the hall at Ightham Mote, was a single, huge, aisled room such as had existed in Roman Britain and was the typical home of the Saxon thegn. The ubiquity of the great hall throughout the Middle Ages is commemorated by the custom which lingers even yet in some villages of referring to the squire's house as 'the hall'. In early Norman England the hall, together with a few out-buildings grouped roughly about a courtyard, constituted the entire accommodation of the manor house. The enormous room was at first always aisled because for technical reasons builders could not roof a wide span. So the hall, like the church upon which it was modelled, took the form of a comparatively narrow, lofty nave flanked by aisles covered by roofs leaning against the nave walls. The majority of

these halls were of timber. No timber hall of earlier date than the fourteenth century remains standing, although numerous medieval barns, like those at Wendens Ambo in Essex or Great Coxwell in Berkshire, survive which are directly related to the hall house. Stone houses were so rare that they were named in deeds to indicate boundaries.

One aisled hall built of stone in the early Middle Ages has been preserved almost in its original state: Oakham Castle in Rutland. Its dependence on parish-church architecture is at once apparent, and its splendour immediately proclaims it the dwelling of one of the most powerful magnates of the period. It was indeed built for Walkelin de Ferrers, one of the great family of the Ferrers, earls of Derby, an exceptionally wealthy man who could command the resources necessary for such an ambitious enterprise. The hall dates from about 1190: it is a fine composition in the Transitional style between Norman and Gothic, with wide round arcade arches, already decorated with the Early English dog-tooth motif, springing from columns with richly carved Corinthianesque capitals. Between the arches, on the nave walls, sit small stone musicians, while looking into the aisles are the heads of men and women with alert, individualized faces quite different from the stylized or grotesque masks of the typical Norman corbel head. Despite the Romanesque treatment of their rope-like hair they already presage the grace and humanity of thirteenth-century sculpture. But the eye is most of all held by the corbels supporting the arches at either end of the hall, so delightful and unexpected is their design, so exquisite the execution. They take the form of animals, emblems of the Evangelists, each resting on the two heads of a man and a woman turned towards each other, silently and eternally communicating beneath a tiny, dog-tooth ornamented arch.

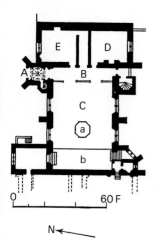

3 Plan of the hall at
Penshurst Place, Kent
(see also ill. 26).
A entrance porch,
B screens passage,
C hall (a, hearth; b, dais),
D pantry, E buttery.

4 Opposite: Rufford
Old Hall, Lancashire,
contains a remarkable
survival in the heavy
movable screen, crowned
by exotic pinnacles, that
separates the hall from
the screens passage. It is
flanked by speres, actual
tree-trunks carved with
shallow panels, which
support the spectacular
late fifteenth-century
roof in typical Lancashire
fashion.

If its architectural grandeur sets Oakham apart from most early medieval halls, its main features are characteristic of all others, of whatever date, down to the beginning of the sixteenth century. The south door, which is now centrally placed, was originally near the east end of the hall. Like the unaltered entrances of Norman churches it is unprotected, but, following ecclesiastical example, it soon became the custom to shield hall doors by porches, which sometimes developed as finely as those of the parish church. There was once a door exactly opposite the south entrance at Oakham. At the same end of the hall the gable wall was pierced by three doors which gave access to the buttery, the pantry and the kitchen, which, as excavations have shown, was detached from the hall as was usually the case in early medieval houses. A splendid detached kitchen, with an octagonal vault, can still be seen at Stanton Harcourt in Oxfordshire. 3

The dormer windows in the aisle roofs at Oakham are later additions: the great room was feebly lit in Walkelin de Ferrers' time from the small windows in the low side walls. At that time the room was warmed by a central hearth, of the kind preserved at Penshurst Place in Kent. The fire was the heart of domestic life for the greater part of the year; its importance is shown by the occasional substitution in medieval documents of the word 'fire-house' for hall. The smoke from the open hearth found its way through a hole in the roof which, from the thirteenth century onwards, was fitted with a pottery louver. Medieval louvers are wonderfully sculptural, beehive-shaped and pierced by two rows of large circular or triangular holes, or like pagodas with tiers of flanged openings, the form taken by the largest example so far found, that of an important fourteenth-century manor house at Dunmow in Essex. 3, 2

In order to prevent sudden gusts of wind from blowing smoke in all directions when the hall doors were opened, two short wooden movable screens, such as can be seen at Rufford Old Hall in Lancashire, were set beside each exit. These screens eventually became a continuous structure reaching from wall to wall, with two doors leading through it from the hall proper into what became known as the 'screens passage'. Such fully developed screens still furnish the halls of Penshurst Place, Lytes Cary in Somerset, Little Sodbury Manor in Gloucestershire and Haddon Hall in Derbyshire. 4, 26

The aisles of the hall, where in earlier periods animals had been stalled, were probably used at Oakham for storage and the accommodation of some of the household servants. At the opposite end of the apartment from the screen was a raised, paved space where the lord of the manor and his family could dine away from the disorder and dirt, the litter of food scraps, straw and rush which turned the floor of the rest of the hall into what was scornfully referred to as the 'marsh'. The floor at Oakham may always have been of stone, but rammed earth was usual even in grand manor houses. The original earth floor of a medieval hall has been preserved at Pallingham, Sussex, now serving as a barn. Even as late as the 1520s Erasmus described the floors of English houses as 'commonly of clay, strewed with rushes under which lie unmolested an ancient collection of beer, grease, fragments, bones, spittle, excrements of dogs and cats and everything that is nasty'.

Despite the filth of the 'marsh' the serving of dinner in a hall such as that of Oakham was a precisely conducted ceremony, knowledge of which was part of a gentleman's education. Such rituals – and indeed the whole organization of the manorial household, with its steward and underlings responsible for the routines of everyday life – foreshadowed the ordered life of the great country house: by the

eighteenth century it had become a masterpiece of smooth, intricate design, with a carefully graded hierarchy of servants, indoor and outdoor, and resources for the satisfaction not only of all domestic wants but of most intellectual desires.

The ritual of dinner began with the laying of the linen cloth on the trestle-table and the setting out of spoons, knives, cups, jugs and platters. Forks were rare even in the time of Queen Elizabeth. Utensils were generally made of earthenware or wood, though among the wealthy it was the custom to make a great display of gold and silver vessels, some of them purely ornamental (such as the 'nef', an elaborate piece of plate in the form of a ship). Pewter, an alloy of tin and lead, for which England was famous, only became common during the fifteenth century. Meat was very often eaten on 'trenchers', thick slices of bread which were afterwards given to the poor or flung to the dogs. Dinner was the most important of the two substantial meals of the medieval day: a contemporary writer declared, 'two meals a daye is suffycyent for a rest man; and a laborer may eate three tymes a day; and he that eate ofter lyveth a beestly lyfe'. It was taken at about 10 or 11 o'clock in the morning, while supper was served at 4 o'clock. Dinner was regularly and ceremoniously announced by 'blowynges and pipynges'.

Of the kind of food served we know a good deal from surviving household rolls, the keeping of which was a normal practice from at least the thirteenth century onwards. Those of the Countess of Leicester, dating from 1265, of Roger Leyburn, general of Edward I, and of Bogo de Clare, brother of the Earl of Gloucester, are among the most revealing, while the Liberate Rolls of Henry III (so called from the Latin writ of 'Liberate', or 'Deliver ye') are as enthrallingly informative in this respect as they are of every other aspect of the life of the time. Poultry was consumed in enormous quantities, beef and mutton were eaten on non-fast-days and a popular simple meal seems to have consisted of dried beans boiled in broth and served with ham. Fish played a great part in the menu because Wednesday, Friday and Saturday were all fast-days throughout the year. The humble salted herring was the staple diet on such days. The fresh herring was considered a delicacy, even by King Henry, who called it 'exquisite'. Salmon pasties were a speciality and we read also of dates, figs, pressed grapes, almonds, ginger and gingerbread, mulberry- and raspberry-flavoured wines and Gascony wine.

Standing in the lofty, church-like hall at Oakham, now no more than a museum-piece, it is difficult to bring the room to life, to see the walls bright with painted figures or patterns, to watch men feasting, playing backgammon or sleeping heavily by the blaze of the central fire. Then the sudden recollection of a tale about a contemporary of Walkelin de Ferrers, a man as powerful as himself, fills the hall with the vivid atmosphere of an evening spent in a room just such as this more than seven centuries ago. It was the spring of 1214; Henry de Pomeroy had been indulging in a 'rere-supper' or late meal (a habit condemned by moralists as leading to gluttony and lechery) with a group of friends in his manor house of Tregony in Cornwall when a serving-man came and told him that he had seen a stranger lurking with bow and arrows in the courtyard. Later Henry called for a candle to light him to bed and as he was passing an unshuttered (and at that time of course unglazed) window 'suddenly there came an arrow close by him, and it flew close to the hand of him who carried the candle'. The danger sharpens the image of revelry.

The impression given by this account is that Henry de Pomeroy was proceeding to a separate chamber for the night. And this may well have been the case, for it was probably early in the thirteenth century that a two-storeyed rectangular building was

5 The fifteenth-century kitchen at Stanton Harcourt, Oxfordshire, as it was in the 1850s. Instead of a central louver there are two rows of vents in each bay of the timber ceiling. The ovens are in the walls.

HIC HAROLD MA

6 A scene from the Bayeux Tapestry showing King Harold and his friends on the upper floor of a two-storeyed house at Bosham in Sussex. The hall is raised over a vaulted basement and reached by an external staircase.

set across one end of the hall at Tregony to provide a private apartment for the master of the house. There is evidence of the former existence of such a block at Oakham. It consisted of the great chamber or 'solar' (a word deriving from the Old French *soler*, an upstairs room, and ultimately related to the Latin word for sun) with either the buttery and pantry or space for storage below it. The solar was reached by steps of wood or stone in a corner of the hall. The source of the two-storeyed block was a type of small independent dwelling, always of stone and thus rare, which may have made its appearance in England in the period immediately preceding the Conquest when, under Edward the Confessor, French influence was strong: King Harold is depicted in an upper hall over a vaulted basement in the 6 Bayeux Tapestry, made about 1077. The prototype of such rectangular, compact little houses was French. In England some of them are associated with the Jewish money-lenders who are first heard of after the Conquest, others, of rather later date, are supposed to have been hunting-lodges of King John, others again are small manor houses, and are peculiar to this country, for the French examples occur only in towns.

Of these manor houses there are two remarkable survivals, Boothby Pagnell in Lincolnshire and Hemingford Grey in Huntingdonshire. Boothby Pagnell is now, 7 like Oakham, no more than a shell, and stands in the grounds of a mock-Tudor house built in 1824. It exhibits the standard plan for such a house and comprises a low, vaulted ground floor divided into two chambers with a hall and solar above it.

An external stone staircase runs steeply up to the hall door set in a round-headed arch, redeemed only by its chamfered jambs and narrow hood-mould from absolute severity. The massive thickness of the rubble walls everywhere asserts itself. Once inside the hall, illumined by a later Tudor window at what must have been the dais end and by two oddly placed, original two-light windows in the gable-end, the eye is instantly drawn to the wall fireplace with its tall, pyramidal hood and plainly corbelled lintel. The wall fireplace was always a feature of the two-storeyed block, possibly because a central hearth would have been dangerous on an upper floor. It was accompanied by a cylindrical chimney, which at Boothby Pagnell is set on a gabled buttress. The pyramidal fireplace hood appeared towards the end of the twelfth century and remained popular until the early fourteenth century. The earliest Norman fireplaces were arched: one of these can still be seen in the hall of
8 Hemingford Manor, where the arch is flanked by shafts with scalloped capitals.

8, 9   Hemingford Manor, unlike Boothby Pagnell, remains a living organism, preserving the arrangements of its Norman origins throughout a long succession of adaptations to changing conditions. It was built about 1150 for Payne de Hemingford, and has been continuously inhabited ever since. And although the four-roomed Norman house has been very modestly enlarged by eighteenth-century additions and altered by the insertion of a gigantic Elizabethan chimney-stack, almost filling the width of the wall between the hall and the solar with its crooked bulk, the hall is still the heart of the house, the focus of its life. The sense of continuity

7 The manor house, Boothby Pagnell, Lincolnshire. The two-storeyed type of house shown in the Bayeux Tapestry is here translated into stone.

17

8 The upper hall, Hemingford Manor, Hemingford Grey, Huntingdonshire. The wall fireplace and unglazed, shuttered window are original Norman features, while the leaning mass of the chimney on the far left belongs to the sixteenth century.

is perhaps stronger in this high, yet homely room than in any other house in England. The windows, like those at Boothby Pagnell, are two-light openings within an embracing arch. Within the deep embrasure of the south window are two stone seats with a foot-rest between them. Such 'sitting windows' are mentioned in Henry III's instructions in the Liberate Rolls for alterations and additions to his palaces of Winchester, Westminster and Clarendon; here throughout the long past of Hemingford Manor two persons must often have sat withdrawn in private converse. Conspicuously protruding from the soffits of the lights, which were formerly unglazed, are two stone lobes, the intention of which was probably to keep shutters in place. Shutters are still fitted to another window in the hall which as 8 it is no longer external, but opens into a bedroom, remains glassless.

A broad, green moat and the River Ouse separate Hemingford Manor from a willowy, stream-threaded expanse which in its essentials has changed little in the long history of the house. More than thirty generations have looked up from the river at the gable of the solar, patterned by the shadows of huge yews, almost black 9 against that dazzling whiteness. For the manor, though sturdily built of stone rubble like Boothby Pagnell, is thickly coated with whitewashed plaster, as was the medieval practice. The irregular, glinting surface of the walls wonderfully contrasts with the stone of the round-headed window openings, each with its chevron-ornamented hood-mould.

The third unit to play its part in the developing plan of the English country house was the tower. The tower, of course, is as obviously related to church architecture as the nave-like hall. It was invested with the same symbolism: it was an aspiring image of power and authority and satisfied the strong medieval predilection for verticality. The domestic tower also had the same practical defensive purpose as its ecclesiastical prototype. It is possible that the domestic form may have been adopted

as a solution to the building of a dwelling on a very restricted site such as a protected mound, where the most convenient way of arranging the usual accommodation of the hall, service and storage space was to up-end it. In the earliest surviving type of tower-house, the stout Norman keep, the essential chambers are piled vertically one above the other, the hall achieving greater prominence by virtue of rising through two storeys. This is the plan of the circular and multi-angular castles of Conisbrough and Orford as well of the rectangular Castle Hedingham. The latter was built in about 1135 for Aubrey de Vere, whose grandfather had been granted the Essex manor before Domesday. Like the Norman two-storeyed house it is entered by an internal stair, though here it leads into the kitchen, furnished, like the great hall above it, with a round-headed, stone-hooded fireplace.

The tradition of the Norman tower-keep persisted as an independent theme, especially in the wilder, constantly disturbed regions of the north. Examples are the tower-house at Corbridge and the beautiful ruin of Edlingham where the noble, rib-vaulted hall is strikingly adorned with caryatids. But it is the varying combination of the tower and the two other types of house just described which affected the evolving design of the English country house. An early instance of the union of the tower and the two-storeyed Norman house occurs at Little Wenham Hall in Suffolk, which like Boothby Pagnell now rises, abandoned though preserved, from the lawns of a modern house. It was begun for Sir John de Vallibus and was probably completed after it had been inherited in 1287 by his daughter Petronella of Nerford, whose patron saint adorns a boss in the chapel. The two components of Little Wenham make an L-shape, the toy-like scale of which is emphasized by giant buttresses. One arm of the L repeats the established plan of the Norman rectangular dwelling with an external entrance and a first-floor hall above a vaulted chamber; the other takes the form of an embattled tower containing a chapel on the

9 Above, left: Hemingford Manor. The original entrance door is at first-floor level.

10 Above: the thirteenth-century manor house of Little Wenham, Suffolk. The hall is on the left; the large traceried window in the tower on the right is that of the chapel, with the solar above it.

same level as the hall, with an arch flanked by traceried windows communicating between the two, while the solar occupies the floor above the chapel and the room underneath it is low and vaulted like that below the hall. It is characteristic of an age of faith that the chapel and not the lord's private apartment adjoins the hall, and that it is upon the chapel, with its rib vault, nervously carved corbels and large east window, that the mason's particular care has been expended.

Another house where tower and two-storeyed block are juxtaposed is Markenfield 11 Hall in Yorkshire. This moated dwelling of coarse limestone makes a more massive impression than Little Wenham Hall with its pallid tapestry of flint, rubble and pink and yellow bricks: it boldly asserts its strength in a potentially unruly countryside. At the same time it is emphatically domestic and alive, for the manorial buildings are ranged about a forecourt which is and always was a farmyard. Licence to crenellate was granted in 1307. This accorded with a decree issued some time before the building of Markenfield that no fortified house might be erected without the monarch's permission, the purpose of the law being to control the possible menace to the state constituted by an unlimited number of strongholds. As at Little Wenham the hall is on the first floor of that arm of the L-shaped building which derives from the Norman two-storeyed house. Traces of the outside stair and the door by which it was originally approached can be clearly seen in the fabric of the wall. The other arm at Markenfield contains the chapel, adjacent to the hall, and another room, probably the solar, opening from it. A hexagonal stair turret crowned by a spire marks the division between this room and the chapel. The spire may have served as a look-out, for, as if to accentuate the tower-like character of the arm to which it is attached, the whole feature soars above it.

Such fusions of the tower and the two-storeyed block prompted William Ryman to build the manor house named after him at Appledram in Sussex during the first quarter of the fifteenth century. The three-storeyed stone tower comprised the solar on the first floor with another room above it, while a chamber with a built-in garderobe, so probably the lawyer's bedroom, occupied the upper floor of a two-storeyed wing in the by this time traditional L-plan. The ground floor of this wing, also divided into two apartments, exactly as at Hemingford Manor, could originally be entered from outside and perhaps it was here that William Ryman conducted his legal business. But there was more to the house than this: on the other side of the tower stretched another wing (rebuilt during the seventeenth century), and this contained a hall rising the full height of the elevation. So at Ryman's all three components of the manor house were conjoined.

12   The tower and two-storeyed block were combined much later at Cotehele in Cornwall, where the solar tower was only added in 1637. But this was not so much due to conscious conservatism or to a sentimental feeling for past traditions as to the extreme remoteness of Cornwall which despite the tin-mining industry endured until the advent of the railway. In the Middle Ages it lay on the very edge of the known world, and its isolation was increased by its people's continued use of a Celtic tongue. Even now the irregular, granite quadrangle of Cotehele with its squat, embattled gateway and inscrutable east and south façades, pierced by narrow windows darkened with iron gratings, seems withdrawn, sequestered in a timeless backwater. It stands on a prominent knoll on the western bank of the Tamar but is so encompassed by trees, especially by Spanish chestnuts of immense size, that it is quite shrouded from the river. The introduction to the house from the water up a

12 Cotehele in Cornwall, confronting the outer world with almost blank walls and with a massive, embattled tower-gate.

13 Squint opening from the solar into the hall of Great Chalfield Manor, Wiltshire, about 1480.

wooded, boulder-strewn slope planted with exotic shrubs is like one of the most luxuriant landscapes of Salvator Rosa. As for the interior (see below, p. 28), it has not only remained as unchanged as if laid under a spell, but the very position of the furniture, the tapestries and embroideries, the armour, the harquebuses and pikes, and the antlers and antelope horns, has not altered since the antiquary William Gilpin described them in the eighteenth century. Cotehele was left uninhabited but untouched in the seventeenth century when its owners, the Edgcumbes, moved to Mount Edgcumbe, a grander house (destroyed by bombs in World War II) built by Sir Richard in 1547.

The combination of tower and great hall is magnificently represented by Longthorpe Tower in Northamptonshire, where in the early fourteenth century Robert Thorpe, the ambitious Steward of Peterborough Abbey, added a stalwart square tower, an awe-inspiringly solid testimony to his authority, to a hall built in about 1260. The tower again contains the solar on the first floor above a vaulted storage room. A third room, reached by a narrow staircase in the wall, preserves stone window-seats like those at Hemingford Grey. But it is the solar which, above all, excites attention at Longthorpe Tower. Here indeed the importance of the owner was unforgettably proclaimed. For this vaulted chamber is covered with paintings 14 of extraordinary quality.

The general colour scheme is vermilion and yellow ochre. The theme of the decorations is the contrast between the worldly and the spiritual life, shown in Biblical scenes, episodes from the lives of the saints and various moralities. These are associated with a dado of birds, minutely observed inhabitants of the near-by Fens including the now-vanished bittern and the rare spoonbill, and with heraldic devices and the figures of Edward II and his brother Edmund. A Virgin, mysteriously spectral because only half recovered from the layers of limewash under which these murals were hidden until 1945, reclines on a high couch of ecclesiastical design clasping the Child. Above her appears a favourite medieval subject, the Wheel of Life, depicting the seven stages of man's earthly pilgrimage. But the most riveting image in the room is that over the fireplace. A figure of regal bearing and proportions rotates a Wheel of the Five Senses – a monkey typifying taste, a vulture signifying smell, a spider's web touch, a boar hearing and a cock sight. The strangeness of the commanding figure is accentuated by his swarthy, blotched complexion, though this is accidental: the flesh colour has worn away leaving the black undercoat. The vehicle used for the pigment was glue, perhaps mixed with egg white.

The fascination of this room lies not only in the fact that it is the most complete example of medieval secular wall decoration to survive but that such elaborate murals must have been a normal feature of the wealthier fourteenth-century manor house. The subject-matter, so closely akin to the great didactic schemes displayed in glass and paint in Gothic churches, testifies as much as the conspicuous chapels to the habit of mind which dominated the domestic architecture of the time. It is likely that the paintings at Longthorpe Tower were commissioned in about 1340 by the son of the builder of the tower, also named Robert and also Steward of Peterborough Abbey. They may have been executed by an artist from the abbey.

The history of the Thorpe family is as relevant to this account as their tower and painted solar, for it illustrates that fluid state of society which I described earlier in this chapter. The first Robert Thorpe was the great-grandson of a villein on the manor of Thorpe who was freed at the beginning of the thirteenth century. His son William was confirmed in his holding of land in Thorpe and his grandson, who was

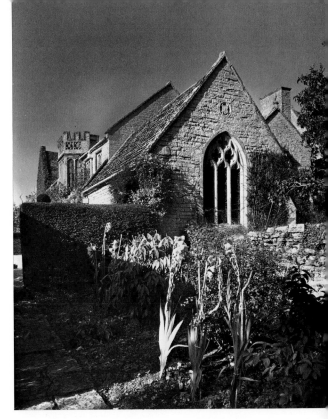

knighted, built the hall to which Robert added the tower. Robert became Steward of Peterborough in 1310 but was not released from service to his overlord until 1324. Of his grandsons one became Chancellor to Edward III and another Lord Chief Justice.

Of all the possible combinations of the three originally independent forms of dwelling the commonest was that which incorporated the hall and the two-storeyed house in a design to which passing reference was made in the sketch of Oakham. The tiny thirteenth-century manor of Old Soar in Kent is an early instance of the relationship, though here the hall has been replaced by a Georgian mansion. The existing two-storeyed block was set across one end of the hall and a spiral staircase of stone led from the north-east angle of the principal apartment to the upper chamber of the cross-wing, which could also be approached by an outside stair. The solar was usually furnished with spy-holes through which the lord, when he retired, could observe what was going on in the hall. There are two such openings, or squints, as they are called, concealed behind masks at Great Chalfield.

13

At Old Soar a further rectangular block is attached to the south-east corner of the solar. It contains a chapel on the upper floor with storage space below it. A similarly placed chapel, some fifty years later in date, leads off the solar at Lytes Cary in Somerset, which takes its name from the Lyte family who owned the manor for five centuries and from the British word *caer*, meaning fortress. Here, however, the original plan is partly obscured by the south wing added immediately behind the chapel in the sixteenth century. At Charney Bassett in Berkshire, the design of a hall house with cross-wings clearly persists despite radical alterations. Here the small thirteenth-century chapel occupied the first floor of a two-storeyed, narrow wing placed alongside the solar block. Indeed, the most popular position for the medieval private chapel came to be in a second two-storeyed building, attached to the solar but under a separate roof.

15

16

14 Above, left: a fashionable young man of about 1340, one of the paintings in the solar of Longthorpe Tower, Northamptonshire.

15 Above: the chapel of Lytes Cary, Somerset, dating from about 1343. Beyond it is a range added in the sixteenth century. The planting in the foreground preserves the tradition of John Cary, a celebrated Elizabethan herbalist.

23

16 The manor house,
Charney Bassett,
Berkshire.

The solar block at Charney Bassett is balanced by another cross-wing at the 16 opposite end of the former hall. This arrangement, the result of a need for more space, prompted also perhaps by a nascent feeling for symmetry, is embodied in innumerable small manor houses in all parts of the country, many of them now reduced to the status of farmhouses. The resulting H-shaped design, with certain modifications, dominated country-house architecture for many decades, in fact until the close of the sixteenth century. A fine early instance of it can be seen at Little Chesterford in Essex, which probably began life in the thirteenth century as a two-storeyed rectangular block of local clunch and flint rubble in the style of Hemingford Manor. In the fifteenth century this house became the cross-wing of a 9 new timber-framed hall with a balancing cross-wing at the opposite end.

It was also in the fifteenth century that one of the most atmospheric of English manor houses, Cothay in Somerset, was built on the site of an earlier dwelling by Richard Bluett, tenant of Thomas Grey, 1st Marquess of Dorset and younger son of a local family who owned two notable houses in the region, Greenham Barton and Holcombe Court. Rose-flushed, tawny stone replaces the plastered timber and clunch of Chesterford Manor, but the basic components of the buttressed, picturesque Cothay are the same – a central hall with a two-storeyed cross-wing at either end – though here, after the passage of more than a century since the emergence of the first houses of this type, the three elements have been more closely integrated by a continuous roofline. The same units also merge to produce the venerable image of Northborough Hall in Northamptonshire, built about 1330–40, and they consort yet again at Great Chalfield Manor, of 1480 (see below, pp. 35–6), where the cross- 28, wings are separately roofed with a conscious archaism which is one of the more IV interesting characteristics of late medieval and Tudor houses.

24

17   At Stokesay Castle in Shropshire, built by a rich cloth-merchant, Laurence de Ludlow, tower, two-storeyed block and hall are all combined in a composition which is superficially even more randomly romantic than that of Ightham Mote. A gabled hall, a cross-wing, a tower with an overhanging timber storey and another free-standing tower are grouped opposite a fantastic Elizabethan half-timber gate-house, dreaming over their own moated reflections in the wooded valley of the

18 Onny. The hall, which there is reason to believe was formerly aisled, with a cross-wing at its south end, was added in about 1285 to a tower built in the twelfth century. At the same time the oddly shaped polygonal south tower, hugely crenellated and buttressed, gave its owner an excuse to call his house a castle. For castle it is not: the tall, beautiful windows, three on each side of the hall, each of two lights with ogee heads below a circle, are not compatible with defence. The timber storey of the older tower is seventeenth-century work, though it may replace an earlier structure. The gatehouse, upon which the glamour of the irregular cluster of buildings so much depends, is a free-standing reminder of the rambling courtyard disposition of which the hall and its adjoining chambers often formed the principal range.

    This chapter opened with a preview of the courtyard theme and the traditional ingredients of the manor house itself as exemplified in the comparatively small and simple Ightham. After glancing at the stages by which this arrangement came into being it seems appropriate to conclude with a brief mention of the most elaborate

19 and the most romantic manifestation of these united elements, at Haddon Hall in Derbyshire. Despite the many alterations which have taken place since this famous house was first built in the twelfth century, its image is still that of some enclosed and battlemented city in a medieval illumination, for its towers, high roofs and

17 Above left: Stokesay Castle, Shropshire. The gabled hall is in the centre, between a half-timbered tower and the great thirteenth-century stone tower. The village church lies near by at the left.

18 Above: the hall of Stokesay. The massive cruck-like braces of the roof belong to the thirteenth century, while the superstructure is later.

25

19 The west front of Haddon Hall, Derbyshire, rises from Norman walls. The embattled gate tower of about 1530, on the left, is balanced on the right by the chapel, dating from the twelfth to the seventeenth centuries.

chimneys crowd above erratic, crenellated walls, and the silvery limestone composition, dramatically pale against a brilliantly green, thinly wooded slope, looks down to the watered silk of a swift, clear stream. It was by that stream that Dorothy, younger daughter of Sir George Vernon, is said to have met Sir John Manners when she eloped with him on the night of her sister's marriage festivities in 1567. There is no evidence for the truth of the story, though it lends piquancy to the staid effigies of Sir John and Lady Manners facing each other across a prayer-desk in Bakewell Church. It was through this union that Haddon passed from the Vernons, who had held it since the end of the twelfth century, to the Manners family.

The house is ranged about two courts divided by the traditional group of the hall with the kitchen and offices placed at one end and a corresponding wing at the other end containing a parlour (now called the dining-room) on the ground floor and a solar on the upper floor. At the highest point of the sloping site rises the twelfth-century rectangular tower built by Haddon's first and almost legendary lord, Peveril of the Peak (celebrated by Sir Walter Scott) and embellished with stepped battlements about two centuries later. The tower shape is echoed by the tall gatehouse and by the crenellated, two-storeyed hall porch soaring above the roof, the former a sixteenth-century addition which, like the Stokesay gatehouse, deliberately exaggerates the picturesque character of the existing buildings. As if in salutation of the stair turret of Peveril's tower a charming embattled octagon was set in the late Middle Ages upon the roof of the chapel which makes up one side of the lower court.

2   THE BIRTH OF AN ART

from the Middle Ages to Henry VIII

IN THE MANOR HOUSES of varying dates glimpsed in the last chapter the merging of originally separate components was already accompanied by enrichments and structural developments in which aesthetic values were playing a growing part. The hall, still the focal point of the manor for social as well as for legal and administrative purposes, had emerged in the fourteenth century as an imposing architectural apartment. It was now only part of the essential accommodation of an important house, and the need for great width and for arcades for storage vanished. It was therefore unaisled, lit by large windows of ecclesiastical design, especially at the dais end, and covered by an open timber roof which, while it never surpassed the finest church roofs, came to rival them before the fifteenth century was out.

The timber roof was a type of construction in which the English showed unique skill and invention. Hall-house roofs follow the same course of development as those of churches, evolving from the simplest king-post type to the intricate hammer-beam composition. They seldom fall into distinct categories, but are delightfully free and individual hybrids. The roof of the early fourteenth-century hall at Ightham Mote, for instance, is basically of the trussed-rafter type. There is no ridge-piece, as there is in the tie-beam roof. Each pair of rafters is halved at the apex and pegged where they meet and they are joined by a short collar-beam near the apex. A straight brace runs from each rafter to the collar-beam, while a vertical strut rises from the wall-plate to support the rafter. But this prescriptive design is given a wholly unexpected aspect by a central arch of stone resting on corbels in the form of groaning grotesques and by timber replicas of this arch and its Atlas figures placed at either end of the hall. Again, the glorious roof at Penshurst, built by Sir John de Pulteney, the rich merchant who bought the manor in 1341, combines the king-post and trussed-rafter types in an entirely idiosyncratic arrangement. It is thought that Sir John may have engaged William Hurley, the King's master-carpenter, who had built the great timber octagon over the crossing of Ely Cathedral. The Penshurst roof is planned in two distinct stages divided by a heavily moulded purlin, as powerful and as conspicuous as the wall-plate. From the latter, separating the roof into bays, rise delicately moulded arched braces, springing from full-length, bowed male figures in fourteenth-century dress. The huge, four-centred arches formed by the braces support weighty tie-beams, a king-post with a moulded capital and struts branching out to sustain the collars and the longitudinal beam which gives them additional strength.

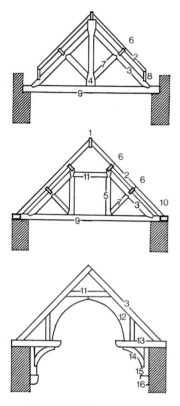

20 Elements of the three main types of timber roof, king-post (top), queen-post and hammer-beam. 1 ridge, 2 common rafter, 3 principal rafter, 4 king-post, 5 queen-post, 6 purlin, 7 strut, 8 sole plate, 9 tie-beam, 10 wall plate, 11 collar-beam, 12 arched brace, 13 hammer-beam, 14 brace, 15 wall-post, 16 corbel.

21 Above, right: the hall of Ightham Mote, Kent. Just visible at the top is one of the stone arches that divide the trussed-rafter roof.

The hall at Cotehele in Cornwall is as conservative as its tower (see above, p. 21), 22 for it was at least a hundred years behind the times when it was begun in 1485. It displays a roof which became fashionable in the late fourteenth century, the arch-braced, collar-beam style, in which the absence of tie-beams enhances the sense of height and space. The slope of the roof is divided at intervals by three purlins; between these and the principal rafters are arched supports known as 'wind-braces', making a complex and surely deliberate pattern of four tiers of interlacing arcadings.

A roof of an utterly different character, though contemporary with that of Cotehele, distinguishes the hall of Great Dixter in Sussex. Its most conspicuous 23 feature is the gigantic, cambered tie-beam, cut from a single great oak, strengthened by tremendous cusped and curving braces and itself supporting a fine octagonal king-post with moulded base and capital. But the individuality of the design lies in the association of the tie-beam structure with hammer-beams – beams which project at right angles from the wall, supported by curved braces and with arched braces springing from them to strengthen the principal rafters. The faces of the hammer-beams at Great Dixter are carved with heraldic devices, the arms of the medieval owners of the manor, the Etchinghams, the Dalingridges and the Gayns-fords. The central rafters, as at Penshurst, are still blackened by the smoke from the open fire that formerly burned on the floor in the middle of the hall. The exceptional sense conveyed by this noble, tranquil room, of long-vanished days, of familiarity with 'the chronicle of wasted time', is intensified by a charming detail: a wood-pecker's nest, cut in half when the braces of the huge tie-beam were fashioned, has been preserved ever since in the woodwork, eloquent witness of a distant spring when our country too was in its spring.

The most highly organized and the most original roofs belong to the period when the manorial system and the whole medieval world of seemingly unchangeable institutions and unchallengeable beliefs was dissolving, when the focus of life was rapidly shifting from the religious to the secular. Caxton's press was replacing the monastic scribe and among the books he published were translations of Virgil's *Aeneid* and Aesop's *Fables*, which were part of the Renaissance of classical scholarship. Just as the slowly emerging vision of the long-lost world of antiquity was revealing horizons beyond the confines of the medieval heaven and hell, so with every new voyage of Columbus and Cabot the material world was opening up vistas beyond the limits of medieval cosmography. Equally disruptive of the past was the work of William Tyndale, as in penury and danger he translated the Bible into words which were to bring millions into daily touch with a new enrichment of the imagination and the compelling power of noble language. Part of this great work was accomplished when Tyndale was engaged as a tutor at Little Sodbury Manor. The English tradition was expanding to embrace those of the two great peoples of the ancient world, the Hebrew and the Greek, and it was upon the solid foundation of common knowledge of these traditions that the culture of the country gentleman was to rest right up until the industrial age. The change was taking place long before the Dissolution of the Monasteries in 1537, as a single arresting event, brought medieval society to a dramatic end.

Meanwhile the villein was achieving his emancipation and new middle classes, encouraged by the commerce and manufacture which were growing with the cloth trade, were thrusting themselves between lord and labourer. Members of this class were joining the ranks of the gentry, all of whom had gained in importance by the

22 Above, left: the hall of Cotehele, Cornwall. The four decorative tiers of wind-braces in the late fifteenth-century roof testify to the growing emphasis on aesthetic values in domestic architecture.

23 Above: the half-timbered hall of Great Dixter, Sussex, is dominated by massive tie-beams in the centre and in the end walls; between them are hammer-beams, of which one is just visible on the left.

24, 25 The late fifteenth-century hall at Athelhampton, Dorset (above), exhibits a spectacular refinement of the arch-braced roof to form a decorative trefoil design, enhanced by cusped wind-braces. The hammer-beam roof at Weare Giffard, north Devon (above, right) is an even more elaborate example of the astonishing development of the timber roof in Tudor England.

26 Opposite: the hall at Penshurst Place, Kent (see the plan, ill. 3). The magnificent roof, tiled floor and octagonal central hearth, surrounded by a stone curb – at the left – survive untouched from the thirteenth century. The screen with its minstrels' gallery was added more than two hundred years later.

decline of their former landlords, the feudal barons. These had succeeded too well in keeping themselves apart; long devoted to no art but war, they fell upon each other and so nearly destroyed their caste that at the end of the Wars of the Roses in 1485 both Yorkist and Lancastrian claimants to the Crown had disappeared and a Welsh gentleman named Henry Tudor, a descendant of the ancient British princes, was enabled to mount the throne of England.

In fact one of the most fantastically ornamented secular roofs in the country dates from Henry VII's accession and celebrates him in its imagery. It is the hammer-beam roof of the hall at Weare Giffard in north Devon, the home of the Fortescues since 25 1450, when the present house was built by Martin Fortescue, son of Henry VI's Chancellor. The large, superbly carved animals on the hammer-beams include the greyhound and the dragon, the heraldic beasts of Henry Tudor. The fashioning of these creatures is unique, for they are grooved and held in position solely by the deep moulding of the braces curving up behind them. The whole surface of this opulent roof is traceried; the huge arched braces and collar-beams, cut all in one piece, are trefoiled and adorned with pendants, the wind-braces between the purlins and principal rafters – three tiers of them – are crossed and cusped, and the wall-plates consist of bands of magnificently and minutely rendered foliage and flowers surmounted by cresting carved in relief.

The developing artistry of the hall roof was matched by that of the screen, which advanced from the primitive plank-and-muntin type still found at Cothay to the traceried panelling, identical with that of church screens, which distinguishes the screens of Haddon Hall, Little Sodbury and Penshurst Place – although at Penshurst 26 the breath of change is already felt in the columns flanking each opening, for they are classical. During the second half of the fifteenth century, following the appearance of the rood-loft above church screens, a minstrels' gallery was introduced over the hall screen. Such galleries are conspicuous features of the halls at Penshurst and Haddon Hall.

27 Lytes Cary, Somerset, from the east.

1 Opposite: the entrance front of Ightham Mote, Kent (see pp. 7–8).

Music had always played a part in the manorial household, even in the ordinary routine of the day. The announcement of dinner by wind instruments has already been mentioned. It was the custom also to summon the attendants by a flourish of trumpets when the lord rode forth; a 'wayte' piped the watch, four times in winter and three in summer; and music was among the chief entertainments of the lord and his lady at night and during bad weather. In wealthy households during the earlier Middle Ages there was often a resident harper. By the end of the period the lord patronized musicians on a more ambitious scale. A surprising number of musical instruments were commonly kept in his house: 'regals' or portable organs, lutes, recorders, virginals (percursors of the harpsichord), flutes, viols, gitterns, shawms and clavichords.

The hall roof and screen are the counterparts of those of the parish church, but houses of the later Middle Ages increasingly showed features which were secular in origin. Conspicuous among them were the bay window and the oriel, a bracketed bay window on an upper storey. The oriel may have developed from the porch at the head of an external staircase, the Cornish name for which still survives as 'orell'. At Lytes Cary in Somerset a fine oriel on the upper floor of the two-storeyed porch 27 is echoed, if not balanced, by the oriel of the wing jutting out from the hall, an addition by John Lyte who inherited the manor in 1523. Inside this wing, the oriel recess yields a splendid view through a stone arch, enriched with traceried panels, down into the hall and up into the arch-braced roof with its quatrefoiled wall-plate and tiers of cusped wind-braces. Such an oriel chamber leading from the hall may have provided a dining-place for the lord of the manor away from the hubbub of the hall itself, before the room below the solar had been made into a parlour, instead of merely being used for storage. The tendency of the lord to dine apart in either

parlour or oriel recess was growing by the end of the fourteenth century, when it was deprecated by Langland in *The Vision of Piers Plowman*:

28 The back of Great
Chalfield Manor,
Wiltshire, seen from the
moat. (For the entrance
front, see colour plate IV.)

II Opposite: the chapel at
Ightham Mote, Kent,
begun at the very end of
the fifteenth century (see
p. 8).

> Wretched is the hall . . . each day in the week
> There the lord and lady liketh not to sit,
> Now have the rich a rule to eat by themselves
> In a privy parlour . . . for poor men's sake,
> Or in a chamber with a chimney and leave the chief hall
> That was made for meals, for men to eat in.

It was a move away from the communal life which was typically medieval and to which we are now returning.

The oriels at Lytes Cary are three-sided like a simple type of bay window, which they in fact resemble except that they are corbelled. John Lyte introduced an actual bay window, two-storeyed and very ornate, into the wing he added to his house; its battlemented parapet shoots up above the eaves, giving it the semblance of a tower, and it is embellished below the crenellations with a typical Somerset open-work frieze of quatrefoils.

IV   Oriels figure prominently in the composition of Great Chalfield Manor in Wiltshire. The elements of this composition are traditional, and have already been met in the previous chapter. The owner of the house, Thomas Tropenell, who took possession of the estate in 1467, chose to build in an outmoded style so that the hall 28 and cross-blocks, which constitute the main bulk of the manor, are still seen as individual, separately roofed entities. Possibly Tropenell, who made his money during the Wars of the Roses at the expense of his former master, Robert, Lord Hungerford, to whom he was Steward, consciously sought to re-create the tradition favoured by the old nobility. Nevertheless he imposed a new design on the familiar

forms. The oriels – one, richly wrought, lighting the solar, the other, furnished with
a semi-pyramidal roof, advancing from the principal bedchamber on the first floor
of the corresponding wing – vary without destroying the astonishing symmetry of
the plan and distinguish the gables of the cross-blocks from the lesser gables of the
porch and the hall bay. Porch and bay are set at either end of the hall and thus make
a balanced composition of it. The pairs of gables are further differentiated by showy
finials: knights in armour crown the gables of the cross-wings, while those of the
porch and hall bay are adorned by griffins clasping the Tropenell arms. If it were not
for the big chimney-breast set in the angle between the hall and its bay, sending its
crenellated top high over the roof, Great Chalfield might be taken for a sixteenth-
century house.

Inside there is more evidence of Thomas Tropenell's awareness of advanced
fashions. His hall is no longer open to the roof, but ceiled, with an attic above it. 29
One of the great innovations of the late fifteenth century was the horizontal division
of the hall, thus making the entire house two-storeyed. For reasons which will
become apparent later in this chapter – a love of ostentation and the beginning of a
new romantic sense of the past – the owners of some of the larger Early Tudor houses
did not always adopt this obvious improvement in comfort and convenience.
Thomas Tropenell cleverly united the internal advantages of the ceiled hall with an
exterior which preserved the aspect of the medieval great hall, for the attic windows,
piercing the end gables of the hall, are invisible from the front.

Gifford's Hall at Wickhambrook, a half-timbered Suffolk manor built by Thomas 30
Higham at about the same time as Great Chalfield, also incorporates a ceiled hall, and
like the Wiltshire house depends for much of its effect on the zigzag of gables,
though here the central and cross blocks are merged under a continuous roof. At

Gifford's Hall, by a further refinement of the customary domestic plan, the solar, a room of unusual distinction with elegantly moulded beams and a four-centred fireplace arch surmounted by crenellations, is directly above the hall.

30 Gifford's Hall, at Wickhambrook in Suffolk. The timber construction, of closely set studs filled with wattle and daub, is typical of East Anglia.

Both this hall at Wickhambrook and that at Great Chalfield exhibit forms of decoration which wholly depart from ecclesiastical procedure. The lower portions of the walls at Great Chalfield are hung with tapestry, a form of wall covering which had come to be the rule in great houses during the fifteenth century. It replaced the paintings on plaster, of which those at Longthorpe Tower are such outstanding examples, and the painted cloths which were usual in the fourteenth century; although woven hangings might occasionally, as the illustrations to the Luttrell Psalter show, adorn the wall behind the high table. A most beautiful armorial tapestry hangs in that position at Haddon Hall. It contains five shields, among them the Royal Arms, on a flower-sprigged background. The fashion for tapestry hangings came from France, where the great centre of manufacture in the fifteenth century was Arras (whence the term, made familiar to us by Shakespeare, by which tapestry was generally known). Apart from heraldry the subjects of the tapestries might include scenes from the Old and New Testaments, but the most favoured themes were battle-pieces, hunting scenes, the seasons, allegories, histories and romances. The inventory of the goods of Sir John Fastolf, veteran of the wars of Henry V, includes pieces of arras showing 'a gentlewoman harping by a castle', the siege of Falaise, the Assumption of the Virgin, hawking, and shepherds with their flocks. Tapestry wall hangings were suspended on pegs and it was the custom for the owner to take them with him when he went on visits to other manor houses to give an air of comfort to the room he inhabited as a guest. Pegs for tapestry can still be seen in the ruined hall of Wingfield Manor in Derbyshire, and at Sudeley Castle.

31 Above: the dining-room at Haddon Hall, Derbyshire.

32 Opposite, above: the long gallery at The Vyne, Hampshire, dating from the 1520s, seemingly panelled with pleated cloth.

33 Opposite, below: a detail of the screen at Compton Wynyates, Warwickshire, of about 1512, where linenfold achieves a climax of refined ingenuity.

Another and more permanent kind of wall covering, again a purely domestic innovation, enriches Gifford's Hall – the extraordinary form of panelling we call linenfold. It had developed from the simplest type of wainscoting, consisting of vertical boards, such as is referred to in Henry III's orders for 'two hundred Norway boards of fir to wainscote the chamber of our beloved son Edward in our castle at Winchester'. This early panelling was usually painted, the preferred colour (again according to Henry's Liberate Rolls) being green, sometimes starred or spotted with gold, to form a background to Old and New Testament figures or heraldic themes. The effect must have resembled that of the glowing painted screens in East Anglian churches, though these consist of the rectangular panels which by the fifteenth century had replaced vertical boarding in houses as well as churches.

In old oak-panelled rooms of this period the echo of the past vibrates with a special intimate insistency, and of all such rooms perhaps the former parlour (now the 31 dining-room) of Haddon Hall is the most memorable. Slight irregularities in the panelling continually divert the eye and the plain rectangles are varied by a frieze of panels, themselves of disparate sizes, carved with coats of arms and geometric patterns, while the wall-plates are enlivened by tiny quatrefoils. What gives this room its unique atmosphere, however, is the juxtaposition of wall panels and carved ornament of a remarkably homely scale and ceiling-paintings of colossal proportions. Plaster ceilings were rare at this date (*c.* 1500) and the boards between the beams were frequently covered with painted designs, a tradition which persisted in Scotland until well into the seventeenth century. Here at Haddon giant red and white chequers form the background to representations of prodigious heraldic beasts and Tudor roses and permit of double readings like the squares and cubes of the 'Op' art of the 1960s, thus magnifying the strangeness of the perspective from the bay at one end of the room to the marvellous window with its seven cusped lights at the

other end. This wide window filled with glass set in sophisticated hexagonal quarry-shapes – no longer open or covered with the stretched and oiled linen of the earlier Middle Ages – itself proclaims the dawning of a new concept of domestic art.

The vitality which was shortly to electrify this art is nowhere more clearly heralded than in the invention of linenfold panelling, where wood was made to assume the unlikely appearance of bunched-up cloth. Sometimes, as at Gifford's Hall, and in the later, inordinate example in the long gallery of The Vyne in Hampshire, lined with linenfold from floor to ceiling, the resemblance to cloth is heightened by the punching and decorating of the edges to counterfeit embroidery. This curious and peculiarly English convention reflects the obsession of the age with drapery, an obsession which induced fifteenth-century painters like Campin, Memling, Van der Weyden and Schongauer to concentrate so intently on the rendering of pleats and folds in flowing robes that the emerging pattern is often the chief point of the picture. But when pleats and folds are translated into wood without any reference to the human figure the effect is as inappropriate as the illusionist marquetry-work in Duke Federigo's library at Urbino or as the inlaid marbles so incredibly simulating rich brocade in the great Baroque Church of the Gesuiti in Venice. The staggeringly detailed decoration of the hall screen at Compton Wynyates in Warwickshire, where tall, thin panels are filled with folds so fine that they suggest silk rather than linen, and horizontal bands, shields and doors are crowded with minutely carved foliage, birds and animals, arouses just such a sense of wonder at the ingenuity of the craftsman, who had only the limited tools of the period, the gouge and the chisel, at his disposal, and just such a feeling of exhilaration at the disregard of 'taste' as those works of Italian virtuosity. In both cases that disregard, allied to superb workmanship, is the exuberant expression of confidence and pulsating creativity.

Fresh impetus was given to this already mounting creativity in domestic design by the reintroduction, after long disuse, of a building material which was not associated with church architecture and therefore freed the artist's imagination. Brick has already made a brief appearance in these pages in the account of Little Wenham Hall. Locally made bricks were used in the fabric of this Suffolk manor house for the first time in Britain since the departure of the Romans. But this was an isolated example. The popularity of brick in the fifteenth and sixteenth centuries was a direct result of the influence of French building in brick on English knights who had been engaged in the wars against France. The very word 'brick' (French *brique*) only became part of the English language in the fifteenth century. Before that time bricks were not distinguished from tiles and were referred to as *tegulae*. Medieval and Tudor bricks were commonly red in colour, but the red varied with the quantity of iron in the clay from palest rust to fiery crimson and deep mulberry. And bricks of other colours were occasionally made. Hengrave Hall in Suffolk is 38 remarkable for the exquisite silvery hue of its brickwork, which was deliberately preferred to red for aesthetic reasons, although both colours were to be had in the locality.

The texture of early brick buildings is animated by delightful irregularity in the surface as well as in the size of the units. The bricks tend to be thinner than the $2\frac{1}{2}$ inches which became normal in the seventeenth century, but the thickness of bricks is never more than an approximate indication of date, for it continued to fluctuate until the standardized size with a thickness of $2\frac{5}{8}$ inches was established at the surprisingly late date of 1936, long after the end of our story.

Brick gave wing to unprecedented flights of fancy in various directions: it encouraged romanticized elaborations of the traditional house of the immediate past, it gave rise to new, extravagant forms of customary features and it also stimulated the feeling for ordered design already apparent in the composition of Great Chalfield Manor. It even led to a structural absurdity – the replacing of the wattle and daub filling of important timber-framed houses with brick. For of course the timber frame becomes redundant in a brick-built house.

Ockwells Manor, at Bray in Berkshire, is as celebrated an instance of brick- 34 nogging as it is an illustration of conscious, emphatic adherence to bygone modes. This emerges even in the timber framing, which is not the close studding of its period but the widely spaced old-fashioned type. The ground-plan is typically medieval, a rectangular block with wings; and although the front has been massively restored, the renovation follows the style of the gabled porch, which is original, in its parade of tracery and very ornately carved bargeboards. The great hall inside is 35 open to the roof and perpetuates all the traditions of the vanishing feudal order. And here, another sign of the growing addiction to display, a tremendous show of heraldic glass proclaims the allegiances and grand connections of the owner. He was Sir John Norreys, Esquire of the Body to Henry VI and Edward IV and Master of the Wardrobe to the former: thus the arms of Henry and his queen, Margaret of Anjou, are prominently represented. Accompanying them are the devices of Sir John's associates and acquaintances, the latter sometimes of the slightest. They include the shields of Henry Beauchamp, Earl and Duke of Warwick, Hereditary Panther to the King, Edward Beauchamp, Duke of Somerset, Sir John Wenlock, Chamberlain to Queen Margaret, Richard Bulstrode, Comptroller of the Household to Edward IV, Richard Beauchamp, Bishop of Salisbury and James Butler, Earl of Wiltshire.

34, 35 Ockwells Manor, Bray, Berkshire. The exterior illustrates the fashionable craze of the mid fifteenth century for brick (above, the west front). The armorial glass in the hall (right) was a rare luxury when Sir John Norreys built his house.

36 The east front of
Horeham Hall, Essex.

At Horeham Hall in Essex and Compton Wynyates in Warwickshire, both 36
considerably later than Ockwells Manor, the medieval trappings are more striking
and more obviously archaic. A timber-framed manor house probably stood on the
site of the present Horeham Hall when it was acquired by Sir John Cutte, Treasurer
of the Household of Henry VIII, after the death of Catherine of Aragon in 1536.
Sir John retained the solar cross-wing of this house and encased it in brick, then added
to it an immense hall with a spectacular dais window and another cross-block with
a crow-stepped gable. The hall, including the projecting two-storeyed porch, is
exaggeratedly crenellated, each big battlement being outlined in freestone, and the
dais window shows four tiers, each of ten cusped lights, surmounted by a frieze of
quatrefoils. The porch is emphasized by stone quoins and the brick fabric of the hall
is varied by diaper patterns, a form of decoration which, like the use of brick itself,
derived from French practice. Even without the pinnacled tower rising beside the
stepped gable and the pretty lantern on the hall roof, both Elizabethan additions,
this façade is richly asymmetrical. Its intentionally irregular and antiquated aspect
is matched by the interior of the hall, which is not only open to the roof but, although
it boasts a wall fireplace, is provided with the louver of the early medieval hall with
its central hearth.

The design of Compton Wynyates (Vineyards) makes yet more contrived and 37
more rambling allusions to the past. Like Horeham Hall it was an old house rebuilt
in the early sixteenth century. It had belonged to the Comptons since the twelfth
century, but the family only rose to wealth with Sir William who became Esquire of
the Body to Henry VIII. His selection of brick for the reconstruction of his ancestral

home was manifestly modish, for the building material of the district is stone. The house is quadrangular and of considered, picturesque irregularity. The word 'picturesque' was of course unknown in the Tudor period, but the impulse which gave rise to Picturesque architecture and landscapes more than two and a half centuries later was already present in this age of increasing aesthetic awareness. As in the eighteenth century it accompanied a nascent interest in the past and inaugurated a change in style, in the one case a change from Gothic to classic, in the other a return to Gothic.

Formerly Compton Wynyates was moated and as if set in silver at the bottom of the hollow in which it lies. It faces south-west, which was unusual: as Andrew Boorde, the much-travelled Tudor physician, said, a house should face east and west, but never south, for 'whilst the Eest wynde is temperate, fryske and fragraunt' the south wind is the bearer of pestilence. The house is turreted and gabled and tall, exotically decorated chimneys rise haphazardly above the battlemented parapet. Two half-timbered gables at either end of the entrance front have the same zigzag pattern and the same large attic oriels, but one is a diminished version of the other; the turrets crowd inconsequently to the east of the front, all of different heights. The square, forward-jutting porch, which, needless to say, is not in the centre of the façade, is flanked by illogical projections which, like the gables, are of odd sizes; the windows, though all square-headed, seem to be randomly disposed and exhibit varying numbers of both cusped and uncusped lights; and the brick fabric, which looks like cloth tightly stretched about the bulges in the walls, is sporadically enlivened with diaperwork.

37 Compton Wynyates, Warwickshire, seen from the south-east. This nostalgic, picturesque house was once uncouthly known as Compton-in-the-Hole, for the reason which the photograph makes clear.

43

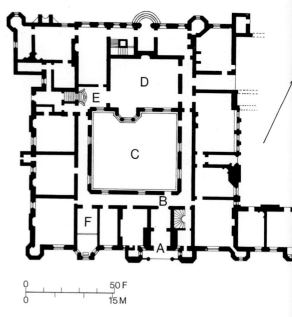

38, 39 Hengrave Hall,
Suffolk: the entrance
(above) and the plan.
A entrance hall, B corri-
dor, C court, D hall,
E main staircase, F chapel.
The house dates from
1523–38.

There could scarcely be a greater contrast to Compton Wynyates than its contemporary, Hengrave Hall in Suffolk. The general aspect of this house is of the kind 38, 39
with which we are familiar in the earlier phases of the Gothic Revival, for its gables
and pinnacles are imposed on a design of perfect regularity. Originally it was also a
design of perfect symmetry, but that symmetry was disturbed by a late eighteenth-
century alteration. The gables of the main façade were then all to have been replaced
by battlements, but the work was never finished, so now we are confronted by a
fascinating juxtaposition of styles representing the meeting-point of two move-
ments in opposite directions: the symmetry of the original left half of the front
springs from the imposition of a new vision of classical order on a Gothic tradition,
while the Gothic ornament along the top of the other half shows the revived interest
in medieval forms invading the classical convention.

The most arresting feature of this façade is the entrance, an outrageously pictur- 38
esque conceit, which in its zestful, unorthodox combination of Gothic and classical
motifs heralds the achievements of the Elizabethans and such excesses of the Gothic
Revival as Knebworth and Harlaxton. It is introduced by a flourish of piers with
pepperpot caps. A stupendous oriel swells between short octagonal turrets topped by
lanterns ornamented with traceried niches and crowned by pepperpot domes. The
oriel is trefoil-shaped on plan, corbelled out from the wall on tiers of multiform
mouldings of classical design. Below these mouldings, in the narrow space between
them and the square frame of the entrance arch, pairs of boldly modelled cherubs,
either nude or clad in Roman armour, support three heraldic shields, the middle
one displaying the arms of the Fishmongers' Company. The three tall windows
billow exuberantly above panels carved with the Royal Arms and they are crowned
by battlements and extraordinary scaly, crocketed half-domes. Slender, clustered
shafts divide the rounded forms, capped by crocketed finials and terminating below
in pendants hanging like richly wrought lanterns between the corbel mouldings.

44

The Fishmongers' arms commemorate the business and allegiance of Hengrave's builder, Sir Thomas Kytson, a typical representative of the upstart nobility. The swagger of his house is characteristic of the man himself; and his braggart gusto declares itself not only in the flamboyance of the oriel but in the actual size of the house. Compton Wynyates contains a bewildering number of rooms by comparison with the traditional manor house, but at Hengrave there were in Sir Thomas Kytson's day forty bedrooms, private dining-rooms and summer and winter parlours; and the buttery and pantry of the medieval house were expanded to embrace still-rooms, a pastry-room, laundry- and linen-rooms. The vast accommodation provided by Hengrave can be measured by the fact that in 1578 the Queen and Leicester and the entire court were housed here, when they were entertained by a spectacle 'representing the fayries'.

The great hall is two storeys high, open to the roof, and was once furnished, as in feudal times, with screen, dais and long dais window. But it is only in this feature that Hengrave's builder indulged in nostalgia for the past, for the arrangement
39 otherwise makes a notable break with bygone conventions. The hall does not, as it always hitherto had done, occupy the full width of the range: there are other rooms behind it. And the hall is not entered directly from the courtyard, but from a corridor which runs round three of its sides, a considerable gain in convenience.

The gallery above the screen at Hengrave and the room leading off it are associated with one of the greatest English madrigalists, John Wilbye. He was appointed Household Musician by Sir Thomas Kytson's son when he was nineteen, and he stayed at Hengrave until his death. An inventory of the furniture in the composer's room was made in 1602. There were two curtains of green and white at the windows, a chair covered with a green cloth, a red and blue coverlet decked the large bed, there was a cushion of tapestry, a pewter water-pot and a staff to 'beate the bed with'. This inventory reminds us that even at this late date the furniture of important houses was sparse and simple. At the time when Hengrave was building the principal
40 article of furniture was still the bed, which consisted of a heavy wooden frame laced with leather thongs or cords and fitted with stout headpieces. The mattress was of feathers. The bed was surrounded by linen hangings, white or coloured, suspended from poles on rings and pulled back during the day when the bed served as a seat. Chairs were more rare than benches and stools, tables were of the trestle type and the only other pieces of furniture were chests and cupboards.

Hengrave was built after a 'frame' or model by John Eastawe. According to the surviving contract of 1523, 'The said Jhon must macke a house at Hengrave of all manor of mason's worck, brick laying and all other things concerning ye masondrie and bricklaying, as well as the laborers concerning the same, according to a frame which the said Jhon has seen at Comby.' (This was probably the Duke of Buckingham's great new Gloucestershire mansion, Thornbury Castle.) The material of the main fabric, pallid brick, has already been described. Its colour blends with that of
38 the stone oriel, the work of John Sparke. The carver was one Davy. The accounts tell us also of Thomas Dyricke, the joiner, and of Thomas Neker from Norfolk, who ceiled and panelled a number of rooms. The workmen, some of whom came from distant places, were 'bordy'd at Thomas Shethe's for XVI d. a week'.

Among the more spectacular and romantic inventions encouraged by the use of brick perhaps the most memorable are those based on the theme of defence. The houses I am going to mention are all essentially mansions masquerading as fortified dwellings. The first, Faulkbourne Hall in Essex, began to take the place of a timber-

40 A bed at Ockwells Manor, Berkshire, though later in date, is still similar in type to early Tudor beds. It has a joined frame, with posts for the curtains which were essential when most rooms were passages to other rooms.

41 The tower of
Tattershall Castle,
Lincolnshire, photo-
graphed in 1857. In the
background is the parish
church, built by Lord
Cromwell just before he
began the castle.

framed house when Sir John Montgomery was given licence to crenellate on his
return from France in 1439. Sir John's son Thomas continued to build, spurred on
by a visit from Henry VII in 1489. Alterations and restorations made during the
nineteenth century accentuate rather than distort the picturesque aspect of this house
in the form of a brick castle. Though less symmetrical in plan than the contemporary
Herstmonceux, Faulkbourne is a controlled design by comparison with a house like
Ightham Mote, for its irregularities are intended. Its marvellous setting, in an
undulating, richly timbered park belonging to the later Picturesque movement,
enhances the picturesque aspirations of Sir Thomas Montgomery. Some of the oaks,
especially one giant, dead except for a single sparsely-leaved branch curving up
from a gaping hole, the socket of a vanished eye, span the whole interval between
the two periods and at the same time link our own age with the deer park of the
original medieval manor.

The entrance front is flanked by towers, vigorously corbelled and battlemented
and each curiously surmounted by a short crocketed spire, all of brick. They contrast
with a huge square tower on the north façade, top-heavy with machicolations and
turrets jutting from the angles. Crenellations and corbel friezes of the same striking
trefoil pattern as that of the tower adorn the bay windows of the main front. One
of these bays lights the dais end of the hall, which is here but one storey high, and
this bay is roofed with an enchanting lierne vault carried out in cut and moulded
brick.

The bay vault at Faulkbourne recalls the even more elaborate vault of an ante- 42
chamber in what was probably the first brick house to be consciously conceived in
a romantic vein – Tattershall Castle in Lincolnshire. A fortified stone house with a 41–43
curtain wall and towers once stood on the site. It had been built by Robert of Tater-

shale and was named after him. Ralph, 3rd Baron Cromwell, Treasurer of England under Henry VI, kept the name when he rebuilt the house in 1434–45. His design proved to be as wholly inspired by the idea of a castle as Belvoir, Peckforton or Castell Coch in the nineteenth century. Originally it was a huge-scale version of the tower and hall-house theme exemplified by Longthorpe (see above, p. 22), but only the tower now stands, its isolation magnifying the splendour of the image in the flat countryside. This soaring building, 110 feet and six storeys high, was planned as a spacious, luxurious mansion disguised as a fortress. Its battlements and arresting machicolations frown in a more intense manner than those of any true castle, its walls, 22 feet thick in the basement, rival those of any Norman keep for strength, and at the same time the large, arched windows piercing the walls of even the lower floors proclaim the essential frivolity of these military devices. Tattershall Castle is indeed a notable instance of architectural ostentation.

Inside the tower, on the first floor, there is a hall, grand even in its present desolation, intended for Lord Cromwell's personal use. Above it is a solar and over that are apartments for the ladies and children of the household, while additional chambers are contrived in the thickness of the walls and one corner turret of each floor contains a garderobe. The second floor of the south-west turret is lined with wattle and daub fashioned into nesting-places for hundreds of doves. Dovecotes were a common feature of the medieval and Elizabethan scene. Fynes Moryson, writing shortly after Queen Elizabeth's death, remarked that 'no kingdom in the world hath so many dove houses'. Pigeons formed a considerable item in medieval and Tudor diet. In the late fifteenth century the Fellows of King's College, Cambridge, disposed of two to three thousand pigeons a year from a huge dovecote on their Grantchester estate.

42, 43 Tattershall Castle contains a rare example of star vaulting in brick (above, left), in an ante-chamber on the third floor. The dovecote (above) was later fitted into a corner room, on the floor below.

The bricks for Tattershall Castle were supplied from a kiln on Edlington Moor about nine miles away by a brickmaker recorded as 'Baldwin Dutchman'; the building was carried out under the supervision of Lord Cromwell's agents, Thomas Croxby, John Southell and John Combe, but the designer is unknown. The choice of material was doubtless suggested by the examples of its use Lord Cromwell had seen during his long service in France during the greater part of the reign of Henry V. The bricks are of a very deep red and measure about 8 × 4 × 2 inches. The magnificent use to which they have been put is apparent not only externally but in the delicate and intricate detail of the interior, in the vault to which reference has already 42 been made, a rare example of the stellar pattern in brick (quadripartite vaulting with intermediate and lierne ribs producing a star design), with the added refinement of quatrefoil tracery fashioned in cut and moulded brick between the ribs. The four sumptuous, sculptured fireplaces are of stone and consist of moulded, four-centred arches surmounted by elaborate friezes of traceried panels or roundels containing heraldic shields, crowned by a moulded cornice with a crenellated top. An emblem, a purse with the arrogant motto *N'ay je droit*, confronts the visitor everywhere in the deserted, echoing rooms, vividly recalling the formidable personality and the office of the owner.

A less overweening expression of individual pride and power, a more romantic allusion to the past than Faulkbourne Hall, Oxburgh Hall in Norfolk translates the III theme of the moated, quadrangular castle into weathered red-brick domesticity with conspicuous success. It is unforgettable because of the contrast in scale between the symmetrical south ranges and the immense, dominating and co-ordinating gatehouse, seven storeys high, and also because towers, battlements, stepped gables, oriels and crenellated chimneys, starting up like carefully positioned castles in a game of chess, rise so directly from the moat upon which the house seems to lie like a galleon becalmed. Like Faulkbourne, Oxburgh owes an intensification of its picturesque aspect to nineteenth-century restoration. The oriels, the dormer 44 windows and the pantiles were all added, with a fine sense of harmony, from about 1835 onwards by Sir Henry Richard Bedingfield, the descendant of Sir Edward Bedingfield, for whom the house was built in 1482.

The house is no longer a complete quadrangle, for the hall range, facing the gatehouse, was pulled down in the eighteenth century. But it is the gatehouse which above all distinguishes Oxburgh. Designed at a time when defence had long ceased to be a necessity, it caricatures that bygone necessity with its enormous proportions and turns military motifs into charming decoration. The machicolation below the ornamental battlements of the turret parapets and above the arch connecting these flanking turrets is no more than a brick frieze of pretty cusped arches, and this theme recurs between each of the seven storeys of the turrets, dividing them into seven tiers. The structure is utterly different from the modest oblong block which comprised the typical medieval gatehouse, such as that at Markenfield or that at Northborough: it is one of the earliest instances of the gatehouse as a showpiece, as the favourite vehicle for the romantic and pompous display which marks the emergence of the country seat as a work of art.

The most stupendous and ostentatious of all such gatehouses is the vast, towered 45 entrance of Layer Marney in Essex, dating from about 1520. It was intended to introduce a courtyard house of equal magnificence, but its builder, Henry, Lord Marney, a staunch supporter of Henry VII and Treasurer to Henry VIII, was dead when the house was only just begun, and his son John died two years later in 1525.

With him the family, established at Layer Marney since the twelfth century, became extinct. The black marble effigies of father and son, the one beak-nosed and lean, the other round-cheeked and large-eyed, lie in the neighbouring church which was rebuilt in brick by Lord Marney as part of the grand, pictorial, irregular group of which the gatehouse was intended to be the dominant feature. Both figures are shaded by astonishing balustered terracotta canopies, that above Lord Henry decorated along the top by huge, shell-shaped battlements, reminiscent of those forming part of the frieze of the church of San Pietro at Modena, but much bigger and supporting dolphin-flanked urns. Similar motifs embellish the gatehouse, where the same craftsman, either an Italian trying to conform to English conventions or an Italian-inspired Englishman, was no doubt at work. For Layer Marney Towers is carried out in brick and terracotta, that finer counterpart of brick introduced into this country by Italians who came here in the service of Cardinal Wolsey and Henry VIII and adorned the great new quadrangle of Hampton Court with terra-cotta busts of Roman emperors which are entirely Renaissance in feeling. The material was unknown in England in the Middle Ages, and is hardly ever found again after the Dissolution until the Lombard Early Renaissance style made its incongruous appearance in Victorian London.

45 The gatehouse is eight storeys high and differs from all other gatehouses of its period in the absolute symmetry of the design in every detail; in the great size and number of its windows, of which there are so many that there is as much glass as wall; and in the striking sophistication of the composition. It is set on a terrace at the top of a flight of steps which diminish in width as they rise and thus exaggerate the dizzy height of the towers or turrets flanking the entrance arch. The dizziness of that height is made to seem yet more preposterous by another outer pair of turrets which are one storey shorter than the main turrets, showing seven instead of eight tiers of arched windows. The effect from the foot of the steps is as if the whole structure were leaning backwards.

44 Above, left: the picturesque character of Oxburgh Hall, Norfolk, was enhanced by the restoration carried out in the early nineteenth century, which produced this great south-east tower, the oriels, dormers and ornate chimneys.

45 Above: the gatehouse of Layer Marney, Essex.

49

46 The entrance front of East Barsham Manor, Norfolk, of the 1520s. The gatehouse, on the left, is echoed by the porch of the house beyond it.

III Opposite, above: though the moat and gatehouse of Oxburgh Hall, Norfolk, look defensive, to their builder in 1482 they alluded romantically to the past, and advertised his own importance.

IV Opposite, below: the entrance front of Great Chalfield Manor, Wiltshire, built about 1470; an archaic composition including a novel oriel window (see pp. 35–6).

Below their crowns of terracotta, shell-shaped battlements and dolphins the turrets are adorned by friezes of trefoiled arches. Three bands of terracotta ornament, again trefoils, enliven each turret; terracotta also forms the material of the unique mullions and transoms of the great five-light windows between the flanking turrets, and of the windows in the range to the left of the gatehouse. From a distance the pale, biscuit-coloured terracotta, which stands out distinctly yet softly against the fiery brick of the main fabric, frames the leaded lights in what appear to be the customary cusped arches of the Early Tudor period, set in the usual square frame. But seen at close quarters the cusps reveal themselves to be strangely and ingeniously formed out of classical scrolls; while the mullions and transoms are thickly covered with Italian Renaissance ornament creating an effect much like that of the decoration of the door jambs of the church of the Corpus Domini at Bologna. An artist trained in the classical tradition is here cleverly counterfeiting Gothic. The work has been ascribed to Girolamo Trevizi or Trevisano, who had been appointed Court Architect by Henry VIII, but there is no proof of this. Whoever the artist the conceit is typical of the whole fantastic spirit of the gatehouse.

Terracotta and moulded brick achieve a very different effect at East Barsham 46 Manor in Norfolk, for here Italian terracotta has been used without a trace of Italian influence in the choice of motif. The house is built in a hollow: the Little Walsingham road runs above it and from there it is an amazing sight. No eighteenth-century folly creates so exotic an impact as East Barsham's clusters of gigantic chimney-shafts and many pinnacles, every one of them encrusted with ornament. The terracotta-work, which is of the same rose-red as the whole fabric and not at first

sight to be distinguished from the carved and moulded brick decoration, is the unifying element of the design. It takes the form of two broad friezes of shields, tracery and heads running below the battlemented parapet and above the ground floor of the long façade, forming a rich, continuous, patterned background to pinnacled buttresses, the irregularly disposed porch and the pinnacled hall bay, which is taller than the gatehouse.

The East Barsham gatehouse is only two storeys high but instantly catches the eye. The entrance arch is flanked by buttresses rather than turrets, surmounted by bedizened pinnacles with domed caps shooting up like the minarets of some Persian or Turkish mosque. Like the ogee and four-centred arches they have a pronounced Oriental flavour and foreshadow the Oriental phase of eighteenth-century Picturesque architecture. The ornament consists of shields, arcading, reticulation, zigzags, lozenges, roses and fleur-de-lis. The groups of chimney-shafts are as profusely adorned with similar motifs. They are superb examples of one of the most striking of Tudor brick conceits, for tall, extravagant chimneys, startling and brilliantly original aerial versions of the components of the column – base, shaft and capital – still dominate many lesser houses all over the country and still advertise the owner's proud possession of a wall fireplace.

The brickmaker's skill is yet further demonstrated at East Barsham by large panels in relief, one above the entrance to the gatehouse and one over the porch which confront each other with variations on the theme of flanking polygonal buttresses and showy pinnacles. Both panels display the Royal Arms, supported above the porch by the griffin and the greyhound and on the gatehouse by the griffin and the lion. They were carved *in situ*. The change in the royal device took place in 1527, so the house itself must have been completed before then. It was built for Sir Henry Fermor.

If the terracotta-work at East Barsham gives coherence to a rather loose composition, at Sutton Place in Surrey, a more famous house, it animates a severely symmetrical plan with delightful caprice. The building, built in the 1520s and thus contemporary with Layer Marney Towers, testifies to as great a concern with form, though here the emphasis is not on verticality but its reverse: Sutton Place already looks forward to the classical, horizontal mode of a hundred years later. It was once a quadrangular house, but the fourth side was destroyed in the eighteenth century. What remains is a balanced, two-storeyed design of three ranges. The surprising thing about Sutton Place is that the symmetry of the hall range is not achieved, as it is at Great Chalfield, by balancing the entrance with another similar structure, but by setting it boldly in the middle of the façade. At either end of this front there project matching, two-storeyed bays, but whereas one lights the hall, the other serves no practical purpose, and is introduced solely in the interests of the composition. The windows, though they are fitted with traditional cusped lights, are all very large and of identical height. The terracotta-work, which is of a pale creamy colour tinged with rose, starkly sets Gothic beside Renaissance motifs with no attempt at synthesis. The parapet shows quatrefoils, cusped arches and lozenge-shapes, but the entrance bay, which rises above the parapet, confronts the spectator with twenty panels, below huge battlements, robustly modelled with amorini more fully Italianate than anything to be seen at Hengrave or Layer Marney. They closely resemble the winged amorini of the frieze in the small cloister of the Certosa di Pavia in Italy. The effect of these purely classical images in improbable conjunction with cusped lights, pepperpot pinnacles and latticed panes is wonderfully exhilarating. Twelve more

47 A detail of the terracotta work at Sutton Place, Surrey. The initials are those of the owner, Richard Weston, who began building the house about 1523, and the tun is his rebus.

v Opposite, above: the entrance front of Penshurst Place, Kent, showing the high-roofed medieval hall and later Elizabethan buildings (see ill. 26 and p. 64).

vi Opposite, below: the courtyard of Kirby Hall, Northamptonshire (see pp. 76–7).

53

49

48, 49 Sutton Place, Surrey: the remarkably symmetrical north front of the hall range (top), and a detail of the terracotta amorini above the entrance door.

such amorini in two rows of panels entertain us from above the entrance and six mark the head of the back doorway of the hall.

This chapter has been principally concerned with the architectural development of the country gentleman's seat, but there were developments in other directions. The increasing patronage of music by the gentry has been touched upon. In addition to their interest in music and encouraged by the example of Henry VIII's court, the gentlemen of England acquired a taste for scholarship and found a new delight in poetry, masques and pageantry, by all of which their lives in their rural homes became enriched.

The cult of the garden also came to the fore for the first time during the Early Tudor period. No great house was now regarded as complete without its garden, which comprised far more than the medieval fruit and herb garden and vineyard. In an age when nature, still unconquered, was regarded as an inimical and fearful power, the garden was inevitably conceived as the antithesis of the untamed natural landscape. It was absolutely formal and artificial. Wolsey's garden at Hampton Court was enclosed and rigidly geometrical in its layout, patterned by clipped box and criss-crossed by straight alleys lined with fruit trees. No flowers but roses are mentioned. Henry VIII introduced symmetrical flower-beds encompassed by green and white palings. He also made the Hampton Court garden more fantastical. He built a 'Mount' on a foundation of brick and rubble and set a pavilion on it and he crammed the whole garden with stone-carved statues of heraldic beasts. Mounts, pavilions and statues all became fashionable, though the statues in lesser gardens were carved in wood.

By the time of the Dissolution of the Monasteries a great secular art had been born. The long predominance of Gothic and ecclesiastical architecture and the habit of mind which had produced it had come to an end. The country house and its setting, fashioned as a conscious work of art to celebrate the pleasures of living, was established as one of the most important influences in the fabric of English society.

3 THE UNIQUE SYNTHESIS

the age of Elizabeth and James I

'IT IS FULL OF IRON MINES, all over it; for the casting of which there are furnaces up and down the country, and abundance of wood is yearly spent; many streams are drawn into one channel, and a great deal of meadow ground turned into ponds and pools for the driving of mills by the flashes, which, beating with hammers upon iron, fill the neighbourhood round about it, night and day, with continual noise.' William Camden the antiquary is describing Sussex in 1585. It was one of many new industrial landscapes in an age which R.H. Tawney, the social historian of the sixteenth century, regarded as a watershed whence the momentum of a downward trend has steadily increased. The change from a religious to a secular attitude, the movement of men's minds away from the absolute and the eternal towards the particular and the ephemeral, the Baconian philosophy which encouraged a mechanical explanation of the universe, all urged the development of science, industry and materialism which has brought us to our present perplexed and endangered standpoint.

At the time the eventual results of these trends, expressive as they were of the splendid vitality, the courage, enterprise and endurance of the Elizabethans, were unimagined. For what strikes us most forcibly about the period is the way in which every tendency in that ferment of creativity and discovery was balanced by its opposite. Wherever we look we come upon a remarkable synthesis. The reasoned, practical endeavours of the first scientists and of overseas adventurers were offset by unrivalled works of imagination. The memorable fact about Elizabethan and Jacobean England in the eyes of the world is that it produced the plays of Shakespeare. It was also the age of Spenser, Ben Jonson, Marlowe and Webster, Nashe and Donne, of the musicians Tallis, John Bull, Dowland and Byrd, and of a school of portraiture that reflected the new self-awareness and pride of the sitters.

Logic was confronted by magic and mystery: the world of natural causes might at any moment be invaded by King Oberon and his invisible army of fairies. It is characteristic of the factual writings of antiquaries such as Leland, Camden, Lambarde and Eardiswicke that the historicity of King Arthur is never questioned, that King Lud is hailed as the founder of London, that Britons are said to have descended from Gomer, one of the sons of Japhet, and that their realm of Britain is asserted to have been founded by Brut the Trojan. It is just as characteristic that Saxon's *Atlas* should be a work of beauty and fantasy as well as of outstanding clarity and detailed information, that it should show ships consorting with sea-monsters in the Irish Channel, and Neptune with his trident embracing a mermaid.

Nor is it surprising to find a new and serious preoccupation with the historical past accompanied by a make-believe revival of the past in the social life of the present. Many noblemen, among them Lords Arundel, Herbert and Cumberland, and Sir Anthony Mildmay, sat for their portraits in full armour, ready for tilting. For the tournament and the pageant of chivalry were among the most colourful and popular diversions of the later sixteenth and early seventeenth centuries. On every Accession Day anniversary, the Queen's knights expressed their loyalty by jousting before her, the combatants assuming Arthurian pseudonyms and appearing as 51 the Knight of the Tree or the Sun, the Frozen Knight, the Red, the Green or the Black Knight. In the Accession Day tournament of 1590 the Earl of Essex wore black armour with a black plume, sat in a chariot drawn by black horses and was followed by a black-clad retinue – an elaborate pageant designed to beg the Queen's forgiveness for his marriage to the widow of Sir Philip Sidney.

The secular bias of the age is undeniable. It is perhaps most forcefully expressed in the ostentatious tombs of the period, proclaiming the importance and wealth of the departed in the very jaws of death. Instead of inviting a prayer for the soul of the inmate, the inscriptions on these tombs ask the spectator to remember the deceased and to be impressed by a recital of his ancestry and his personal achievements. The effigies scorn the look of death: they lie under canopies supported by bulbous posts, for all the world as if they were stretched on their own beds, they lean on their elbows or they kneel in their finest array, their eyes, cheeks, lips and hair painted to counterfeit the hue and freshness of life. Many a village church is dominated by the overweening presence of Elizabethans. At Snarford in Lincolnshire the de Pols so crowd the interior that they distract attention even from the altar, an eloquent testimony of the change which had transformed both Church and society. Even the discreet and sober William Cecil, Lord Burghley, the builder of Burghley House (see pp. 81–2), announces his worldly importance from a marble six-poster in 50 St Martin's at Stamford, in Lincolnshire, where he lies in state dress clasping his staff of office.

50 The sumptuous effigy of William Cecil, Lord Burghley, Queen Elizabeth's confidant and adviser, who died in 1598 and is buried in St Martin's, Stamford.

Yet the affirmation of the importance of the individual, the extrovert delight in the glitter and symbols of that importance, the zest and exhibitionism, the worldliness, were united to an acute, poignant awareness of the brevity of life. A skeleton grins beneath Robert Cecil's lifelike effigy surrounded by figures of the Virtues at Hatfield. Elizabethan poetry and the falling cadences of Elizabethan music are haunted by the sense of the transitoriness of all earthly joy and success.

This awareness of mortality was anything but spiritual, however, and the Church of England which resulted from the Act of Supremacy in 1559, steering a middle, synthesizing course between Catholicism and Puritanism, inspired no enthusiasm for church-building. Domestic architecture, on the other hand, flourished as never before: to the Elizabethans architecture meant neither churches nor public buildings but houses. And though industry had already made its impression on the landscape, that landscape was transfigured by an extraordinary outburst of domestic building of surpassing harmony and by the appearance of great houses of arresting individuality and dynamic beauty which, despite grievous losses, still stand in such numbers as to form an uplifting and consoling part of England's eroding environment. At the same time the building of these houses was accompanied by disquieting elements. Recent studies of sixteenth-century masons have shown that there were

51 George Clifford, 3rd Earl of Cumberland, was Queen's Champion from 1590 and headed the challengers at the Accession Day Tilts. Nicholas Hilliard depicts him wearing an elaborate allegorical costume with the Queen's glove pinned to his bonnet.

57

revolutionary changes in the building trade: high-pressure work with much over-time became normal for the first time in England, owing not so much to the great number of ambitious new buildings as to the impatience of the owners to have them finished. It was now too that the word 'architect', as applied to a specific person, made its appearance in the English language. It occurs on the title-page of a book by John Shute of 1563, the only work in English on architecture to be published during Elizabeth's reign. The term is used again in the church register of deaths at Blickling, in Norfolk, where Robert Lyminge, dying in 1628, is described as 'the architect and builder of Blickling Hall' (see pp. 104–6); and Robert Smythson had also been called 'Architector' on his tombstone in 1614. This marked the beginning of the divorce between the architect and the craftsman, and the emergence of the system whereby the designs and specifications for a building are made not in carpenters' shops and masons' yards but in drawing-offices far removed from the materials to be used and from the men who shape and joint them, though the full, disastrous effects of the rupture did not make themselves felt until the nineteenth and twentieth centuries. 103

The uses to which the Elizabethans put the discredited and despoiled monasteries are as illuminating as the wealth of their new building. Monastic lands were purchased by country gentlemen of immensely increased power and riches. Huge quantities of dressed and rough stone from the disestablished religious houses formed the fabric of magnificent mansions either in the immediate neighbourhood of the ruins or within easy reach of them. Some large and noble convents, among them Vale Royal Abbey, Cheshire, entirely disappeared. Even more typical of the altered focus of men's thoughts, of the desire for profit in this world rather than the next, was the appropriation of monastic buildings for industrial purposes. Having acquired the priory of Robertsbridge, in Sussex, Sir William Sidney (who at the same time obtained the lease of Penshurst Place from Edward VI) set up an iron-mining business within the walls; he built a forge in the former gatehouse and steel forges in the monks' brewhouse, while the miners were housed in the abbot's lodging. Sir William's contemptuous indifference to the former character and significance of his property is highlit by the use to which he put the priory psalters: he dismembered them to make covers for his accounts- and forge-books.

It is surprising how many of the great Elizabethans sprang not from the aristocracy but from the ranks of landed proprietors. Camden, Eardiswicke, Lambarde, Sir Walter Raleigh and Carew were of their number, and many of them, among them the Cecils and the Sidneys, either built or were associated with the houses shortly to be described. Some of these men came of families long established as gentry. This was the case with Sir Philip Sidney, Spenser, Bacon, Hakluyt, Raleigh, Sir William Sheldon and the maritime explorer, Sir Humphrey Gilbert, who went out from his ancestral home, Compton Castle in south Devon, to take possession of Newfoundland in the name of the Queen. With the typical versatility of his age, Sir Humphrey was also the author of the *Discourse on the North West Passage to Cathay*, and put forward an ambitious, idealistic scheme for a London academy for the education of the sons of the nobility and gentry.

Other leading spirits of the age were recruited into this landed class from the ranks of merchants and yeomen, soldiers or sailors. Sir Francis Drake was of this company, and if Lord Burghley was the son of a knight, his grandfather was but an inconspicuous man-at-arms in the reign of Henry VIII who changed his name from the original Welsh Sityllt to Cecil, to suggest an association with the great Roman 50, 73 family of the Caecilii. The spectacular rise of the Cecils is an indication of the social aspirations of the families who had been exalted in the stead of the feudal nobles – families who included the Russells, the Cavendishes, the Seymours, the Dudleys and the Herberts.

The mobility of society which was already noticeable in medieval England was immensely accelerated during the sixteenth century, stimulated both by the distribution of the monastic estates and by the vitality of commerce and the new industries. Sir William Petre, for example, the younger son of a yeoman from Torbryan in Cornwall, built up a huge estate out of Church property, became Secretary of State to Henry VIII, Edward VI and Mary, and was a Privy Councillor under Elizabeth I. He left his native county and settled at Ingatestone in Essex, on a manor which he had acquired from the nunnery of St Mary's, Barking. The Roberts of Truro, again, were (according to a Royalist diarist, Richard Symonds) originally villeins who made a considerable fortune in tin-mining. They bought a chapel and tithe barn on land which had belonged to the priory of Bodmin. Richard Roberts, son of the purchaser, changed his name to Robartes when he was knighted in 1616, and five years later paid Buckingham £10,000 for a peerage. He built the grandest
113 Cornish mansion, Lanhydrock, on the site of the abbey tithe barn.

The inscriptions on the monuments of many Elizabethan and Jacobean squires record their origins as 'Citizen and Mercer' or 'Citizen and Haberdasher' of London or some other town. It is striking also what a large proportion of the 'new men' who purchased land, built fine houses and founded county families were successful lawyers, who had benefited from the inevitably litigious consequences of the
1, 72 Dissolution. Montacute in Somerset, Barlborough in Derbyshire, Prideaux Place in Cornwall and Ingatestone Hall in Essex are but four of the lovely houses paid for by money made in the Courts of Law.

With a background of social fluidity it was only natural that the gentry should be prone to harp on their gentility. We have already encountered changes of name made in the interests of greater gentility. It is not difficult to augment the list: Thomas Writhe, on being appointed Garter King of Arms, decided that Wriothesley (pronounced Risley) would be a more aristocratic and impressive name than his
77 own; and the builder of Wollaton, though far from being a *nouveau riche* – his family had been gentry since the thirteenth century – was nevertheless born with the patronymic of Bugge, which, with the unashamed snobbery of his age, he exchanged for the nobler name of Willoughby. Another expression of this ridiculous but high-spirited snobbery was the fanatical preoccupation of the gentry with heraldry and pedigree. The College of Arms was inundated with applications for heraldic devices; even Shakespeare was not above applying for a coat of arms. There was naturally much illegal traffic in pedigrees and devices, and it is amusing to find the Garter King of Arms, Sir Gilbert Dethick, who followed Wriothesley, constructing an illustrious descent for himself as having sprung from the Dethicks of Dethick Hall in Derbyshire, when in fact his origins were Dutch and obscure.

The houses built by the rising and shifting class of Elizabethan landowners are among the most exciting and important of their rich contributions to their own and future generations. The character of these buildings, their originality, their extravagant ostentation and ebullience, their backward glance at tradition in conjunction with astonishing innovations, their conjoining of the practical and the fantastic, their resolution of conflicting elements into a synthesis of unique harmony, bodies forth all the trends and the temper of the society of which they were part.

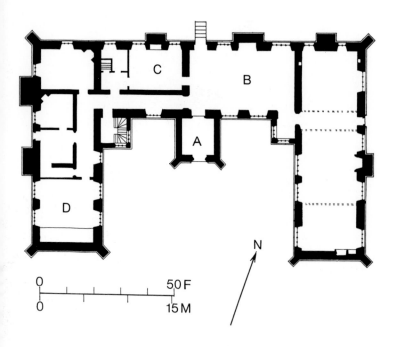

52, 53 Barrington Court, Somerset: the entrance front (above, right), and the plan, which is, like the entrance front, almost perfectly symmetrical. A entrance porch, B hall, C buttery, D kitchen.

A house completed as early as 1514 already points to this remarkable architectural synthesis. For at Barrington Court in Somerset, traditional motifs are elaborated 52, 5 and controlled by a grasp of classical symmetry in a more richly satisfying and stimulating way than in any of the houses considered in the previous chapter. The house was built for Lord Daubeney, Henry VII's Chamberlain, who had played a notable part as a commander of the royal forces in the rebellions of 1497, and completed in the year of his marriage. The old plan of a principal block with cross-wings has evolved into a varied, unified composition of which the central feature is the three-storeyed, gabled porch standing out between two gabled bays to give the house the E-shape which was to become the most popular domestic plan later in the century. In the angles between the main block and the wings gabled staircase projections advance rather less boldly than the porch, caught up in the great forward rush of the wings with their broad gable-ends. So the whole house moves to an advancing and retreating measure. But it also has an upward movement, through its twisting chimneys and the finals that spiral up like miniature Baroque columns from the apex of every gable and from the tops of the buttresses that flank them. The word 'Baroque' has been used deliberately: the Reformation in England and the later Counter-Reformation in Italy were each productive of a dynamic architecture of movement, the one secular, the other religious, the one stately and predominantly angular, the other frenzied and swirling, yet each a fusion of the soaring Gothic and the orthogonal classic.

53 At Barrington Court the only hint of classical influence is in the symmetry of the design. When classical themes are introduced into sixteenth-century houses they are so transformed by intensity of imagination that it is only possible to speak of stimulus, not of influence. Invention was not hampered by the principles and disciplines of the classical orders and foreign, classicizing ideas provided material not to be copied, but to be absorbed into the hybrid fabric of some of the most exotic, most daring buildings in the history of Western architecture. This development and the postponement of the day when the orders would triumph in this northern land were aided by the fact that with the break with Rome England was cut off from direct contact with Italy, the fountain-head of the Renaissance. French and Netherlandish versions of classical proportions and ornament were known from handbooks, the forerunners of the pattern-books of the Georgian period. They included books by the Fleming Vredeman de Vries, especially his *Variae Architecturae Formae* of 1563, in which classical forms are shown bedizened with strapwork and curious ornament. The craftsman-architect John Thorpe shows in the collection of designs and surveys he left behind him that he knew the work of the French sixteenth-century architect Du Cerceau, *Les plus excellents bastiments de France*. Copies of Serlio's *Architettura* provided inspiration for chimney-pieces and ornaments, though there is little direct connection between Serlio's work and English practice before the seven volumes of the *Architettura* were published in translation by Robert Peake in 1611.

The hold of the past on the imagination of sixteenth-century Englishmen has already been noted. Architecturally this preoccupation with the past is not only manifest in certain features of new houses but in the ways in which existing houses of earlier date, dismantled abbeys and abandoned castles were adapted and altered. Conversion was almost as great a passion of the age as the designing of new houses. Sir William Sharington's work at the Augustinian abbey of Lacock is an outstanding instance of the sixteenth-century conversion of a major medieval building. He bought the property for £750 in 1540, at the same time appropriating the north-east chapel in the parish church, where his fine monument, a richly decorated tomb-chest, instantly catches the eye. His character showed the disquieting duality of that of so many men of his century. His undeniable feeling for architecture was allied to a deplorable lack of scruple. Sir William was Vice-Treasurer of the Bristol Mint and he took advantage of his office to finance his activities at Lacock from the State coinage. He was found out and deprived of his property in 1549. His wife managed to obtain his release and buy back the estate in the following year and work at Lacock was immediately resumed.

Like several of his contemporaries and like some remarkable landowners of succeeding ages Sir William was himself responsible for the plan and the picturesque aspect of the converted abbey. He kept the entire cloister of the medieval structure with its lierne vault and lively bosses, and the chapter-house and warming-room, but above the east range he introduced a gallery with Italianate pilasters. He skilfully harmonized the fifteenth-century gatehouse with an outer courtyard built of stone but with half-timbered dormers and a pretty half-timbered clock turret and cupola, and concentrated his interest in classical form on the south front of his house.

If Barrington Court prefigures the great Elizabethan developments of traditional

54, 5

55

54

design, this Lacock façade for the first time stresses the classical element which was an inseparable part of those developments. The proportions of the design and the prominent balustraded parapet masking the roofline – an essentially classical convention – are completely novel and untraditional. The oriels are Gothic Revival additions by the later owner of the abbey, Fox Talbot, the pioneer photographer, and must be discounted in any estimate of Sharington's conception. The sharp discord between this balustraded, horizontal front and the medieval survivals at 54 Lacock is beautifully resolved by the corner tower. This is polygonal, with a Renaissance parapet, and the fenestration of the top room is absolutely regular. Yet the stair turret is crowned by a pepperpot dome and below the parapet beast heads snarl and grimace like medieval gargoyles. Inside the tower in the two top rooms and contemporary with them are two extraordinary stone tables as revealing of Sharington's interests as the building itself. They are polygonal like the tower. One is supported by fauns carrying buckets of fruit, the other by four terms and four niches enclosing allegorical figures. But the Gothic past is not forgotten: the Renaissance-derived niches are provided with rib-vaults. The tower was built to command a view and it also performed the essential service of drawing attention to Sharington's mansion.

In the case of existing houses, as distinct from monastic establishments, Elizabethan alterations and modifications almost without exception exaggerate and glamorize the character of the building as well as transforming it by the introduction of classical themes. Shortly after 1580 the rambling aspect of Haddon Hall, which strikes us as 6, 87 so essentially medieval, was intensified by the addition of a long gallery, oriels and castellated bays and by the glorious terraced garden, which calls attention to the sloping nature of the site.

54, 55 Opposite: Lacock Abbey, Wiltshire. The house seen from the south-east, with Sharington's polygonal tower in the centre, and the medieval cloister.

56 Above: the south front of Haddon Hall, Derbyshire, showing Sir John Manners' Elizabethan long gallery and terraced garden. At the right is Peveril of the Peak's twelfth-century tower; at the far left is the chapel, which forms the junction between the south and west fronts of the house (compare ill. 19).

63

57 The long gallery of Penshurst Place, Kent, is part of the wing added to the house in 1574–5. The finely ribbed ceiling showing quatrefoils and square shapes breaking into leaf is typical in its freshness of this first great period of the plasterer's art.

At both Knole and Penshurst Elizabethan work is so woven into the earlier fabric that the dominant sensation in both these famous Kent houses is of an enriched, deepened medievalism which embraces and sustains all diversities of actual style as well as century-long accumulations of rare possessions – though here the spell is made more potent by three or four hundred years of unbroken ownership. The pensive faces of generations of auburn-haired Sidneys looking down from the walls of the gallery at Penshurst accentuate the sad, nostalgic harmonies of the place, 57 while the portraits of the Sackvilles in the Brown Gallery at Knole, all in oval, identical frames hung opposite a panelled wall pierced by very small windows, make, in conjunction with the lozenge-patterned ceiling, a sophisticated, amusing composition which is like an abstract of the assemblage of quadrangles and the intricate maze of rooms and galleries which bewilder the visitor to this great house. Knole's architectural flavour is chiefly due to Sir Thomas Sackville to whom Queen Elizabeth had granted the lease in 1566, though he did not gain possession for more than thirty years. He then invested the medieval structure, formerly the residence of Thomas Bourchier, Archbishop of Canterbury, with irresistible fantasy by adorning it with obelisks, heraldic beasts, shaped gables and mullioned windows.

The additions made to Penshurst by Henry and Robert Sidney (son and grandson v of the owner of the iron-mine at Robertsbridge) are similarly responsible to a considerable extent for the present picturesque aspect of the house. Sir Henry Sidney added the whole of the range of buildings on the west side as well as the entrance front to the courtyard with its gatehouse, all of which is battlemented and intensifies the character of Pulteney's great hall. Sir Robert built the long gallery 57 with pronounced dependence on medieval idiom, despite the fact that the shape of the room was dictated by fashion. The Sidneys retained the internal arrangements of the medieval hall at Penshurst unchanged.

26

58   At Knole, Sir Thomas Sackville remodelled Bourchier's hall by introducing a flat ceiling with a gallery above it, but he preserved the traditional plan by furnishing the apartment with an exuberant screen, profusely carved with rollicking terms, strapwork and heraldic devices and surmounted by prancing Sackville leopards whose curling tails merge with the flurry of leafy loops and scrolls beside them. Knole was always a grand house: for a short time, when Cranmer handed it over to Henry VIII, it even became a royal palace.

  It was not only great historic mansions which inspired genial conversion in the sixteenth century. Little Moreton Hall, in Cheshire, is an instance of the enlargement and alteration of a modest manor house built in materials once commonly used for all but the finest houses in every district where wood was available – timber framing with a filling of wattle and daub. Early timber-framed houses show few local variations: it was in the Elizabethan period, in response to a new sense of the possibilities of varying materials and with a conscious striving for effect, that marked regional styles developed. Little Moreton Hall is the most spectacular example of the so-called black-and-white manner of the West Midlands, in which the timber frame is divided into small square or rectangular panels patterned with diagonals,

58 The hall at Knole, Kent, a room of the 1460s remodelled in about 1605.

65

59 The fantastic bay
windows at Little
Moreton Hall, Cheshire,
added in 1559.

stripes, quatrefoils and cusped lozenges all aggressively black against a background
of blindingly white plaster. It is not entirely fanciful to see these walls as arrangements of playing-cards, spades and clubs, for the images on the court cards of our
packs originated in the sixteenth century.

The original Little Moreton was a moated hall house; about 1559 William
Moreton added grotesque hexagonal bays, an east range and an elaborately deco- 59, (
rated gatehouse to his grandfather's house. Each facet of these bays is crowned by a
steep little gable and the upper storey of each overhangs so that the swelling forms
jostle each other and nearly fill the tiny courtyard. The windows, beneath the zigzags of the gables, are shaded by wavy pelmets of wood painted black and outlined
in white and inscribed in staring white lettering: GOD IS AL IN AL THING THIS WINDOVS
WHIRE MADE BY WILLIAM MORETON IN THE YEARE OF OURE LORDE MDLIX. Under the
bulging upper half of the parlour bay adjoining the hall, white on black we read:
RYCHARDE DALE CARPENTER MADE THIES WINDOVS BY THE GRAC OF GOD. Not only
is every inch of the timber-work embellished with painted and carved designs,
including a Renaissance acanthus motif along the bressummers, but the leaded lights
of all the windows are of the most intricate geometric and floral patterns. In the
gatehouse nearly every opening shows a different wiry, angular device. The
immense variety in lead glazing in Elizabethan houses is a minor symptom of the
astounding fertility of invention of the age. By 1589 there were fifteen glass-works
in England and a book published in the reign of James I, entitled *A Booke of Sundry
Draughtes, Principally serving for Glasiers*, contains over one hundred designs for
leaded lights.

60   The gatehouse of Little Moreton Hall is the most extraordinary feature of the whole house. Familiarity never dims the excitement aroused by this startling image and its reflected counterpart. It must already have been a remarkable sight in William Moreton's day, jettied and covered with zigzags, lozenge-shapes and ball-ended crosses, but when his son added another storey in about 1580 to make room for a fashionable long gallery, the soaring, top-heavy, glittering black and white structure entered the realm of the fabulous. It abounds in the illimitable vitality of the period; it exaggerates and exalts the typical and humble medieval timber-framed dwelling, making of it a bizarre, unforgettable phenomenon.

60 The gatehouse of Little Moreton Hall. On the top floor is the continuously-glazed long gallery (ill. 62).

THE · SPEARE · OF · DESTINYE ·

WHOSE · RVLER · IS · KNOWLEDGE ·

61, 62 Opposite and above: the long gallery at Little Moreton Hall.

The interior of the gallery also evokes a vision of a transmogrified Middle Ages. 62 The timber roof is a variant of that already seen in the hall at Lytes Cary, a combination of the arch-braced and collar-beam types with tiers of cusped wind-braces. 20 But this Gothic theme is strangely diversified by the great length and narrowness of the apartment, by the continuous range of windows along the walls and by the sense of being tremendously high up, of hovering airily above the moat, the house and the landscape. And the gable-ends of the long, long room are plastered and ornamented with coloured reliefs and mottoes which are redolent of the atmosphere of the sixteenth century. A Botticelli-like figure precariously balanced on a globe beneath a wheel between two lettered panels proclaiming THE WHEELE OF FORTVNE WHOSE RVLE IS IGNORAVNCE faces a similar figure at the other end of the room holding up an armillary sphere and clasping a pair of dividers amid coils of naturalistic foliage, accompanied by the legend: THE SP[H]EARE OF DESTINYE WHOSE RVLER 61 IS KNOWLEDGE. It is almost a translation of Bacon's apothegm *nam ipsa scientia potestas est* – knowledge itself is power – and might stand as the watchword of intellectual history in Elizabethan England. The faith it expresses is that of Marlowe's Faustus:

> Oh what a world of profit and delight,
> Of power, of honour and omnipotence
> Is promised to the studious artisan!
> All things that move between the quiet poles
> Shall be at my command; emperors and kings
> Are but obeyed in their several provinces,
> Nor can they raise the wind or rend the clouds;
> But his dominion that exceeds in this
> Stretcheth as far as doth the mind of man.

68

The conversion and restoration by Elizabethans of some of the medieval castles which, either whole or in ruin, were common sights of their countryside, displays the same enthusiasm for the past and the same brilliantly fantastic play upon medieval features in combination with new invention as their adaptations of abbeys and old houses. That grandest of castle ruins, Kenilworth, owes its poetry more to Elizabethan allusions to its medieval origins than to any of its actual extensive medieval remains. Elizabeth I gave the castle to Robert Dudley in 1563, the year before he became Earl of Leicester, and it was he who converted the Gothic apartments and enhanced the pictorial effect of the buildings by the addition of a gatehouse, a cliff-like new wing and a courtyard to introduce the keep. The general impression of these additions is medieval, but a closer look reveals a liberal sprinkling of classical detail. The pillars and round arches of the little courtyard, the pilasters and shell-topped niches of the gatehouse (which is yet turreted and battlemented) all speak the language of the Renaissance, while the façade of Leicester's Buildings is animated by the wholly Elizabethan feature of tall canted bay windows, nearly all glass, so that the castle has become a romanticized version of the original stronghold.

Lumley Castle, in County Durham, is an interesting example of the sympathetic adaptation of a Gothic quadrangular fortress in the spirit of a more sober antiquarianism. It was the work of Lord John Lumley, descendant of the builder of the castle, Sir Ralph Lumley. His ardent medievalism (which did not prevent the introduction of a chimney-piece with Doric pilasters in the first-floor hall nor the insertion of large square-headed windows in the courtyard) and at the same time the hyperbole to which his whole age was prone are seen in the extraordinary display of shields on the gatehouse and above the entrance door of the hall.

63   By contrast with both Kenilworth and Lumley, the Old Castle of Wardour in Wiltshire is so overlaid by Elizabethan fantasy that it is more like one of Spenser's allegorical castles than a medieval building, an effect aided by ruin (for it was half demolished during the Civil War). The impression is helped by the site, high, wooded and overlooking an artificial sheet of water. The castle, originally built in the late fourteenth century by Lord Lovel of Titchmarsh, was altered by Sir Matthew Arundell in the 1570s. It was always a courtyard house rather than a fortress, and of a curious hexagonal plan which could not fail to appeal to the Elizabethan predilection for ingenious invention. One side of the hexagon projects to embrace the entrance which is recessed between two tower-like wings. The windows are two-light mullions with four-centred arches enclosed in a square head, thus consciously Gothic and intended to harmonize with the medieval building, but the portals of both the entrance and the stair going up to the first-floor hall are classical and there is high poetry in the juxtaposition in the first of these portals of shell-headed niches, a fan vault, a coat of arms and the head of Christ with the inscription *Sub nomine tuo stet genus et domus*. The designer of the conversion was Robert Smythson.

Knowledge of planning and building construction was doubtless encouraged by works of renovation and alteration such as these, as it had been earlier fostered by the detailed surveys of convents and their estates which had to be undertaken before they could be re-allocated. This, and the availability of large numbers of skilled masons, in part accounts for the sudden advance in the purely technical quality and the scale of the domestic architecture built during the fifty or sixty years following the accession of Elizabeth I in 1558. Without that advance the singular poetry of the great examples of that architecture could not have been expressed.

63 Opposite: Wardour Old Castle, Wiltshire.

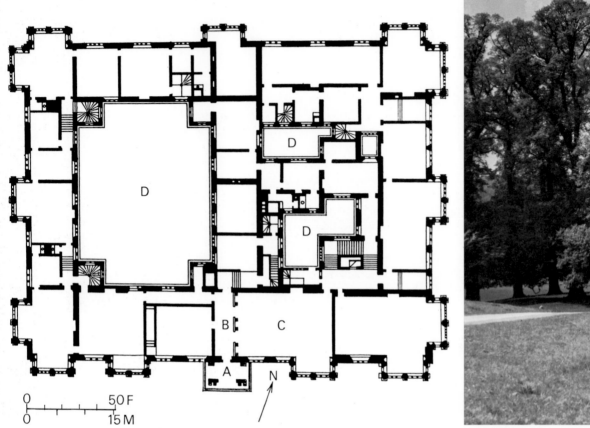

64 Plan of Longleat
House, Wiltshire, after a
sixteenth-century drawing
at Hatfield which shows
the house as its owner
intended it to be.
A entrance porch,
B screens passage, C hall,
D internal courtyards.

The first newly built house to embody the High Elizabethan style was Longleat, 64–6
which probably dates from 1567 after a fire had destroyed an earlier house, a
converted priory Sir John Thynne had purchased in 1541. Sir John's origins were
obscure, but his uncle William Thynne had entered the royal service and it was
perhaps with his help that John was taken into the house of the Duke of Somerset
and eventually became a Clerk Comptroller of the Royal Household. He was one
of those landowners whose chief passion was for building. His letters show that
apart from architecture almost his only interest was money-making, though he
writes intelligently and with some enthusiasm of his reading, which included
Froissart's *Chronicles*, the works of Chaucer, 'Plutarch's Morells in French', 'a boke
of Morell Philosophie', Fox's sermons and Erasmus's *Colloquies*.

Among the craftsmen Thynne employed at Longleat was Robert Smythson,
who seems to have been largely responsible for the final form of the house. At the
same time it is certain that Sir John Thynne himself directed all the operations and
concerned himself with the minutest details. Smythson and Alan Maynard, a
naturalized Frenchman, were the head masons; the principal joiner was Adrian
Gaunt, who made a model of the design upon which the present appearance of
Longleat is based. Maynard seems to have been the chief author of the delicate
architectural ornament both inside and out.

65   Seen from Paradise Hill, across the vast expanse of rolling green (landscaped by Capability Brown in the mid-eighteenth century and remodelled in the early nineteenth century by Humphry Repton), Thynne's silvery palace looks for a moment almost wholly classical except for its huge mullioned windows; but only for a moment. The symmetrical façades, set upon a high basement, in à manner quite novel at that time in England, and crowned by a parapet and sculpture in true Renaissance style, are soon recognized for what they are: mere screens behind which irregularly disposed pepperpot domes, heraldic finial beasts, exotic chimneys and strapwork cresting create a restless skyline, agitated still more by the gesticulating figures in fluttering drapery or classical armour on the parapet. The dome-capped turrets, commanding a prospect over the countryside, were used as 'banketting houses': here on summer evenings a lady and gentleman might withdraw to take their banquet, a word which then meant a dessert of sweetmeats, fruit and wine. Thus the defensive turret of the medieval castle was transformed into a charming frivolity.

64   Castle architecture is recalled in the courtyard plan of Longleat, and there is a faint but suggestive allusion to it in the tower-like, jutting bays running through several storeys, in which the real originality of the house consists. The great size of

66 the windows derives directly from that of the Perpendicular church window, but

65 Longleat House, seen from the east across its park.

73

66 The south front of
Longleat House.

the classical pilasters are a new, Renaissance invention. There are thirteen projecting bays at Longleat, grouped in pairs on the main façades and disposed centrally and at either end on the east and west fronts. They are set at a little distance from the corners of the building so that the angle in each case projects sharply between them, quickening the stately tempo of the bays into a sudden, short *vivace*. The whole composition is an unexpected juxtaposition of the old and the new, of the vertical and the horizontal.

The interior of Longleat was largely remodelled in the early nineteenth century by Sir Jeffry Wyatville, who also rebuilt the north front, but the unique way in which it united novelty with tradition can still be made out. The principal entrance, in the centre, still leads into a screens passage opening into the hall, which, like the 67 medieval hall, runs parallel to the façade. The roof of this hall was originally open; it was ceiled in the late seventeenth century when Bishop Ken of Bath and Wells was deprived of his see and a room was constructed above the hall to house his library. The hammer-beams of the Elizabethan timber roof, the rich pendants and arched braces, all continuing the medieval tradition, are still visible. They consort with a screen which is mainly classical in character, for it has rusticated round-arched openings, flanked by fluted Ionic pilasters, and between the panels of the gallery above them are little caryatids. But apart from the powerful roof the feature of the hall which immediately draws the eye is the stone fireplace. It has a square-headed opening between pairs of Ionic columns supporting a classical frieze. Over this two paired caryatids, male and female, and a central mermaid, whose twin tails entwine to make a spiralling column, balance baskets of rounded fruits on their heads below a further classical frieze. Between the caryatids and the mermaid are round-headed arches with angel heads in the lunettes above bold, writhing cartouches, now containing a clock and a wind-direction indicator. This exuberant composition is attributed to Maynard.

An inventory compiled in 1639 gives some idea of the further original arrangements at Longleat. The hall, as was usual by the time the house was built, had lost its old importance in the life of the family. The steward and numerous servants (all men at that period) took their two main meals of the day, dinner, served at 10 a.m. and supper, at 5 p.m., in the hall, but Sir John Thynne, his family and their guests ate in the great chamber on the first floor, where there was also the with-drawing-room to which the Thynnes retired after meals. There was to have been a gallery on this floor, but it was never built. On the ground floor there was a parlour suite comprising the parlour, the outer parlour and the 'shovell-board parlour'. The last was given over to the popular pastime of shove-ha'penny. (An old shovell-board table, a very long table with appropriate markings incised at one end, can still be seen at Beeleigh Abbey in Essex.)

That most emphatically Elizabethan of apartments, the long gallery, has been referred to a number of times in this chapter. Such long, narrow rooms, which are among the most attractive and striking innovations in the internal planning of sixteenth-century houses, may have suggested themselves to builders as an exciting use of space when they no longer needed to satisfy only basic functional requirements. Early examples of such a use of space, heralding the long gallery, occurred at the end of the fifteenth century in the remarkable plan of the Prior's Lodging at Much Wenlock and in the rebuilding of Richmond Palace. The first of such long chambers to be put to some of the uses the Elizabethans eventually found for it was the Galerie François I at Fontainebleau, built in 1528 and given over to gentle exercise and the lavish display of pictures. Serlio defines a long, narrow room above an open loggia, 'in France called a gallery', as *una saletta per spasseggiare* – a room to stroll about in.

Apart from the gallery at Hampton Court, dating from about 1530, the earliest instance of the fully-fledged long gallery in England is that at Ingatestone in

Essex, probably completed in 1543. Here, as in the great mansions built later in the century, the apartment was decorated with the framed portraits which were then considered essential to the furnishing of an important house; but the principal use to which the Ingatestone long gallery was put was the making of music. In the upper ranks of Elizabethan society the members of the family and their guests were all expected to be active musicians; and the present fluctuation of light in the shadowy lengths of such splendid galleries at those at Hardwick, Chastleton or Penshurst was VII then matched by vibrations of sound from the singing of madrigals and the playing 88, of lute, viol or virginals. Ingatestone Hall has a special link with the great age of English music, for Sir William Petre's son John was a close friend of William Byrd, who frequently visited both Ingatestone and Sir John Petre's own seat, Thorndon Hall. Sir John's name was attached by Byrd to his Tenth Pavan and Galliard in the book of his compositions given in 1591 to Lady Nevill.

Each of the Elizabethan prodigy houses combines the traditional and the classical, the vertical and the horizontal, in a different way. At Kirby Hall in Northampton- VI shire, which is contemporary with Longleat, the classical elements consist of details applied to a traditional frame rather than of general ideas of proportion and organization such as are embodied in the façades of the Wiltshire mansion. For Kirby is quadrangular in plan with a courtyard in the middle, and the principal range, in accordance with custom, comprises the hall rising to the full height of the building and a porch leading into the screens passage. But the treatment of these familiar features transfigures them utterly; and this house is one of the great poetic experiences in architecture. The poetry is heightened by ruin and by the proximity of the solitary building to the ironstone-mining industry which has marked the landscape with slag-heaps and livid pools.

The designer of Kirby is unknown, but the mason is thought to have been Thomas Thorpe, father of the famous John Thorpe. The house was built for Sir Humphrey Stafford of Blatherwicke. Despite the conventional disposition of the hall the range is externally of perfect symmetry. The lofty projecting porch is centrally placed between tall windows, and the even taller dais window has its counterpart at the other end of the range, even though there is no functional justification for it – one of many instances of the predominance in this period of aesthetic over practical considerations. With its steep roof rising above the parapet and its conspicuous areas of glass the hall instantly recalls the nave of a Perpendicular church. But the buttresses normally set between Perpendicular church windows have been replaced by giant classical pilasters with Ionic capitals enlivened by delicate carvings of flowers and foliage, while above them runs a narrow cornice embellished with the same motifs. The giant pilasters accurately reproduce an illustration in the *Architecture* of Philibert de l'Orme, published in 1567, but it is their conjunction with an English traditional hall and with structural dependence on the English Perpendicular style which gives Kirby its special quality.

The interior of the hall sustains the unique mood of the exterior: it is roofed with an oak barrel-vault, divided into rectangular compartments crossed by wavy diagonals like medieval wind-braces and with flowery bosses at the intersections; and while this construction looks back to the Middle Ages, the tenderly carved foliage on the diagonals, the design of the cornice and all the mouldings are classical.

The vigorously jutting hall porch with its spontaneous assemblage of classical 69 themes brilliantly infuses the wonderful, restrained mixture with a burst of wild fantasy. The round-arched entrance is flanked by coupled, fluted Ionic pilasters

with so strong an entasis that they visibly taper upwards. A third pilaster is set round the corner on each side of the porch, thus imparting a strongly lateral movement to the predominantly vertical composition. The pilasters support a floral frieze like that on the façade itself, dividing this stage of the porch from the next. Here on the first floor there is again an arched opening with a balcony in front of it set on coarse brackets. The opening is crowned by a broken segmental pediment bearing the date 1638; it none the less entirely harmonizes with the aspiring tendency of the whole porch and especially with the flanking columns. These columns taper as dramatically as the pilasters, and their boldness is accentuated by their extraordinary bases which take the form of colossal leafy brackets. Again the floral frieze, advancing and withdrawing with the motion of the pillars, intervenes between this stage and the final attic storey. This storey rises far above the rest of the building, in the form of a curving Dutch gable decorated with a shell ornament, flanked by stone balls and supported by a screen of seven Corinthian colonnettes; these are once more placed on brackets, which bulge dramatically from a frieze of strapwork containing the family's motto (*Je seray loyal*) and the date 1572. The gable exists purely for effect: behind it there is nothing but a pair of unusually tall, square-shafted chimneys.

68 A masque at the house of Sir Henry Unton, who was Queen Elizabeth's envoy to France and knew the composer John Dowland. To the accompaniment of music, the winged figure of Mercury presents the goddess Diana and her train. Notice in the background the servants, and the sideboard with its display of plate.

The fresh, unacademic character of the Kirby porch has another parallel only a few miles away, in the amazing bay window set like a sculptured relief against the 70 east wall of Deene Park, the home of the Brudenells, bought by them in 1514 and altered between then and the nineteenth century. The bay electrifies the most picturesque and animated façade of the great courtyard house. It bears the initials of Sir Edmund Brudenell, who inherited Dèene Park in 1549, and of his wife Agnes who died in 1572, so the composition is contemporary with the Kirby porch. It consists of two enormous windows, each of eight lights, divided by alternately fat and thin Ionic columns. The capitals of the columns in each row support a broad frieze, boldly panelled like the base from which the whole structure rises, and decorated with robust cartouches and strapwork. The double grid of mullions and transoms is surmounted by a shouldered gable, abruptly truncated, pierced by a three-light window and ornamented with a rosette like a medieval wheel window in a square frame.

Longleat and Kirby show the two directions in which the Elizabethan synthesis of Gothic and classical was to develop. The former is an essentially new conception though it alludes to the past; the latter is essentially traditional but incorporates Renaissance imagery and Renaissance notions of symmetry.

The most inspired successor of Kirby is Montacute, in Somerset, completely 71 traditional in plan but fusing the vernacular with Mediterranean influence in a new, strange and unforgettable harmony. Whereas Kirby is an unselfconscious expression of enthusiasm for classical motifs used to embroider a native design with fortuitous

69, 70 The hall porch at Kirby Hall, Northamptonshire (below) and the east wall bay at Deene Park near by, both of about 1570, show the inventive Elizabethan use of classical forms. The Deene Park bay is probably not in its original place.

rather than calculated felicity, Montacute is a sophisticated work of art in which every effect is deliberate. The house was built in about 1590 for Sir Edward Phelips, a West Country lawyer, later Speaker in the House of Commons and Master of the Rolls. Its architect is thought to have been the Somerset mason William Arnold, who later contrived the exquisite symmetry of Wadham College, Oxford, and turned the Gothic hunting-lodge known as Cranborne Manor, Dorset, into an evocative Arcadian fantasy.

71   The east front is what matters most: the west front no longer looks as it did originally, for the porch and balustrade of a great Dorset house, Clifton Maybank, were grafted on to it towards the end of the eighteenth century, and though the porch is individually interesting as a fine example of a local style, it has no connection with the transforming vision which shaped the east façade of Montacute and its setting. The resemblance of the basic design of Montacute to that of the medieval
53 hall house is as clear as in the case of Barrington Court: the traditional central block, projecting porch and advancing wings are all there. But the theme is metamorphosed by the builder's firm grasp of classical art and his personal, impassioned interpretation of it. This is not an English E-type house embellished by classical detail, but a new synthesis rich in suggestion and allusion. Obelisks, classical figures and friezes, a balustraded parapet, circular and shell-headed windows, semicircular pediments and curly gables are resolved into a single austere concord with tall chimneys, heraldic beasts, steep roofs and huge rectangular grids of leaded glass.

72 A corner of the garden forecourt at Montacute House.

73 Above, right: William Cecil, Lord Burghley, the builder of Burghley House. Of himself he remarked, 'I have gained more by my temperance and fore-bearing than I ever did by my wit.'

The forecourt confirms and enriches the perfection and rarity of this synthesis. Little open rotundas interrupt the enclosing obelisk-adorned balustrades, and in each corner stand pavilions upon whose square plan swelling oriels impose a quatrefoil shape. Fantastic ogee cupolas surmount both pavilions and rotundas, but those of the rotundas are merely outlined in stone, and are airy, skeletal versions of the solid pavilion roofs. They all taper up to finials in the guise of intersecting circles, emblems of the overruling harmony of the spheres.

Within the walls, though the flower-borders are Victorian, the garden remains a fascinating relic of a type of architectural garden design favoured at the time. A description of Leicester's new garden on the north side of Kenilworth by Robert Laneham, a court official who accompanied the Queen on progress, shows that it had close affinities with this enclosed garden at Montacute:

Close to the wall is a beautiful terrace ten feet high and twelve feet broad, quite level and covered with thick grass which also grows on the slope. There are obelisks on the terrace at even distances, great balls and white heraldic beasts, all made of stone and perched on artistic posts, good to look at. At each end is a bower, smelling of sweet flowers and trees. . . . There are also four parterres cut in regular proportions; in the middle of each is a post shaped like a cube, two feet high; on that a pyramid, accurately made, symmetrically carved, fifteen feet high; on the summit a ball ten inches in diameter.

The combination of geometric shapes in this layout, as at Montacute, where square and quatrefoil, sphere and ogee consort with classical columns, obelisks and balusters, is characteristic of the Elizabethan passion for ingeniously contrived pattern, for what was called a 'device', whether expressed in stone or in print. For poetry as well as architectural plans and architectural ornament might take the form of diamonds, circles, ovals or even, as in George Puttenham's *Art of English Poesy* (1589) a pillar. The Elizabethan device usually expresses more than pure delight

in what is 'curiose': it is a symbol, either verbal, like John Thorpe's well-known design for a house on the plan of his own initials, or visual. Thorpe's circular house arranged as three rectangles grouped round a hexagonal courtyard and enclosed within a circle alludes to the Trinity, and also to current philosophical theories about the orderly structure of the universe and the supremacy of the circle. New House at Redlynch in Wiltshire, where three wings radiate from a central hexagon, likewise symbolizes the Trinity. It was built by the Gorges family, of whom Sir Thomas, a man given to the study of astrology and the occult, caused Longford Castle to take the form of a triangle in allusion to the Trinity.

If Montacute can be seen as the noble offspring of the kind of synthesis achieved at Kirby, Burghley House stems directly from Longleat. Like Sir John Thynne, with whom he corresponded about architecture, William Cecil, created Lord Burghley in 1571, supervised the designing and building of his two great mansions, Theobalds (destroyed a century later) and his Northamptonshire seat. His interest in architecture is further shown in a letter to Sir Thomas Smith, English Ambassador in Paris, and the designer and builder of Hill Hall in Essex, asking him to obtain a copy of Philibert de l'Orme's *Nouvelles inventions pour bien bastir*. Again, letters to Sir Thomas Gresham, English Resident in Antwerp, testify to Cecil's feeling for architecture and also inform us that Flemish masons were among those he engaged to work on his own ambitious projects.

William Cecil cuts a sober figure against the glittering background of his age. Reticent in both character and dress, he protested that he was no courtier; and he was indeed a secret man, preferring the quiet routine of his own house to the formality and glamour of court life. Yet it is only necessary to glimpse Burghley House to realize that even he could not escape the spirit of his age and that he deeply shared its passion for extravagant display.

74 Burghley House, William Cecil's great Northamptonshire mansion, seen from the south-west. The entrance front with its gatehouse is on the left; the obelisk-spire marks the fantastic hall porch in the courtyard.

The mansion is one of the largest of the period, and its size was only partly dictated by the expensive honour Lord Burghley accepted as a condition of his pre-eminence – that of entertaining his Queen, which he did a dozen times at a cost of some £2000 to £3000 for each visit. Cecil had inherited the monastic manor of Burghley from his father. As early as the 1550s he began to enlarge and add to the original medieval buildings; and it was not lack of accommodation but the impossibility of adapting the older house to the proud conceit which eventually possessed his imagination which led him to destroy the existing structure, start afresh and create the present stupendous pile.

Burghley House was completed during the 1580s at enormous expense. Cecil's chief mason-designer may have been John Symondes, Clerk of the Queen's Works and Master Plasterer. The result is clearly related to Longleat. It is informed by the same receding and advancing movement set up by bays, it shows the same regular fenestration, the same horizontal moulding dividing the storeys and powerfully knitting the composition together, and it exhibits the same quivering skyline. But Burghley presents a more unified image: Renaissance form and Renaissance details have been welded surely and smoothly with traditional elements in a superb architectural chimera. Its effect is immensely furthered by its landscape setting, one of the most perfect achievements of Capability Brown. The house, built of Barnack stone, is constructed about a courtyard. The castle fantasy is more strongly in evidence than at Longleat, for here there are square corner towers and a gatehouse in the Early Tudor style, the latter five storeys high with flanking turrets. Pepperpot domes, tall chimneys in the form of clustered columns and parapets consisting of arches and obelisks impel the design more emphatically upwards and complete the metamorphosis of the defensive theme into a fairy-tale fortress.

The interior of Burghley was greatly altered at the end of the seventeenth century, but enough Elizabethan work remains to show that the temper of the conception matched that of the exterior. The double hammer-beam roof of the great hall combines Gothic spandrel tracery with classical forms in the pendants; it rises above spiralling columns and a conspicuously ebullient classical fireplace, with a curving pedimented chimney-breast and huge fluted volutes supporting a swelling frieze.

Gothic and classic are knit into a yet closer and more idiosyncratic whole in the most astonishing feature of the interior, the Roman Staircase. It is of stone, which is in itself unusual, for with the remarkable exception of Hardwick, the material of Elizabethan stairways is almost invariably wood, and their composition is usually based on the square-well design mounting in flights at right-angles to each other, as at Burton Agnes, Knole and Hatfield. In all these cases it is the intricacy of the structure and decoration which is arresting. At Burton Agnes there are no less than eight newel posts, joined in pairs by arches, every inch of the surface of which is covered with carving, while at Hatfield and Knole each of the heavy, square newels is lavishly ornamented and surmounted by a figure. The Burghley House staircase is entirely different in character: not only does it make an impression of monumentality and dignity instead of merely inviting wonder at the craftsman's skill, but it has solid walls and is roofed by stone tunnel-vaults patterned with squares and circles. This suggests a typical Italian Renaissance stairway, but it is nothing of the kind, for the landings are rib-vaulted and adorned with pendants, and their conjunction with the generally classical form of the composition is peculiarly expressive of the Elizabethan imagination.

The castle theme, merely adumbrated at Longleat and not more than suggested

at Burghley, dominates the whole design of Sir Francis Willoughby's great house
, 78 at Wollaton. It was begun in 1580. The architect, Robert Smythson, had not only
worked at Longleat, but, it will be remembered, had been in charge of the conversion
63 of Wardour so that the predilection of the age for sham medievalism was reinforced
in him by intimate contact with a genuine Gothic fortress. Sir Francis Willoughby
was the brother-in-law of Sir Matthew Arundell of Wardour, and it seems likely
that Arundell was responsible for Smythson's employment at Wollaton.

Sir Francis's mansion is set like a true castle on the top of a hill, but no traveller
sighting its theatrical silhouette from afar would take it for a medieval stronghold,
despite its central 'keep', 'curtain walls' and square angle towers. For the walls are
gridded with glass which turns the solid masonry into an airy palace glittering
through the smoke of the coal-mining landscape; and the largest of all the many
windows are precisely those in the keep, filled with traceried lights in the Gothic
style. The keep soars above the rest of the building, in the form of a giant tower with
round, pepperpot-crowned corner turrets. It contains the hall, furnished with an
elaborate classical screen in the traditional position and a hammer-beam roof, and
above it the so-called Prospect Room, a vast lantern commanding spectacular views.
This room, which has no fireplace and which was dedicated wholly to the pleasures
of *looking*, is an even more forceful example than the Elizabethan long gallery of
the increasing concern for aesthetic rather than practical matters in country-house
design of the period.

75 Above, left: a landing
of the Roman Staircase at
Burghley House, of the
1580s.

76 Above: the oak
staircase at Hatfield
House, Hertfordshire,
begun by Lord Burghley's
son Robert Cecil in 1607.
The gates prevented dogs
from going upstairs.

77, 78 Wollaton Hall, Nottinghamshire, designed by Robert Smythson and built in 1580–85: the south front, and the plan (in which the south front is at the right). A entrance porch, B screens passage, C hall, D pantry, E buttery, F kitchen.

The conscious medieval revivalism of the Wollaton composition is combined with absolute symmetry, with Doric friezes and pilasters, classical niches, cartouches, balustrading, obelisks and statues and with busts in roundels of Plato, Virgil, Aristotle, Diana and Hercules. The design is based on that of a villa published 78 by Serlio. Perhaps the superabundant ornament spread over the frame of the house reflects the character of its owner just as the severity of Hardwick mirrors the personality of the Countess of Shrewsbury. The lavish, restless display at Wollaton, 79, 8: the juxtaposition of motifs derived from such disparate sources – from the Netherlands, from Italy, from classical antiquity, from Gothic England – may express Sir Francis's lack of ease in life, his jealousy, suspicion and muddle-headedness, as well as his pretentiousness and his undeniable erudition. But this ornament is more than decoration, more than exuberant ostentation: it accelerates the rhythm of the expanding, contracting, and above all aspiring movement of the whole design and imparts an essential, theatrical flourish to a castle which despite the monumentality of its shape is all fantasy, semi-transparent, brittle and defenceless.

Barlborough Hall, in Derbyshire, resembles Wollaton in its general conception. Its design is also attributed to Robert Smythson, and the dates 1583 on the porch and 1584 on an overmantel show that it was built at the same time. It is again a quadrangular building with castle features, but here a cupola takes the place of the great tower, and the dramatically advancing corner turrets of Sir Francis Willoughby's mansion have been replaced by hexagonal bays set in from the angles of the house, shooting up one storey above the roofline and crowned with alternately square and semicircular battlements. As at Longleat the kitchen and offices are relegated to the basement, but the most unusual feature of the interior plan is the

corridor running round the sides of the courtyard on each floor. This may show the
39 influence of Hengrave (see Chapter 2, p. 45). Barlborough is a deeply romantic,
exciting house. That it has none of the grandiosity of Wollaton is somewhat
surprising, for its builder, the lawyer Francis Rodes, was largely a self-made man,
and his career, which culminated in a Judgeship of the Common Pleas in 1585,
proved so lucrative that he was enabled to buy land in Derbyshire, Nottinghamshire
and south Yorkshire. His high-sounding pedigree, unlike that of Sir Francis
Willoughby, denoted new ambitions rather than ancient gentility.

The Elizabethan synthesis of Gothic and classical, of old and new, achieves its
79–83 most intense and perfect expression at Hardwick Hall in Derbyshire. The plan can
81 be seen either as a traditional H-design with the cross-bar of the letter projecting on
either side of the uprights, or as a radical departure from past practice in the form
of two squares (which to the sixteenth-century mind equalled the circle in significance) imposed on two Greek crosses joined by a central rectangle, a composition
as complex and as fraught with symbolism as that of any church in Rome.

The exterior of this great house is as sensational as its plan. Three arms of each
of the Greek crosses take the form of immense square towers, at once investing
the building with a castle atmosphere. They rise one storey higher than the already
exceptionally lofty core, projecting sharply from the middle of the narrow north
79, 80 and south façades and set away from the corners of the house on the long west and
east fronts, on either side of a central shallow bay across which they are connected by
a classical colonnade. The drama of advance and recession produced by this
imaginative arrangement is far more powerful, more three-dimensional and more
66 dominant than the movement of the bays at Longleat, though it is based on the

79 Hardwick Hall, Derbyshire, by Robert Smythson, built in 1590–97. Seen from the south-west, the great square towers mass together in one concentrated upward thrust.

same principle of the repetition of a projecting unit. The effect of these changing images is further enhanced by the vast diamond-paned grids of the windows, severely rectilinear like the house itself and increasing in size as they ascend, reaching their heroic, flashing climax on the upper storey which is nearly all of glass.

The vertical tendencies of the design have been deliberately exaggerated by the siting of the house on abruptly rising ground. It towers and the flicker of its open-work parapet, which brandishes the initials of its owner and builder, E. S. – Elizabeth Shrewsbury – against the sky, can be seen from every side, surging above tree-shaded hollows and above the exotic, evocative survivals of the original gardens – a wall startlingly crenellated with trefoil-shapes topped by obelisks, pavilions with bizarre crowns and curious triangular lodges. Hill-top sites appealed to Elizabethan builders, to flaunt the magnificence and novelty of their architecture, but no other combination of structure and terrain is more grandly eloquent of pride and gratified ambition than Hardwick, just as none more movingly embodies the unerring sense of harmony of the age.

The fine quality of both the exhibitionism and the poetry at Hardwick reflects the personality of the builder, a personality at once representative of her age and yet modelled on a larger scale. Elizabeth, Countess of Shrewsbury, usually known as 85 Bess of Hardwick, was a parvenue, a truly formidable, uncomfortable character. Edmund Lodge, in *Illustrations of British History* (1791), described her thus: 'A woman of masculine understanding and conduct, proud, furious, selfish and unfeeling, she was a builder, a buyer and seller of estates, a moneylender, a farmer and a merchant of lead, coals and timber; when disengaged from these employments she intrigued alternately with Elizabeth and Mary, always to the prejudice and terror of her husband.' This man, George Talbot, 6th Earl of Shrewsbury, Bess's fourth and last husband, wrote in 1589 that she had 'called him knave, fool and beast to his face and mocked and mowed at him'.

Elizabeth was born in 1520, the daughter of an insignificant country squire, John Hardwick, who lived in a small manor house standing but a stone's throw from the present mansion. When she was only thirteen Bess was married to Robert Barlow, himself no more than fourteen years old. The boy died soon after the wedding and some years later his young widow became the wife of Sir William Cavendish, a rich landowner and Treasurer of the Chamber to Henry VIII. His properties lay in Suffolk, but Bess induced him to sell them and to buy the great Chatsworth estate in her native Derbyshire. Here, in 1549, she embarked on her first building enterprise, a huge courtyard house with lofty, consistent ranges. The faintest ghost of this structure survives in the unusual composition and unusual height of the classical Chatsworth which replaced it (see Chapter 4). In a period 136 when great houses were conspicuous for their vertical emphasis, the Elizabethan Chatsworth was outstanding; it drew special comment from Charles Cotton in 1681:

> The noble front of the whole edifice
> In a surprising height is seen to rise.

Sir William Cavendish died in 1557, leaving all his property and fortune to Bess, although he had children by two former marriages. Three years later Bess married Sir William St Loe, Captain of the Queen's Guard and Grand Butler of England. His death a few years later left her in possession of yet greater wealth. Then, in 1568, despite her age and lack of feminine charm, she secured an even richer and more influential husband in the person of George Talbot, Earl of Shrewsbury.

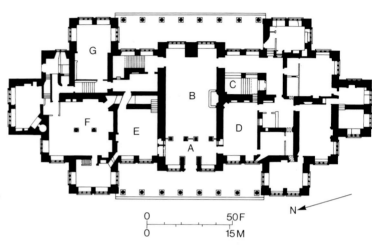

85

80, 81 The west front of
Hardwick Hall, and the
plan of the ground floor,
which shows the novel
position of the hall.
A screens passage or
vestibule, B hall, C stair,
D pantry, E buttery,
F kitchen, G chapel.

No doubt her astonishing vitality and intelligence, qualities which radiate from the
hard-featured face in the long gallery at Hardwick, seemed irresistibly attractive to
this conscientious, low-spirited man. For him the marriage was disastrous. For
Bess it was a tremendous worldly triumph, for she contrived that its celebration
should coincide with the wedding of two of her six children by Sir William Cavendish
to two of the Earl's children by a former Countess.

Bitter quarrelling between the Earl and Countess of Shrewsbury soon ended in
separation. Bess lived for a short time at Chatsworth, then returned to the manor
house in which she had been born. This modest dwelling was quite inadequate to
her sense of her own importance and to the standards she had acquired with increasing affluence, so she at once set about transforming it. In 1590 work was arrested
by the death of the Earl. Bess inherited an immense fortune and she instantly
abandoned the Old Hall for an entirely new project, a grander and much more
original house, the present Hardwick Hall. The grim, gaping masonry of the Old
Hall still gloomily confronts the glittering new building across a wooded declivity,
the contrast of dark and light magnifying the already potent romance and sensation-
alism of the place. Bess moved into her new mansion on 4 October 1597 to the sound
of music. She was seventy-seven years of age.

The triumphant exterior of this wonderful house has already been described.
Within, despite certain inevitable changes, it is a remarkably preserved relic, most
eloquently enshrining the spirit of its age and still filled with the strong presence
of its first owner. In her eighty-first year Bess compiled an inventory of the contents
of her house and many of the pieces can be seen today in their original positions.

Robert Smythson was probably responsible for the general design of Hardwick, but the guiding mind behind it was that of its owner. The most revolutionary feature of the interior had already been introduced by Bess into her conversion of the Old Hall: the great hall, instead of running parallel to the front of the house in 81 accordance with the medieval custom which had persisted in Elizabethan planning, was centrally and symmetrically placed at right angles to the front. Thus the great hall of the Middle Ages assumed the guise it was to wear in all classical mansions: it had become an entrance hall, running centrally across the house, differing from its descendants only in that the staircase is excluded from the composition.

On passing through the main entrance, the visitor is confronted by a screen of 82 Roman Doric columns supporting a gallery and transforming what would have been the screens passage in a medieval house into a vestibule. Anyone still inclined to the once-prevalent view of Elizabethan architecture as 'barbarous' or 'quaintly irregular' in its 'uncomprehending' use of Renaissance motifs need only glance at these columns to realize that the designer perfectly grasped the principles of classical art. English sixteenth-century builders and sculptors departed from a strictly literal reproduction of Renaissance forms deliberately, in the interests of greater variety. If the proportions of the screen had governed the whole design of the hall at Hardwick, it would have been a tame affair: as it is, the effect of the screen is entirely subordinated to the electrifying impact of the colossal overmantel of coloured plaster, a riot of scrolls, swags and aggressively muscular strapwork against which two dusky stags hold up Bess's arms embellished with wild roses and a coronet.

The purpose of this hall is not to charm the senses with classical harmonies but to introduce the emotive theme of the whole great house – the pride, ardour and assertiveness of the old woman who created it. The monstrous scale of the stags and their turbulent background announce and exaggerate a motif which recurs again and again at Hardwick, but which like so many manifestations of that age is ambiguous: its temporal character is given another mysterious dimension by the Hardwick motto of which it is the visual counterpart,

> The redolent smelle of eglantine
> We stagges exalt to the Divine.

The hall is flanked by buttery and pantry with the kitchen beyond the buttery, so that although a staircase leads directly up to the dining-room above the buttery and kitchen, the hall could still have been used for either of the two main meals of the day. The inventory of 1601 lists its furniture as 'three long tables and six formes'. Two of these forms remain.

The principal rooms of the house lie on the top storey, where they are planned as the culmination of the spectacular stone staircase which starts from a chamber to 83 the right of the hall, mounts with an impressive absence of balustrading that recalls the night-stair in Hexham Abbey and yields vistas as stirring as those afforded by the ascent to the chapter-house at Wells. But the Hardwick stair departs utterly from Gothic practice: it comes closer to the daring architectural conceits of Baroque Europe in the part it plays in the design and atmosphere of the house, giving unity to the composition and urgency to its drama.

The plan of Hardwick creates rooms of a delightful variety in size: with their superb tapestries and needlework, plaster and marble reliefs, their striking chimney-pieces and springy, uneven floors, they are astir with rumours of the life which filled them nearly four hundred years ago. The most evocative of all the apartments

82, 83 Hardwick Hall:
the hall (above), looking
towards the screens
passage or entrance
vestibule, and the stone
staircase. The lanterns are
part of the original
furnishing.

are the two principal ones, the High Great Chamber (or Presence Chamber) and the long gallery.

In the High Great Chamber the soft glow of rose and gold, dull green and muted VIII blue from the painted plaster frieze and the tapestried walls may owe something of its harmony to the passage of time, but plaster and tapestry have always presented the same illuminating contrast in their treatment of classical subjects, and have always stimulated the eye with their unique proportions. For the plaster frieze is so deep (twelve feet) that the high, echoing room is divided horizontally almost in half by the strongly moulded cornice between it and the tapestries. The latter, woven in Brussels and purchased by Bess in 1587, two years before Hardwick was begun, interpret the story of Ulysses with academic Italianate correctness. The frieze above them, by an English artist, Abraham Smith, is based on equally 'correct' designs by the contemporary Flemish painter Martin de Vos. In it outworn classical forms and motifs – its subject is Diana and her court – are clothed with fresh, invigorating fantasy. The tapestry figures are no more than pallid ghosts below the coarsely modelled, boldly projecting forms of Diana, Ceres, Venus, huntsmen, dogs and wild creatures; and these images are set among smooth-stemmed trees and giant foliage seen with equally dynamic enthusiasm. The embowering forest is not the conventional landscape background of the tapestries: it is as important as the figures and determines the mood of the room.

The enchantment of the long gallery is of another order, though again the VII proportions of the room, its immense length and great height, are decisive for its

84, 85 Bess of Hardwick (below, right, a portrait at Hardwick), and a page from her Account Book, covering a fortnight in November 1593. As well as materials it lists craftsmen and labourers, with the number of days worked and their wages. At the bottom Bess has written out the total, 'thre pende hyghttene shyllynges' (£3 18s 0d), above her confident signature.

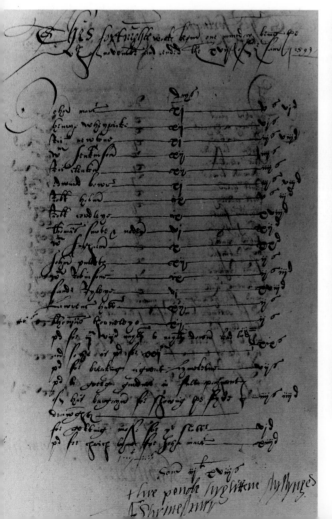

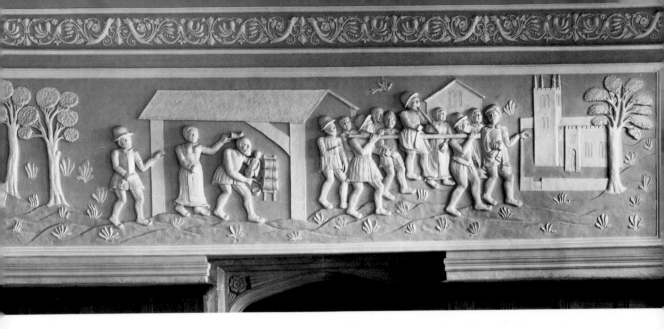

character. But the special quality of the apartment derives from the extraordinary effects of light from the three gigantic bay windows on the garden side. On sunny days rectangles of crystal brilliance shiver on the rush matting, alternating with mysterious areas of shadow and imparting a livelier measure to the slow rhythm of the long vista. In grey weather opalescent light suffuses the whole gallery, enhancing the amazing richness of its texture. It is then that the two splendid architectural chimney-pieces best reveal the extent of their author's departure from his model, Serlio: the bold use of strongly contrasting local alabaster and marbles, and the vigorous, idiosyncratic strapwork surrounding the central figures of Justice and Misericordia express the personality of their Elizabethan designer, Thomas Accres. It is above all in the even light of a grey day that the portraits of many familiar figures of the sixteenth and seventeenth centuries glow like jewels against the blue and umber tapestries. They include Bess of Hardwick herself, three of her husbands, Mary Queen of Scots, the 1st Duke of Devonshire in Garter robes, by Kneller, and Queen Elizabeth I, perhaps by Richard Stevens, shown full length in a rose-coloured, embroidered dress against a background of darker pink. The tapestries behind are half hidden by the pictures, although it was for their exhibition that the room was planned. They illustrate the story of Gideon and were woven in Brussels for Sir Christopher Hatton in 1578. Bess bought them from his heir for £326 and covered the Hatton arms in the borders with cloth painted with her own device, cleverly adding antlers to the Hatton does to turn them into Cavendish stags. Dwarfed by the height of the room, the furniture – a virginal bearing the date 1653 and the name of its maker, Thomas White, carved chairs and stools and a number of day-beds – seems to lie on the long stretch of rush matting as if held down by a spell.

    Some idea of the tremendous range, freshness and gusto of Elizabethan plaster-work can be gained when one compares the bold, geometric pattern and strapwork frieze of the plaster ceiling of the Hardwick long gallery with the forest frieze of the High Great Chamber, the surprising plaster panel in the hall at Montacute realistically depicting the fate of a henpecked husband forced to 'ride the skim-mington', and the fantastically agitated reliefs of religious subjects above the hall fireplace and over the screen at Burton Agnes in Yorkshire. The fact that plaster could be manipulated without the labour which invariably deadened carving in

86 The story of a hen-pecked husband, on a plaster panel in the hall at Montacute House, Somerset: he tries to get some beer, is beaten by his wife with a shoe, and is finally paraded by his neighbours astride a pole.

91

stone was in itself inspiring, especially where a repeating pattern was involved. The Hardwick ceiling is exceptionally restrained, and contrasts with the intricate, flower-filled quatrefoils, lozenges, rectangles and heraldic devices of the long gallery at Haddon Hall or the complicated, ambivalent design in the hall at Knole. The latter can be seen as octagons enclosing triangular-headed crosses or as squares within irregular, eight-pointed stars. Fruit-like pendants set in coronals of leaves mark each alternate starpoint or, if you choose to read the pattern thus, the tip of each cross. The mouldings at Knole and Haddon recall the moulded ribs of Gothic architecture, but the shapes they assume are entirely new.

The plasterwork in the long gallery at Hardwick consists of double ribs: such double ribs developed into a single wide ribbon which lent itself to graceful, interlacing designs like those in the long gallery at Chastleton, where loops and twists adorned with beads and lozenges burgeon into rosettes and fleurs-de-lis. In the ballroom at Knole the bands are broader and more richly decorated, the curving forms are allied to angular shapes and flower-sprays fill the spaces between them. This broad-banded style is seen in its final, exaggerated form in the gallery at Blickling Hall in Norfolk. Here immensely widened bands of plaster, encrusted with spiralling flower forms, describe rectilinear and curving shapes. The intervening spaces are filled with strapwork, coats of arms set in swirling foliage, and mythological and symbolic figures in high relief, setting up a counter-rhythm to the emphatic measure of the main pattern, while leafy pendants and voluptuous scrolly brackets in the form of high-bosomed female half-lengths give a sudden vertical accent to the predominantly horizontal movement of the restless composition. The broad bands of a ceiling such as this at Blickling would have been cast in plaster of Paris (sulphate of lime) from reverse moulds, while the strapwork and figures were modelled by hand.

87, 88 Opposite: the long galleries at Haddon Hall, Derbyshire, of about 1600 (above) and Chastleton House, Oxfordshire, begun a few years later.

89 Above, left: the plasterwork above the screen at Burton Agnes Hall, Yorkshire; its reliefs, which include the four Evangelists, the elements and the virtues, are three-dimensional versions of Flemish engravings.

90 Above: a detail of the long gallery ceiling at Blickling Hall, Norfolk, made between 1616 and 1627.

Chastleton House in Oxfordshire, begun about 1602, is built round a small court- 88
yard and is far less ambitious in scale than Hardwick, but like the great Derbyshire
mansion it relies for its effect upon the striking way in which the grouping of
vertical, angular forms shifts as one walks round the house. And although it is
gabled, Chastleton alludes almost as powerfully as Hardwick to the castle motif,
not only in the crenellated towers projecting from either end, but in the energetically
projecting bays of the main façade. Between them the central recession lies in caver-
nous gloom. The house was built for a wool-merchant, Walter Jones, and bears a
certain resemblance to Burton Agnes in Yorkshire, which is known to have been
designed by Robert Smythson.

Burton Agnes, built in 1601–10 for Sir Henry Griffiths, is also a courtyard house. 89, 9
As at Chastleton, the entrance is in the side of one of the two projections on the main
front. The advancing and retreating movement of the building is again greatly exaggerated, but the vertical stress, so much emphasized at Chastleton, is less pronounced.
Five-sided, square and semicircular bays – the latter more prodigiously swollen than
any Regency version of the theme – stand in assertive contrast; steep, finialled gables
vie with battlements and soaring chimney-stacks; and the front of the house is a
storey taller than the rest, so that the sides are surprisingly asymmetric.

At Hardwick and Chastleton the balance between the new and the traditional is
perfectly maintained. But that perfection of synthesis could not continue. Just as the
harmony achieved in other spheres of life, in religion, science and politics began to
dissolve after Elizabeth's death and the succession of James I, so in architecture there
was a definite slackening of the exciting tension which distinguishes the great
sixteenth-century houses. For all its flamboyant poetry Bolsover Castle in Derbyshire, begun in 1612, has no unity: its keep, in which the fashionable preoccupation
with the castle theme becomes obsessive, creates a discord with the amazing range 92, 9
alongside it. And the traditional elements of the huge mansions of Audley End and 97
Hatfield are no longer seen with the transforming eye of high genius, but are merely 100
exaggerated, caricatured.

91 The entrance front of
Burton Agnes Hall,
Yorkshire, one of the
later creations of Robert
Smythson, is dated 1601
above the porch. The
sash windows in the
centre are later insertions,
replacing stone
mullioned windows like
those at either end.

Within the engraving: *La galerie* · *Bolsover* · *Monseigneur le Marquis à cheual* · *Grenpades furles Voltes a main gauche*

Bolsover was designed by John Smythson, the son of Robert Smythson, but its form was dictated by the architect's patron, Sir Charles Cavendish, Bess of Hardwick's third son, who was passionately addicted to castles. He was concerned with the building not only of Bolsover, but of other castles at Slimsby, Blackwell-in-the-Peak and Ogle. Bolsover owes much of its effect to its site, on a lofty promontory of the same ridge from which Hardwick rises. The extravagant romance of the architecture is heightened by its remoteness in both space and spirit from the wide landscape over which it towers – fields, farmhouses, industrial developments, scarred hillsides and slag-heaps, all submerged in colliery smoke.

The nucleus of the castle is its massive keep, consciously recalling its Norman prototype, a high, almost square block with three angle turrets and a great staircase tower soaring a stage above the thick walls topped with crenellations. But when this is said it is necessary to add that no one could mistake the date of the keep. It is crowned by a pretty cupola and lantern filled with mock-Gothic tracery and it is adorned with a projecting bay and balconied windows between rusticated columns. In front of it, accentuating its impressive height, is a small, stony forecourt enclosed by battlemented walls and entered between two stout, squat pavilions decorated with battlements and obelisks. The keep is approached from this courtyard by a balustraded stair and a round-arched door beneath a pedimented window.

92 Bolsover Castle, Derbyshire, seen in an illustration from *The Book of Horsemanship* (1658) by William Cavendish, Duke of Newcastle, who inherited the keep – on the left – and built the gallery range. He himself is riding the sprightly horse.

92, 94

93 An Ionic chimney-piece from Book IV of Serlio's *Architettura*, which may have suggested the design of a chimney-piece in the Elysium Room of the keep at Bolsover.

94 Above, right: the Pillar Parlour in the Bolsover keep. The bizarre horse-head motifs on the pendant in the vault allude to the Cavendish passion for riding.

Internally, the plan of the keep is based on that of the traditional tower house, with the kitchen and offices and a cellar for storage in the vaulted basement. On the ground floor are the hall and the parlour, known as the 'Pillar Parlour', and above 94 them the Great or Star Chamber and withdrawing-room, the Marble Closet (together with a bedchamber and two inner chambers), the Heaven Room and the Elysium Room. At the top, a group of small rooms lead off a lobby under the cupola. In that mysteriously ill-lit interior Gothic and classic are fused for the last time in the period in a potently fantastic and original synthesis.

The rooms are vaulted, but the elaborate decoration suggests a medieval atmosphere by means of classical motifs, and the ornate chimney-pieces – which are the most powerful visual elements in the whole building – are of completely successful hybrid character, although they are directly related to designs by Serlio. Smythson 93 made use of the classical orders and of Serlio's ideas only in the most general way. In shape the chimney-pieces are immensely varied: some are square, some are polygonal, and others, set in the angles of rooms, are quadrant-shaped with conical hoods, the hoods enriched by complicated, deeply moulded panelling, crested with strapwork and volutes and studded with jewel-like roundels of coloured marbles. The lintels are never horizontal, but arched in the Gothic manner, and in one instance the opening is trefoil-shaped. Each chimney-piece is set against a rectangle of stone and enclosed by a stone moulding. Thus framed and cut off from the rest of the room it makes the impact of a bold relief, an effect which is intensified by the designer's marvellous colour sense, by his juxtaposition of yellow, indigo, slate-grey, rose and amethyst-coloured alabasters and marbles. These profoundly exciting compositions are the last manifestation, in miniature, of the whole style and spirit of the art which is the subject of this chapter.

There is no doubt that the Bolsover keep makes its indelible impression on the imagination precisely because it so strangely contrasts with the ravaged façade of the now-ruinous building added in 1629–33 by John Smythson and his son Huntingdon for Charles Cavendish's son William. To look along the 170 feet of this stupendous composition towards the keep, from the broad terrace in front of it, conscious of the precipitous slope on one's left dropping down to the landscape already described, is one of the great architectural experiences. This grand façade is as eccentric in its use of the classical idiom as one of the wilder works of Sicilian Baroque. The colossal windows are surmounted by pediments broken into three instead of the more usual two parts; and the main entrance, approached by a double stair, is heavily rusticated and crowned by a broken pediment of the more orthodox kind but with a detached, segmental pediment hovering oddly above it. The immense wall is further animated by unique rounded projections, extravagantly banded and vermiculated. They cannot be called shafts, for they do not support anything. Yet they do serve a purpose: they control the rhythm of the mighty composition and they refer picturesquely (if unchronologically) to the defensive theme of Bolsover, for their shape is that of upright cannon with the bolt at the lower end.

Huge, thrusting waterspouts and pedestals set at regular intervals along the parapet quicken the movement of the façade, and that movement is impelled towards the keep by a singular device: instead of turning at right angles, the end nearest the keep makes a diagonal turn in its direction, and the gesture is accentuated by a curved and pedimented gable. The two buildings are also physically connected. A doorway beneath one of the curious Bolsover broken pediments leads from the keep on to the top of a battlemented wall enclosing a garden and over an archway into the terrace building. The door is in itself an unforgettable object, for the fan-

95 The idiosyncratic gallery at Bolsover, built by John Smythson in 1629–33 and ruined in the eighteenth century. Beyond it on the left is the keep (compare ill. 92).

96 The screen in the hall
at Audley End, Essex.

shaped panelling of the semicircular top and the rectangular lower panels are all
rusticated and vermiculated. John Smythson was fascinated by rustication, and
made many drawings of this form of decoration while in London at his patron's
expense in 1618, but the notion of applying this ornament to the panels of a wooden
door is peculiarly his own.

The Fountain Garden inside the wall-top walk is named after the fountain in its
centre, a composition as bizarre and as mysteriously poetic as the doorway. A lofty,
tiered pedestal carved with lion masks and with corner bastions pierced by circular
openings rises from a sunk basin surrounded by alcoves. Upon the pedestal, one
knee raised, one foot resting on a tall block of stone, stands an enchanting statue of
Venus, the rounded figure of a young girl freckled with lichen, with short flying
locks and a monumental neck, pressing a piece of inadequate drapery to her bosom
with her left hand. Box hedges encircle the fountain and edge the walks leading to it;
and the thick encompassing wall is pierced by alcoves and little rooms, lovers'
retreats. One in a sequence of three miniature rooms boasts a hooded corner
chimney-piece like those in the keep.

At Bolsover the traditional and the classical are contrasted rather than fused,
despite the synthesizing details which we have noted. At Audley End mansion in
Essex we meet a similar juxtaposition rather than union of vernacular and Mediterranean influences. Here the confrontation takes place in the great hall, still in its
medieval form and position though the house was laid out between 1603 and 1616.
The screen had already become an anachronism when Haddon Hall and Hengrave

96–9

96 were built, yet at Audley End it dominates the apartment. It is massive and of oak, two-storeyed like the screen in the Sackvilles' great house, with pairs of coarse, robust terms commanding the design in both stages. Male and female, crowned with Ionic volutes, these half-figures stare boldly from garlanded panels of diverse shapes, which, fantastically crested, soar up to a central feature with twin arches filled with open strapwork.

This rich screen faces a second screen, of stone, simple, dignified and severely classical. The composition consists of two tiers of three arches supported by chaste Ionic pilasters above and by Tuscan pilasters below, with a noble staircase going up in parallel flights from the two outer arches. This screen and stair are the work of Sir John Vanbrugh, and belong to the period a hundred years later when the style which is the subject of this chapter had been replaced by an addiction to the rules of classical architecture. But the interesting thing about it is that while Vanbrugh's screen is opposed in form to the Jacobean screen, both possess a theatrical sense of movement: in this hall the two forms of English Baroque, one preceding the European mode and the other following on its heels, are brought into fascinating proximity.

At both Audley End and Hatfield the plan of the traditional manor house is preserved and preposterously magnified: these are among the largest houses ever
98 built in England. The palatial river front of Audley End is like a blown-up version of the homely façade of Great Chalfield. The porch leading into the archaic screens passage is balanced by a totally unfunctional porch, so placed that both projections are equidistant from the dais window of the hall. Enormous though it is the present
97 Audley End is only part of the mansion built, possibly by the mason and sculptor Bernard Janssen, for Thomas Howard, 1st Earl of Suffolk, who ruined himself by

97 Henry Winstanley's view of Audley End from the west, done in 1676, shows the vast quadrangle that originally preceded the hall range, and the courtyard beyond. The entrance, then as now, was in the left-hand porch of the hall range. This range, and part of the wings extending back away from it, are all that now remains (see ill. 98).

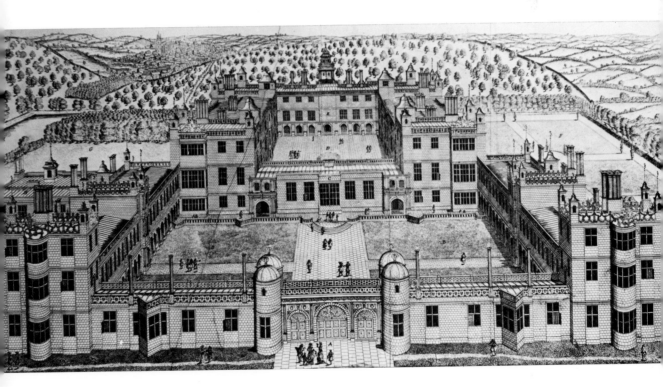

98 The west front of Audley End (compare ill. 97).

VII, VIII Opposite: the long gallery with its original tapestries (above) and the High Great Chamber at Hardwick Hall, Derbyshire (see pp. 90–91).

IX Overleaf, above: the west front of Petworth House, Sussex (see pp. 132–3).

X Overleaf, below: Dyrham Park, Gloucestershire, seen from the south (see p. 140 and ill. 140).

spending public funds on his giant enterprise. Before Vanbrugh reduced the huge pile to more manageable proportions in 1721, the façade towards the Cam looked into a great quadrangle, and the wings behind the existing building were closed by a vast gallery above an open arcade reminiscent of that at Hatfield. 97

Even in its more compact state the general impression made by the mansion, in spite of its turrets crowned by copper, convex roofs and spirelets, is of a heavy, widespread mass of stone in which the horizontal elements predominate. And this effect is not mitigated by the sudden surprising complexity and heightened intensity of the south-east aspect. Jutting bay windows, canted, square and polygonal run through the three storeys of the house, creating a powerful advancing and retreating movement, enriched by strong chiaroscuro. 98

Hatfield, designed by Robert Lyminge and begun in 1607, is an immensely expanded version of Barrington Court: the wings of the E-shape are broadened to a thickness of two and, at their ends, of three rooms. So far extended is the house that the upward movement of the central stone tower and cupola, the shouldered, segmental gables and three-storeyed porch is considerably weakened. 99–1 52

In the hall at Hatfield the screen, closely akin to that at Audley End, is accompanied by a similar feature at the opposite end of the hall, a projecting gallery corbelled out from the panelled wall on grotesque brackets swelling upwards to terminate in the fiercely vital heads of men and beasts. Though it could not differ more sharply from the Vanbrugh screen in the Essex mansion, it seems to look forward to the wilder eighteenth-century Baroque work of the Continent rather than to belong with the characteristic products of the Elizabethan period. The brackets are first cousins to 99

99 Overleaf: the hall at Hatfield House, Hertfordshire, looking towards the gallery.

100 Above: Hatfield, designed by Robert Lyminge and begun in 1607. The plan (opposite, below) is traditional, but the classical loggia in the centre of the south front, originally open, represented a new fashion.

the prodigiously dynamic corbel figures supporting the balconies of the Palazzo Dorata at Noto, in Sicily, while the arcaded gallery itself with its fretted infilling and voluptuously carved pilasters surmounted by heraldic beasts and the Cecil arms resembles the enclosed, cage-like balconies of seventeenth-century towns in Andalusia.

The Hatfield garden, later much altered, was, like the house, a magnification of an earlier Tudor conception. Flights of steps leading down from the mansion were adorned with gilded lions carved in wood, and an elaborate fountain designed by the French engineer de Caus was surmounted by a statue of Neptune 'painted to represent copper', while the fish in the basin were of lead. There was a maze, a rose garden and knot gardens. At the same time, however, the garden was distinguished by many new plants brought from Belgium, France and Italy by Robert Cecil's gardener, the celebrated naturalist John Tradescant; a gardener's image is carved on one of the newel posts of the staircase. The vineyard at Hatfield was the largest ever 101 planted in England prior to the Victorian period.

Blickling Hall in Norfolk was, like Hatfield, the work of Robert Lyminge, and 103 though its scale is rather more modest than that of either Hatfield or Audley End, it is again ostentatiously traditional. It was built between 1616 and 1627 for Sir Henry Hobart, Lord Chief Justice. Originally it was conceived with two wings open to the north forming a deep courtyard. The central turret and lantern and the central

101 Left: the figure of a gardener, carved on a newel post of the great stair at Hatfield (see ill. 76).

102 Below, left: the plan of Hatfield. The entrance front is at the top, the side seen in ill. 100 at the bottom. A open loggia, B screens passage, C hall (a, gallery: see ill. 99), D main staircase, E parlour, F upper part of kitchen, G chapel.

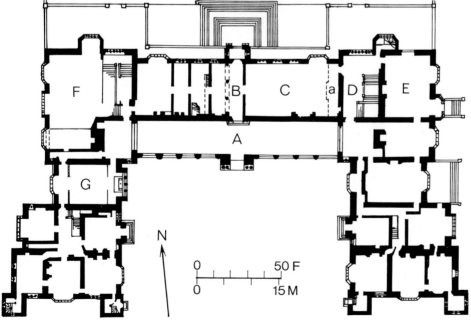

103 Blickling Hall in Norfolk, built in 1616–27 to the designs of Robert Lyminge. Exactly contemporary with the Queen's House by Inigo Jones (ills. 109, 110), it includes only a few classical elements, such as the pediments over the tower windows.

door, with its Tuscan columns and figures of Victory in the spandrels, have a classical look, but the main features of the house – the curly gables, the steep roofs, the square corner turrets with their ogee caps, the design of the chimney-stacks and the red-brick fabric – deliberately refer to Tudor houses of some sixty or seventy years earlier.

In May 1633 Charles I was lavishly entertained at Bolsover with a banquet in the terrace range and a masque by Ben Jonson, *Love's Welcome at Bolsover*, staged in the Fountain Garden with the spectators watching from the wall-top. The theatrical character of the architecture made it an ideal setting for such pageantry. In his masque, where a surveyor, a carver, a mason and a carpenter take part in a 'Dance of Mechanics', Ben Jonson ridicules the architectural theorists of the time, in particular Inigo Jones, who appears as Iniquo Vitruvius, the surveyor. And thus in this fantastic building embracing the old and the new, where the taut harmony of the finest sixteenth-century architecture is already threatened, we are introduced to the most arresting figure of the following chapter, the figure who more than any other individual ensured the triumph of the classical orders in this northern land and the final disruption of the Elizabethan synthesis.

4 CROSS-CURRENTS

the seventeenth century

THE HAPPY UNION in the great Elizabethan houses of incongruous elements was only one expression of the balance achieved in an age of peculiarly intense and exuberant imagination. Already in the houses described at the end of the last chapter the transience of that balance was apparent. During the seventeenth century trends and attitudes which had been fused developed along widely diverging paths, and the scene in every sphere of life is one of unstable equilibrium accompanied by an acceleration of materialism.

The underlying philosophy of the century which witnessed the founding of the Royal Society and the discoveries of Newton and Boyle was a technique of investigation rather than an account of Being; it was preoccupied with How rather than with Why and Whence. Reason banished the phantasms and fairies of Elizabethan England together with the notion that poetry might convey profound intuitions and glimpses of truth. 'The influence of poetry', wrote Bishop Sprat, 'is now exhausted and our present concern is with the serious work of trying to behold face to face, through science, what was formerly seen in a glass darkly.' 'The course of things', he went on to declare, 'goes quietly along its own true channel of natural causes and effects and the new philosophy of the physical sciences shall enrich us with all the benefits of fruitfulness and plenty.'

It is extraordinary to think that it was in so cold a climate of general opinion that Milton produced his great heroic poem on the Fall of Man, and could achieve a state of such high-wrought exaltation that he was expecting an imminent divine event in an England 'standing on top of golden hours', when 'thou, the eternal and shortly expected King, shalt open the clouds to judge the several Kingdoms of the World.' Though political notions inspired the Cromwellian revolution, the religious background of the struggle, the whole phenomenon of Puritanism and the rise of such fanatical sects as the Ranters, the Baptists and Congregationalists seem curiously out of key with Bishop Sprat's reasoned outlook, while the hideous mania for witch-hunting, which reached its height during the Long Parliament (1645–7), is in as violent contrast to it as the lonely figure of Bunyan's Pilgrim bearing his great burden of sin on his back.

There is, however, no lack of evidence of the practical application of the new philosophy. It was with an eye to material benefits that many landowners became promoters of the emigration movement. They did not themselves become colonists: their object was to create a permanent market beyond the Atlantic for English goods in exchange for the products of the New World. The institution of the money-market, after an Act of Parliament had legalized the lending of money on interest, was but one sign of the times. The notion of using money to beget money appealed to merchants and shopkeepers; but it also encouraged a new and eventually disastrous tendency in landowners – to live from investments instead of from the judicious management of their estates. Men who looked upon property as a source of profit and not, as they had hitherto done, as a means of maintaining a given state of society, embraced every opportunity of increasing their land, buying up needy squires, a process analogous to the absorption of small businesses by large which has contributed to the malaise of the modern industrial world. The dukes of Bedford added manor to manor, acre to acre until they were so 'spacious in the possession of dirt' that most of Bedfordshire seemed to be theirs. At the same time these great landowners were far more than rent-collectors, and were animated by a fine sense of responsibility: not only did they labour to improve their Bedfordshire properties, but two of them, Francis Russell and his son William, successfully initiated the drainage of the Fens.

An increasing proportion of squires and noblemen began to interest themselves in the advance of industry, especially the development of the coal trade. Fourteen times as much coal was produced in Cromwellian and Restoration England as in the sixteenth century. Coal became the regular domestic fuel in all regions accessible by water (with a consequent effect on the design of fireplaces) and was used in many processes of manufacture. Pits were deeper, miners spent much more time underground, exposed to ever more danger from explosion; and between them and their employers there arose an impassable barrier such as had never previously existed between landlord and tenant. The future widening rift between the classes was further ensured by another short-sighted enthusiasm of country gentlemen – their excessive zeal for the preservation of game. A law was passed in 1671 which prevented all freeholders of under £100 a year from killing game on their own land: thus farmers and yeomen were sacrificed in order that the squire might have abundance of partridges to shoot.

Yet the grave social consequences of the growing materialism of the gentry did not make their full impact for some generations, and the English country house of the seventeenth century was as much a centre of contented domestic industry, in which every member of the family and every servant played an essential an honoured part, as it had been in the reign of Elizabeth I. The picture of life at Claydon House in Buckinghamshire given in Lady Verney's *Memoirs of the Verney Family during the Civil War* is of a self-contained community. The members

brewed and baked, they churned and ground the meal, they bred up, fed and slew their beeves and sheep and brought up their pigeons and poultry at their own doors. Their horses were shod at home, their planks were sawn, their rough ironwork was forged and mended. Accordingly the millhouse, the slaughter-house, the blacksmith's, carpenter's and painter's shops, the malting and brewhouse, the woodyard full of large and small timber, the sawpit, the outhouses full of all sorts of odds and ends of stone, iron and woodwork and logs cut for burning – the riding-house, the laundry, the dairy with a large churn turned by a horse, the stalls and styes for all manner of cattle and pigs, the apple and root chambers, show how complete was the idea of self-supply.

The stewponds full of fish, the decoy for waterfowl and the dovecots were as important. Wool and flax were spun by the women of the household, who were also engaged in needlework, embroidery, cooking, curing, preserving, wine-making and the preparation of medicines from herbs.

All this domestic activity was carried on in increasingly comfortable surroundings. The houses of the period, in some of which the furnishings have remained almost untouched, are pervaded by an atmosphere of intimacy and quiet luxury. The sounds of the lute accompanying verses celebrating the charms of ringleted, silken-clad, sloping-shouldered beauties addressed as Anthea, Saccharissa, Lucasta or Castara seem but just to have died away in the richly plastered and carved interiors
104, of Ham in Surrey, Belton in Lincolnshire or Dyrham in Gloucestershire, where the
127 walls are adorned with framed pictures and sometimes hung with damask or gilded leather, and the floors are enlivened by the glowing colours of carpets from Turkey or Persia. It is peculiarly indicative of the temper of the age, of the inclination for retirement and the solitary pursuit of scholarship, that the most notable additions to the rooms of the country house were the library and the closet. John Evelyn, the diarist, mentions a number of libraries, including those of Lord Spencer and the Duke of Norfolk, and it was during the seventeenth century that the noble collection of the Cotton family – now among the treasures of the British Library and Bodleian Library – was assembled. One of the first alterations carried out by the Duke and
104 Duchess of Lauderdale at Ham was the addition of a library to house their rare books, among them works printed by Caxton and Wynkyn de Worde. The closet, used for reading and writing, for privacy and warmth, was attached both to bedrooms and to living-rooms and had become general by the end of the century. Unaltered examples survive at Ham and at Dyrham.

104 The library added to Ham House, Surrey, in the 1670s, described by the bibliophile Dibdin about 1800 as 'a very wonderful book paradise'. The pattern of the fine plaster ceiling, with a central oval wreath of tightly packed foliage and flowers, is typical of the period.

105 The fantastic topiary garden at Levens Hall, Westmorland, is a rare surviving example of the seventeenth-century taste for living, evergreen sculpture.

The addiction to the pleasures of the library was accompanied by a passion for garden-making. It was in the seventeenth century that the particularly English form of topiary, the art of evergreen figure sculpture, was developed. Gervase Markham, writing at the time, comments on hedges simulating battlements which support the leafy shapes of beasts, birds, 'creeping things and shippes', and William Lawson, author of *A New Orchard and Garden*, tells of yews clipped to resemble men armed in the field, ready to give battle, or 'swift-running greyhounds; or well-scented and true running Hounds to chase Deere or hunt the Hare'. Kip's views of country seats at the beginning of the eighteenth century show cocks, hens, fans, plumes, discs and balls in yew and box. At least two astonishing seventeenth-century topiary gardens can still be seen: the wonderfully impressive array of huge monoliths at Packwood in Warwickshire symbolizing the Sermon on the Mount, and the dark mass of fantastic shapes crowding the walled court at Levens Hall in 105 Westmorland. Against a soft, light background of deciduous trees an utterly illogical and immensely solid company of giant hats, corkscrews and umbrellas, birds, balls, mammoth sets of weights and abstract forms pierced by holes advance in close ranks towards the old stone house, their startling scale making havoc of its proportions, their vitality draining the pale walls of their substance.

Such topiary is not the only glimpse of the English taste for gardening in the seventeenth century. The first gardening books make their appearance. Two of their authors, Markham and Lawson, have just been mentioned. A splendid book by Louis XIV's head gardener was translated into English as *The Compleat Gardener*, and there were also Rea's *Flora, Ceres and Pomona*, Temple's *Gardens of Epicurus* and John Evelyn's *Sylva. The Garden Book of Sir Thomas Hanmer*, written by a Welsh landowner, reveals the wealth of new plants introduced during the period, including

106 Sir Edmund Verney
of Claydon House,
Buckinghamshire,
Charles I's standard-
bearer who lost his life at
Edgehill in 1642.

the tulip, laburnum, nasturtium, the crown imperial, love-in-a-mist, honesty, the
tulip tree and the red maple. Aesthetically the garden remained formal and Italianate,
though modified by Dutch and French influences, until Vanbrugh revolutionized
the surroundings of the country house by conceiving the approximation of gardens
to painted landscape. But there was a hint of later irregularity in such innovations
as the 'wilderness of high, large trees, in which there are many agreeable shades',
extolled by a sightseer at Dyrham, and the wilderness planted at Ham, through the
trees of which could be seen the perspectives, the array of statues, the parterres and
fountain which delighted Evelyn in 1678.

The ideal family life of the country gentleman was rudely, and in many cases
tragically, disrupted by the victory of the Parliamentary forces. Husbands, brothers
and sons fell in battle and houses were sequestrated from their owners. It is this
situation which gives such poignancy to Lady Verney's *Memoirs*, already mentioned
here. Sir Edmund Verney and his son Ralph were divided in their loyalties, yet
Puritan and Cavalier lived in harmony and affection at Claydon, both alike concerned to protect their home and lands in an evil season. Both were drawn into the
struggle between the King and his enemies, and the devotion of Sir Edmund,
Charles's standard-bearer at the Battle of Edgehill, has become legendary. He so
defended his charge that even in death his hand refused to relinquish the standard.

The rhythm and imagery of architecture inevitably vary with the prevailing
state of scepticism or confidence about ultimate issues, and the underlying rationalist
philosophy of the England of Charles I, Cromwell and the Restoration fostered the
tendency towards ever greater horizontality and classicism. But just as the establishment of this philosophy was impeded by religious attitudes, so tradition in country-
house design, the romantic habit of evoking the past and delight in the variety of

N

107 Plan of the first floor of the Queen's House, Greenwich, before the spaces flanking the bridge were filled in. A hall (upper part, surrounded by a balcony), B Tulip Staircase, C drawing-room, D bedroom, E bridge over the London–Dover road, F loggia.

108 Above, right: a portrait of Inigo Jones after Van Dyck.

regional materials, delayed the development of an architecture based on order, proportion and formal canons which often bore no relation to locality. In the same way, although the new word 'architect' denoted an artist rather than a trained craftsman, a man whose patron was expected to take an intelligent interest in plans conceived according to rule, Peter Mills, the creator of Thorpe Hall near Peter-borough, was trained as a bricklayer, and the three best-known seventeenth-century architects were all amateurs. Inigo Jones was first recorded in 1603 as a 'picture- 108 maker', and achieved fame as the designer of royal masques, beginning with *The Masque of Blackness* in 1605; his name was not associated with building until his appointment as Surveyor of the Works to James I in 1615, when he was already forty-two. Sir Christopher Wren had been Gresham Professor of Astronomy in London and Savilian Professor at Oxford before entering upon his architectural career, and Sir John Vanbrugh was a regular soldier and playwright until the age of 144 thirty-five when the Earl of Carlisle commissioned him to design Castle Howard.

Inigo Jones had travelled in Italy with Thomas Howard, 2nd Earl of Arundel, and there he had conceived a passion for Palladio. He acquired a copy of Palladio's *Quattro libri dell'architettura*, which, filled with his notes, still survives at Oxford. The great Italian architect followed a strict system of harmonic proportions based on the direct study of surviving Roman remains; the four parts of his book – the fundamentals of architecture and the orders; domestic design; public and urban design; and temple design – were practical rather than theoretical in intention and were addressed to the practising architect.

Fortunately, Inigo Jones's royal patron, James's wife Anne of Denmark, shared his enthusiasm, and enabled him to introduce the fully realized classical ideal in the Queen's House at Greenwich, which was begun as early as 1617. The cool, white

109, grace, the austerity and absolute horizontality of this building with its level skyline,
110 make an indelible impression even upon eyes which have looked at hundreds of subsequent English Palladian houses. What must have been its effect when first it rose in an England where steeply pitched roofs and half-timber predominated, and where the orders had been applied only as aids to poetical imaginings.

It seems incredible that the Queen's House and Lanhydrock, the Cornish home of the Robartes family, were contemporary. In fact building at Lanhydrock probably did not start until 1620, while the gatehouse was not added until 1658, more than twenty years after the completion of the Queen's House. Although perfectly symmetrical and although the gatehouse exhibits Renaissance details, the spirit of Lanhydrock is wholly that of the previous century. It is partly battlemented, the windows are mullioned, and fantastic outcrops of obelisks occur in the free manner
113 of the Elizabethans. The most distinguished room of the interior is a long gallery embellished with a flamboyant plaster ceiling in the style of that of the Blickling gallery. Broad, floral bands describe coils and geometric patterns about boldly modelled scenes of the Creation and pendants like richly adorned armillary spheres hang down at regular intervals. The wall panelling, it is true, is classically proportioned, but the fireplace, surmounted by a plaster panel filled with large figures in the strongest relief, has the same hybrid character and brims with the same abundant
VIII vitality as Abraham Smith's chimney-pieces at Hardwick.
107 The plan of the Queen's House originally took the shape of an H, but it was an H which owed nothing to that of the English traditional house. For the cross-bar (normally the great hall) assumed the form of a bridge over the London–Dover road, which divided the building into two blocks; and the hall occupied the north upright of the H. Later in the century the two blocks were united by Inigo Jones's

109 The north front of the Queen's House, Greenwich, begun by Inigo Jones in 1617. A comparison with other houses built in the first third of the seventeenth century (ills. 97, 100, 103) emphasizes the boldness and novelty of the new Palladian mode.

pupil and nephew by marriage John Webb and the house acquired its present aspect. Later still the road was moved. The severity of the square building is enlivened only by the rustication of the ground floor and by the first-floor loggia on the garden side, with its elegant Ionic columns, a sterner version of Palladio's Ionic loggia at the Villa Pisani at Montagnana.

111   Inside, the hall makes no pretence of being part of the living accommodation, and is plainly a vestibule: it rises to the full height of the house and is divided horizontally by a balcony giving access to all the rooms on the first floor, which, as in an Italian villa, is also the *piano nobile*. The ceiling inaugurates the style of plaster ornament 113   which succeeded the crowded decoration exemplified in the gallery at Lanhydrock. The vigorously patterned ribs are of such great size that they are as deep as the cornice, and they frame only a few simple rectangular panels of huge dimensions, arranged about a vast central circle which once enclosed a painting by the Venetian Artemisia Gentileschi. A double cable motif, acanthus leaves and berries luxuriantly adorn the ribs. Despite the scale of the plasterwork, there is nothing ponderous about this ceiling – as there is, for instance, about the basically similar design in the 112   dining-room at Forde Abbey in Dorset, where leaves and fruits in high relief riot over every inch of the massive ribs, and the compartments are filled with coarsely executed volutes and roundels, so that the dazzling plaster oppresses the panelled room, destroys the calm of its classical proportions and reduces the furnishings to doll's-house size. In the lofty hall of the Queen's House, the giant circle seems to revolve gently above the echoing circle of the black and white marble floor, which is itself set in motion by the skilful diagonal arrangement of the tiles. This symmetrical, chastely classical apartment dates from the same decade as the halls of 99   Audley End and Hatfield. That is the measure of its strange novelty.

110, 111 Opposite: The Queen's House, Greenwich, from the south, showing the open loggia (above), and two-storeyed hall (below, left). The plaster ceiling is of the purest Italianate type.

112 Opposite, below right: a rustic version of the new style of plaster ceiling. Putti and grotesques surround the goddess Flora in the centre of the dining-room ceiling at Forde Abbey, Dorset, of about 1650.

113 Left: the long gallery at Lanhydrock, Cornwall, clings to the Tudor tradition although it dates from 1636 and later.

114 The Tulip Staircase in the Queen's House, Greenwich.

115, 116 Opposite: the south front of Wilton House, Wiltshire, as it appears now and as it might have been. The drawing by Isaac de Caus shows a façade twice as long, with the present ornamental motifs doubled. It also gives a vivid impression of the formal garden, planned by de Caus with the advice of Inigo Jones.

The main staircase departs as radically and more spectacularly from tradition. It is 114 circular, but it no longer winds about a newel like the circular staircases of earlier houses: it has, in Jones's words, 'a vacuum in the middle'. The steps are tailed into the wall, so that the treads rise seemingly unsupported, a device which had never before been seen in England. The inspiration was Italian; but this original and peculiarly English design differs from the Mediterranean models: at the Queen's House tulips of wrought iron parade their undulating, decorative silhouettes against the white walls. Just as Palladio transformed the pedantic rules of his classical authority, the mediocre Roman architect Vitruvius, by his genius, so Inigo Jones informed the tenets imposed by the orders with the individual, poetic temperament which we encounter so directly in his sketch-books, where lively figures play a more conspicuous part than buildings.

The drawings remind us that Inigo Jones's influence was wielded not only through actual buildings but through his presentation of architectural themes in his masques. The scenery of these masques is by no means always so restrained as the design of the Queen's House. An ornate quality, which is more in evidence in Palladio's mature works than his later imitators seemed to realize, is strikingly displayed in Inigo Jones's theatrical drawings, and it dominates the interiors he designed at Wilton. XI

117 Design for a chimney-piece from Jean Barbet's *Livre d'architecture, d'autels et de cheminées*, which inspired Inigo Jones's chimney-piece in the Double Cube Room at Wilton (opposite).

XI Opposite: the Double Cube Room at Wilton House, so called because it is exactly 60 feet long, 30 feet wide and 30 feet high. The overmantel and wall panelling were designed to take portraits by Van Dyck, most notably his famous Herbert family group on the end wall. The magnificent gilded furniture is by William Kent (see p. 166).

The work at Wilton was commissioned by Philip, 4th Earl of Pembroke. The exterior of the south range dates from after a fire of 1647–8, and is largely the creation of John Webb, but there was much of Inigo himself in the original design of 1632, for which a drawing survives at Worcester College, Oxford. The façade in the drawing, which is by Isaac de Caus, the architect in charge, is wider than the present façade and more unrelentingly horizontal, for the angle bays do not rise up above the parapet. The central feature consists of a portico with six giant Ionic columns.

The state rooms at Wilton were decorated by Inigo Jones in his old age when the Civil War was at its height. The Double Cube Room must be one of the best known of all country-house interiors, but its white and gold magnificence can never be confronted with easy familiarity. The influence here is not wholly Palladian, for the heroic chimney-piece, with its broken pediment, scrolled cartouches and reclining gilded figures, and its theatrical gilt-draped, columned and figure-flanked frame for a Van Dyck painting, was based on an engraving in Jean Barbet's *Livre d'architecture, d'autels et de cheminées* (1633). The splendid central doorway with its broken pediment and festoons appears in a drawing Inigo Jones made for an immense palace at Whitehall which never materialized. The motifs of the lavishly gilded, deeply carved wall ornaments, pendants of fat fruits, scrolls and cartouches, are from the same source. They reappear enormously magnified and translated into a tilting, loosely flowing idiom in the broad, steep coving of the ceiling painted by Edward Pierce. The sense of movement and of extreme vitality imparted to the room by the change in scale gathers force in the illusionist painting within the central oval of the ceiling, depicting a lofty dome supported on a colonnade and animated by classical figures. This *trompe l'oeil* masterpiece was the work of Emmanuel de Critz.

In the Double Cube Room as in Elizabethan architecture the vertical and the horizontal are once more brought into harmony. Though the language of the Elizabethan houses is an imaginative compound of the traditional and the classical,

115
116

XI

117

and that of Wilton purely classical, the latter can be regarded as a development of the former.

The static horizontality and severity of the exterior of the Queen's House were premature, and more than fifty years were to pass before the full impact of their influence was felt. Inigo Jones's followers and collaborators, while they sometimes yielded to Italianate fantasy, were unable to break completely with tradition and at the same time could not always resist French and Dutch fashions. The taste for homely red brick encouraged by Wren later in the century was a further impediment to the proliferation of strict Palladianism.

A translation of the symmetry and horizontality of the Queen's House into a more acceptable red-brick idiom was effected by Hugh May. Little is known about his early years, but he held a post in the Office of Works and was appointed with Wren a Surveyor for rebuilding the City of London after the Fire. He designed Eltham Lodge, now marooned on a golf course in the heart of Woolwich, in 1663–5 for Sir John Shaw, a vintner of London, who had amassed a large fortune before the Civil War and was thus able to be of help of Charles II during his exile. On the Restoration he was rewarded with an annuity of £800 and later with a baronetcy. Through royal favour he obtained a long lease of one of the parks attached to Eltham Palace, and there built a house in the latest fashion. This hip-roofed building, especially the entrance front with its centrepiece adorned with stone pilasters and a pediment enclosing a garlanded coat of arms, has a distinctly Dutch air, probably the result of a tour of Holland May had made with the painter Sir Peter Lely in 1656. There is no backward glance to the vernacular style in this composition. The traditional smaller English house was gradually adapted to conform to its shape and arrangements, and Eltham can therefore be regarded as the prototype of the typical Georgian dwelling.

118 The entrance front of Eltham Lodge, Kent, designed by Hugh May and built in 1663–5. The roof was originally balustraded, as at Ashdown (ill. 119), and the windows were mullion-and-transom crosses.

XII Opposite: the staircase balustrade at Petworth House, Sussex, the work of Salvin in the nineteenth century, reflects the idiosyncratic classicism of the house without recourse to imitation. The allegorical paintings, in which the Duchess of Somerset joins in celestial revels, are of about 1720 and probably by Laguerre.

119 The garden front of
Ashdown House,
Berkshire, designed about
1650. In the background
are the two pavilions
that flank the entrance.

120 Opposite, above:
Raynham Hall, Norfolk,
seen from the south-west.
Begun for Sir Roger
Townshend in 1622, it
introduced the Palladian
style to Norfolk.

Ashdown House, Berkshire, was designed in about 1650 for the 1st Earl of Craven, 119
almost certainly by John Webb. Its fabric is fully expressive of its Berkshire down-
land locality – pale, luminous chalk stone, with quoins, window surrounds and a
basement of darker limestone. Ashdown is related to Eltham Lodge (which it pre- 118
ceded) in its affinities with Dutch building and also with the style advocated by
Inigo Jones. It displays the same steep roof in the form of a truncated pyramid,
though here the flat central area is balustraded and adorned with a cupola. But there
are other forces involved in this astonishing image, which differs in spirit almost as
greatly from the Queen's House and Eltham Lodge as from Lanhydrock. The start- 109
ling height of the building is indeed more in key with the Elizabethan habit of mind
than with the outlook of Cromwellian England. The vertical movement is assisted
by the diminishing height of the windows on each successive storey, by the two
great symmetrically placed chimney-stacks thrusting up from the roof and by the
extraordinary contrast between the tall house and the low, steep-roofed rectangular
pavilions standing on either side and slightly in advance of it on the entrance side.
These pavilions foreshadow the wings which were to become important components of the eighteenth-century country house; they also turn Ashdown into a
parody of the earlier hall house, with wings detached from the central structure and
set parallel instead of at right angles to it. Their chimneys are remarkably tall, and
originally rose right up to the eaves of the main building, like huge, free-standing
square pillars. The effect of such powerful vertical accents must have been as
grotesque as that of the fantastically lofty chimneys of the Château de Chambord.

Another of Webb's houses shows him under quite different influences, although
it is equally eloquent of his delight in movement. Lamport Hall, still the Northamptonshire home of the Ishams for whom it was built between 1654 and 1657, was
clearly conceived as an Italian villa in the manner of the architect's master, but the
feeling behind it is more that of the Inigo of the Double Cube Room and the XI
masques than of the Queen's House. The front is hugely and wholly rusticated, and
invigorated still further by the amazingly disproportionate pediments over the

door and above the ground-floor windows, colossal alternating triangles and segments on great brackets. The segment over the door bursts open to counteract the immense weight of the window-heads. As if unable to sustain the classical idiom throughout, Webb planned the hall in the outmoded, traditional manner with its entrance close to one end. The decoration has been altered but the agitated 121 fireplace is Webb's. Fat swags and garlands of fruit, cornucopias and three-dimensional swans, one on each side of the mantelshelf, carry the composition vividly upwards to a triangular pediment jutting up from a broken segment.

120   Raynham Hall, in Norfolk, is another house which moves vertically as well as horizontally and which is marked by a refreshingly personal fantasy within the classical convention. Its kinship with houses of the previous age is clear. Its shape, to begin with, immediately recalls the traditional H-plan. According to a drawing at the Royal Institute of British Architects in London there were once two entrances in the west front, each leading into a screens passage at either end of a hall running parallel to the façade: thus, as at Audley End, symmetry was persuaded to co-operate fully with the traditional. The present doorway, though it accords well with the spirit of the house, took the place of the original entrances in about 1680. A strong horizontal emphasis is provided by the cornice and the wide panelled band between the windows of the ground and first floors. This movement is counteracted by the large keystones pushing up through the lintels of the lower windows of the wings, and still more by the shaped and pedimented gables of these wings and by the central double pediment, in which a triangular pediment rises from a broken segmental one. The swelling shapes of the gables are accentuated by flanking Ionic volutes, and it is the treatment of these volutes which makes this façade so memorable. They have been conceived as supports for the pediments in which the gables end: thus they have been given Ionic capitals, which instantly turn them into pilasters – but pilasters which look as though they were made of icing-sugar rather than stone, pilasters cut loose from their bases, swaying and coiling as they carry the pediment aloft with a smooth floating movement contrasting with the sharp thrust of the pediment itself.

121 The hall chimney-piece at Lamport Hall, Northamptonshire, designed by John Webb and probably made by Caius Cibber.

122 Groombridge Place, Kent, seen from across its moat.

123 One of the north gate-piers of Thorpe Hall, Northamptonshire, designed by Peter Mills, of about 1653–6.

The general tendency to build according to classical rules was furthered by the publication and increasing use of guides and pattern-books. They included Inigo Jones's annotated edition of Palladio's work; two books by the Dutch-born courtier and amateur architect Sir Balthazar Gerbier, *A Brief Discourse concerning the Three Chief Principles of Magnificent Building* (1662) and *Counsel and Advice to all Builders* (1667); Sir Henry Wotton's *Elements of Architecture* (1624); and technical works by Joseph Moxon (1678) and William Leyburn (1668) which illustrated the orders with their propositions and details. Engravings published during the second half of the seventeenth century made English architects familiar with Italian buildings, and Dutch books on the work of such men as Philip Vinckeboons, Jacob van Campen and Hendrik de Keyser were also circulated.

A characteristic modification of the traditional country house by the tendencies of the age and the new architectural influences can be seen at Groombridge Place, 122 Kent, a house associated with the poet Edmund Waller, whose beloved 'Saccharissa' was Dorothy Sidney of Penshurst. The warm, russet-coloured old brick building drowsing above its wide square moat conveys a deep sense of security and continuity. Built about 1661 by Philip Packer, Clerk of the Privy Seal to Charles I, it stands within the courtyard of the original medieval house which Packer's father had bought in 1618. The hall-house design still clearly controls the composition: the plan is H-shaped, with a central block only one room thick containing the hall and a chamber above it, and projecting cross-wings. But the steep gables of the vernacular hall house have been transformed by the hipped roofs introduced at Ashdown and 119 Eltham Lodge, which create a continuous eaves-line and increased horizontality. 118 The eaves cornice with modillions corresponds to the wide Italian eave, and classical influence has dictated the large brick quoins and the conspicuous, pedimented Ionic portico of sandstone. The windows – which were originally transomed rather than sashed (an arrangement still visible at the side), with lead glazing-bars and swinging iron casements like those of the dormers – are symmetrically placed only on the main front.

The place of the medieval gatehouse and the Elizabethan entrance pavilions has been taken at Groombridge by classical gate-piers topped by pineapples, a modest example of one of the most visually exciting innovations of the seventeenth century. The walls generally enclosing the much-extended grounds of the period are pierced by openings flanked by massive piers, superior to many of their Italian and French counterparts in the variety and boldness of their design. Peter Mills's gate-piers at Thorpe Hall in Northamptonshire, for instance, are as brilliantly individual and inventive as any Elizabethan conceit, especially those to the north and south: eagle-topped, heavily rusticated and held down by huge entablatures, they are adorned with tall niches each half-filled by a fat round pedestal supporting a covered vase on which is poised an Ionic capital.

Sophisticated versions of the classically-disguised traditional house can be seen at Ham in Surrey, Honington in Warwickshire, Ramsbury in Wiltshire, Hanbury in Worcestershire and Belton in Lincolnshire, each with a different emphasis. Ham, of brick, like Groombridge, but with stone dressings, was originally built in 1610 by Sir Thomas Vavassour, Knight Marshal to James I. The appearance of the north façade of the house at that time is shown in a miniature by Alexander Marshall of Catherine Bruce, Countess of Dysart, with a prospect of Ham in the background. Bay-windowed wings advance on either side of a central block, onion-domed turrets shoot up in the angles between these components and a roof-high projection surmounts the entrance. The few alterations which took place in this composition later in the century were all made with a view to reducing its vertical accents. Thus the exotic, aspiring turrets were brought down to the level of the eaves and the tall bay over the door was entirely removed. The front was ennobled by the addition of oval niches adorned with classical busts, an Italianate device which had been introduced in the previous century.

The south front of Ham, meanwhile, was turned into a long, low, classical rectangle simply by filling in the space between the wings. (The balconies and the Venetian and sash windows belong to the eighteenth century.) The Duke of

124 The north front of Ham House, Surrey, a Jacobean design attuned to the classical taste in the 1670s, when it was given a fashionable roof and cornice. Projecting at the far right is a new wing, built on to contain a library (ill. 104) and staircase.

123

124,
128,
130

124

Lauderdale, who with his Duchess was responsible for most of the alterations at Ham, refers in a letter of 1673 to two German joiners who 'have wroughte much for the finishing of this house, and have made the double chasee for the windows'. The word 'chasee', a corruption of the French *châssis* (frame), is the source of the word 'sash'; but the sashes of the Duke's time were of the early type, still found occasionally in cottages, which slide sideways.

The personalities of the formidable Duke and Duchess are so imprinted upon the interior of Ham that the visitor is as uneasily aware of them as of the high interest of the architecture and decoration. Ham had become the property in 1637 of William Murray, 1st Earl of Dysart, and he bequeathed it to his daughter Elizabeth. The likeness of her in youth by Lely shows an exquisitely fair, large-eyed girl whose features suggest uncommon wit, vivacity and, above all, determination: this face already reveals the traits which later made her a fit partner for the coarse and sensual but ruthless and brilliantly clever John Maitland, member of Charles II's Cabal Ministry and afterwards Duke of Lauderdale. In the double portrait of the pair at Ham the Duchess, though middle-aged, preserves her beauty, as pale, fair people often do, but her expression is cruel and rapacious. Before her father's death she had married Sir Lionel Tollemache of Helmingham Hall in Suffolk, a gentle unassertive man who shared neither her quick intelligence nor her thirst for power. She formed a close friendship with John Maitland and when Sir Lionel, whose health was never robust, fell ill, she almost certainly hastened his end. Three years later, in 1672, the Earl of Lauderdale's wife died and after only six weeks he and Lady Tollemache were married. Both had an insatiable appetite for luxury, and though the splendour of Ham has tarnished and faded with time it is still so eloquent of the taste of the Lauderdales that their successors seem scarcely to have left a trace of their shadowy tenancies.

The Duchess inherited her strong visual sense from her father, who built the striking staircase at Ham in about 1638. It already heralds the type of staircase which reached its full development in grander country houses towards the end of the century. The balustrade is composed of carved panels instead of balusters. The forceful reliefs consist of trophies of arms, counterparts in wood of the decoration on Palladio's Loggia del Capitanio in Vicenza.

125 Below: a portrait of the Duke and Duchess of Lauderdale by Sir Peter Lely, in the Round Gallery at Ham House.

126 Below, right: the staircase at Ham, of about 1638. The rich wood-carving is set off by chaste plaster ceilings with garlands of crisp leaves.

104   The numerous rooms at Ham are small by comparison with the spacious chambers of Elizabethan houses. They still include the traditional great hall, though it was not used as such after 1638, and a long gallery, a low-ceilinged apartment without a fireplace articulated by the most delicately carved, garlanded Ionic pilasters and distinguished by two superb gilded tables of Dutch character supported by Negress caryatids. But the unique richness of Ham, a richness of marble, plaster, wood, tapestry and leather, of silver and gold, of velvet, damask and sarsnet, is all concentrated in the smaller rooms, where the feeling of secrecy and intimacy is as all-pervading as the consciousness of acute visual discrimination. The very chimney furniture of the Duchess's Bedchamber, the Marble Dining-room, the North Drawing-room and the Queen's Bedchamber is of silver. The Marble Dining-room
127 flaunts gilded leather; the North Drawing-room exhibits gilded chairs carved with dolphins and covered with rose-red brocaded satin, while flanking the fabulous fireplace are writhing, spiral-fluted columns like those in Raphael's tapestry cartoon *The Healing of the Lame Man*. This is but one of the Baroque details which impart movement to the sumptuous interiors. In the White Closet, within the central, deeply moulded oval of the ceiling with its acanthus ornamentation, a painted colonnade seems to revolve against an illimitable vista of soft clouds populated by nymphs, shepherds, and flying *putti*; and in the Queen's Closet, where the eagle soars with Ganymede into a blue distance overhead, the wainscoting is carved and gilded in the full Baroque style and the fireplace is of that typically Baroque, make-believe material, stucco counterfeiting veined marble. The difference between the comparatively sparse furnishing of the previous period and the luxuriousness of the seventeenth century is underlined in this room by two amazing chairs, 'sleeping chayres, carv'd and guilt frames, covered with crimson and gould stuff with gold frieze', as they are described in the inventory of 1679. They have wings and adjustable backs and the feet take the form of sea-horses, while the cross-bars are vigorous scrolls ornamented with finely carved cherubs and fruits.

127 The North Drawing-room at Ham, of the 1670s. The vigorous Baroque chimney-piece includes climbing cherubs in its decoration; it may be due to the German artist Francis Cleyn, who painted the overmantel picture. The tapestries, based on paintings of the seasons by Teniers, were added some decades later.

127

128, 129 The entrance
front of Hanbury Hall,
Worcestershire (above),
scarcely prepares the eye
for the full Baroque
impact of the illusionist
paintings in the staircase
hall, by Thornhill.

The highly developed visual discernment of the Lauderdales is as apparent in their choice of pictures and decorative paintings as in their furnishings. They commissioned sea-pieces by Willem van de Velde for the overdoors of the Duchess's Bedchamber, and two other Dutch painters, Bega and Dirck van den Bergen, who were both visiting London in the early 1670s, were asked to execute fourteen pastoral scenes and meticulous studies of plants, insects and animals above doors and fire-places. Henry Danckerts, an immigrant Dutchman, is represented by romantic pictures of classical ruins in landscapes. This is a theme for which the Duke and Duchess seem to have had special feeling, for some of the most exciting pictures at Ham are based on this motif – the dramatically lit *Classical Ruins* and *A Sorceress among Classical Ruins*, by a Scots artist who won little recognition in his own life-time, William Gowe Ferguson. Another interesting commission was that given to Francis Barlow for paintings of birds in a room which was originally a bedchamber, and which the Duchess made into a 'Volary Roome' or aviary after the Duke's death. Barlow's drawings are often found in country-house collections, but he was less often patronized as a painter.

Honington Hall in Warwickshire, unlike Groombridge Place and Ham, was a house newly built during the last quarter of the seventeenth century. The owner was a rich London merchant, Sir Henry Parker. Honington no longer looks exactly as it did in the Restoration period. A broad canted bay was added to the west front and a canted stone veranda with Tuscan columns was built on to the south side of the house in the eighteenth century. But the east front remains as Sir Henry knew it. The cross-wings of the vernacular house have here become shallow projections, so that the building is an almost square, symmetrical block, the type of house in fact
118 which was foreshadowed by Eltham Lodge. The exceptionally tall chimneys at Honington belong to a past tradition of verticality. Seen in conjunction with the motif of imperial busts in niches, they are piercingly eloquent. The combination is as powerful as that in Milton's poetry of antique gods and English hedgerows, daisied meadows and upland hamlets steeped in morning mist. The busts infuse an unremarkable composition with a strain of epic and nostalgic grandeur, which is reinforced by the dramatic and prominent doorway with its conspicuous columns and heavy segmental pediment breaking open to make way for a huge urn.

It is ornament again which gives individuality to the main front of Hanbury
128 Hall in Worcestershire, built for a barrister, Thomas Vernon, in 1701 at the close of the reign of William and Mary. Although the long, horizontal lines of the house and its careful symmetry and regularity control its aspect, it embodies most of the disparate influences of the age: its relation to the old H-plan is clear despite its Palladian proportions; the prodigious half-columns supporting the pediment over the central bay, the volutes on either side of the window above the entrance and the conspicuous keystones of the windows show a faint stirring of the Baroque spirit; the oval *oeil-de-boeuf* window in the pediment is French in flavour; and the general inspiration behind the red-brick house with its sash windows and hipped roof is Dutch.

The hint of Baroque feeling in the main façade at Hanbury is reinforced im-mediately inside the house by the rich, illusionist paintings by Sir James Thornhill
129 covering the walls and ceiling of the staircase hall. The ceiling is transformed into a cloudy firmament in the recessions of which floats an assembly of the gods, sitting, recumbent and entwined and moving in perspective so that they continually draw the eye upwards. On the walls, below an illusionist cornice with coarse brackets

130 The south entrance front of Belton House, Lincolnshire, built between 1684 and 1688. To the left of the house are the stables.

and roundels, and between fluted pilasters – also in paint – are scenes of classical subjects in settings that recede to infinity. The ceiling and walls are linked by the descending figures of Mercury and a cherub, Mercury clasping the portrait of Dr Henry Sacheverell, the fanatical High Churchman. This animated decoration, annihilating the barriers between painting and architecture, though not of the same order as the tempestuous adornment of the Würzburg Residenz is nevertheless at once recognizable as of the same genre.

Belton House, near Grantham in Lincolnshire, is closely related to Hanbury, 128, repeating the main features of that brick façade in stone. It is now thought to be the 130 design of William Winde or Wynde, 'the learned and ingenious Captain Wynne' as Colen Campbell called him a few decades later in *Vitruvius Britannicus*, and was built for Sir John Brownlow. As at Hanbury the adaptation of the classical mode to the traditional H-plan is carried out with assured smoothness. Belton differs from the Worcestershire house chiefly in the Dutch-derived detail of the balustraded roof; the steps mounting to the central entrance also give slightly more impetus to the vertical tendency of the cupola.

The unruffled harmony of Hanbury and Belton has none of the exuberance and unexpectedness of the syntheses imagined and made concrete by the Elizabethans; instead it is subdued, reticent and urbane. It is the domestic style associated with the great name of Wren. And though very few domestic buildings can actually be ascribed to him, popular opinion persists in attaching his name to a number of houses with the attributes of Hanbury, Honington and Belton. He may have had no hand in them, yet the serene logic of the designs and the skill with which tradition and novelty have been blended in each case are typical of Wren's unique genius for assimilating and co-ordinating ideas from widely varying sources, always preserving a sympathetic awareness of the past and at the same time subordinating it to his firm grasp of classical principles.

131, 132 Sudbury Hall, Derbyshire, a Jacobean house 'modernized' about 1670. The entrance front (above, left) shows a new porch and roof, and the interior received a magnificent staircase carved by Edward Pierce.

Such a resolution of the conflicting trends of the period was rare. In the last decade of the seventeenth century, before Lord Burlington had established a static Palladianism, these trends made individual and extreme appearances. The Dutch-inspired brick cube of Eltham Lodge was copied at Uppark for Ford Lord Grey by William Talman, who designed the palatial, half-Italian, half-French east front of , 138 Dyrham and the grander south and west fronts of Chatsworth, both Baroque in spirit and anticipating the full-blooded Baroque of Hawksmoor and Vanbrugh. 131 Meanwhile at Sudbury Hall, in Derbyshire, the local architect and sculptor Sir William Wilson worked in the Elizabethan manner, achieving a synthesis of the traditional and the classical less interesting, it is true, than great masterpieces such as Hardwick or Wollaton, but fascinating as a personal combination of the E-plan with the new Continental decorative idiom.

Sudbury was begun about 1613 for Mary Vernon; the Jacobean builder already imparted a strong advancing and retreating movement to the house in its plan, and gave a sparkle to the fabric by using brick of two colours to make a diaper pattern. Sir William Wilson, working for George Vernon from about 1670, encouraged the sense of animation and contrast in several ways: he designed a splendid two-storeyed classical centrepiece, he added a balustrade, dormers and a cupola, and he stressed the scintillating effect of the texture by setting the quoins of the upper storey in bold relief and by inserting arrestingly unconventional tracery (round-headed lights surmounted by ovals) in some of the windows. The frontispiece carries the eye straight up to the cupola through two tiers of tall, high-based, coupled columns supporting huge broken entablatures and curving pediments, in which cartouches seem to be precariously suspended rather than fixed.

The interior of the house matches the energetic frontispiece in both style and 132 feeling. The naturalistic imagery of the opulent plaster ceilings and the woodwork, 126 of breathtaking perfection, moves to convoluting Baroque rhythms. The staircase

133 The long gallery at Sudbury. In the memorable plaster ceiling closely ordered wreaths of flowers and fruit (compare ills. 104 and 112) are contrasted with loosely flowing scrolls.

is the most memorable example of the type already seen at Ham. Minutely rendered acanthus leaves and flowers, the work of Edward Pierce, whose gifts as a painter have been glimpsed at Wilton, fill the balustrade with palpitating undulations. In the drawing-room we encounter for the first time the incredible carving of Grinling Gibbons, surrounding the portrait above the fireplace. The motifs, the minutely 134 observed flowers, fruits, dead game and fish arranged in lavish festoons, and the sheer plentitude of them proclaim the materialist philosophy of Bishop Sprat. The wood is lime, which Gibbons was the first in England to use for sculpture. The most effective of all the plasterwork at Sudbury is that of the long gallery, where the 133 combination of the traditional apartment with a cove of great shells, leaf fronds and flower-swags, and ceiling-wide roundels and geometric shapes adorned with naturalistic flowers and foliage, is intensely exciting. This plasterwork was done by two London craftsmen, Bradbury and Pettifer. The wiry leaf tendrils were modelled upon lead with plaster while it was still soft and were twined into position before the plaster had set. Before Sudbury was restored and redecorated, when, after the death of the 9th Lord Vernon, it became National Trust property, it was possible to see the lead where the plaster had broken off.

Meanwhile, in total contrast to Sudbury, the unknown architect of Petworth in Sussex created an image even more overwhelmingly horizontal and reticent than the Queen's House. The predominating feeling behind the immensely long, pale IX rectangle of Petworth's west front is French, though whether it was the invention of an Englishman fired by French ideas, as Sir Anthony Blunt has suggested, or whether it was the work of Pierre Puget or Daniel Marot is unknown. In any case it reflects the taste and wishes of Charles, 6th Duke of Somerset, who in 1682 had married the heiress of the Percy family whose castle stood on the site.

134, 135 Carvings by
Grinling Gibbons at
Sudbury (above, left), of
about 1677, and Petworth,
done some fifteen years
later. This is still-life
sculpture applied to the
wall, breathtakingly close
to nature yet marvellously
composed.

The projections in the centre and at either end of the composition are so slight that
they cause no break in the even rhythm of the façade. Yet subtle variety, too delicate
to disturb the horizontal spirit of the house, is yielded by its fabric, which is of local
sandstone, sandy green in colour, with shining Portland stone for the window-
frames and the panels between the windows of the end bays. These panels are recessed
and thus make niches for precisely carved ornaments, busts and eagles. Originally a
shallow saucer dome hung above the central projection, and while this must have
unified the design it could not have given more than a slight vertical counter-
direction to the building. This reserved and refined façade nobly embodies the
rational bias of the age, and the nobility is sustained by the setting, a rich landscape
garden of a later date with a serpentine lake, perfectly placed thickets, undulating
vistas, temples and glorious stone urns, fluted at the base and carved with masks and
flower-sprays.

One of the most celebrated of the Petworth interiors, the Grinling Gibbons
135 Room, affords a startling foil to the severe exterior. The extraordinarily delicate
and skilful carvings framing the sixteenth- and seventeenth-century portraits in
134 this room surpass those at Sudbury Hall. They were done in 1692 when Gibbons,
at the height of his fame, had just begun his stone-carvings for St Paul's Cathedral.
They convey an irresistible and uplifting sense of joy and freshness which reflects
the mood of Restoration England, liberated after a time of oppression and unrest.

136 This seventeenth-century view of Chatsworth House, Derbyshire, from the south-east, shows the whole grandiose layout of parterres and water-works. In the right foreground is the domed temple from which the famous Cascade shimmers down towards the house.

At Chatsworth, in Derbyshire, the note of exuberance struck in Gibbons's carvings informs the whole princely house. Here again, as at Petworth, the relationship between the building and its environment approaches the sublime, and all is on a grand scale. Though the grounds were landscaped in the mid-eighteenth century, when the fine pictorial view of the house from the bridge over the Derwent was created, and though great changes were made by the 6th Duke of Devonshire after 1811, the basic character of the setting was determined by the same late seventeenth-century spirit which prompted the design of the mansion, an eager, aspiring Baroque spirit. For the images associated above all with memories of Chatsworth are those of the Cascade and the Long Canal. The latter is higher than the ground on the south side of the house, so that the silvery building appears from a distance to float on the shining water. The Cascade, carried out by a pupil of Le Nôtre, recalls the two-mile-long ribbon-vista of sparkling water at Caserta, which is one of the great expressions of the Baroque mood. The prospect from the temple at the summit of the Cascade is not on the same stupendous scale as the scene from above the waterfall at Caserta, but the fantasy of the quicksilver, strait-jacket composition in the gentle English landscape is as exhilarating. Water (supplied by natural pressure from a series of man-made lakes) streams out from the temple, a delicious niched and rusticated structure with a stepped dome which is itself a circular waterfall. Fountains and jets shoot up in the temple forecourt, and it is through their snowy spray and to the accompaniment of their plashy thunder that anyone standing inside the building looks down endlessly moving, glittering steps of water to the house and beyond it to the western wooded slopes of the park.

The house, like the Cascade, was a product of the enthusiasm and imagination of the 4th Earl of Devonshire, a direct Cavendish descendant of Bess of Hardwick. The

136
138

137

136

Cavendishes supported the Royalist cause in the Civil War, but the 4th Earl was no friend to Charles II and still less to James II. He put his name to an invitation to William of Orange, nephew and son-in-law of James II, and marched with five hundred men to Nottingham to meet him. When William became William III in 1689, Cavendish's reward was a dukedom. He had already started to rebuild the Elizabethan Chatsworth. He shared his ancestress's passion for bricks and mortar, and although his house emerged as wholly classical it was instinct with the drama and movement which characterized all Bess's buildings.

137 137 The south front of Chatsworth seems to rise directly from the waters of the Long Canal.

The façades at Chatsworth differ from each other, and each is meant to be looked at from a directly frontal viewpoint in the pictorial Baroque manner. The Duke himself may have designed the most spectacular front, to the west, a truly grandiose composition set in agitated, angular motion by the exaggeratedly vermiculated and rusticated double staircase mounting steeply to the high terrace on which the house stands. The ground floor of the façade is boldly rusticated; above it, massive fluted columns and pilasters rise the whole height of the building to support a frieze carved with restless, scrolled ornament. The vertical movement of the pilasters is hastened by the urns vibrating directly above them on the balustraded parapet. Giant keystones thrust up from the windows, the two central ones of which are framed by voluptuous garlands, and a tall figure of Athene on the pediment of the entrance projection emphasizes the ascending character of the design.

The south and east fronts, which predate the west façade, are the work of William Talman. His early life and origins remain obscure, but when he began work at Chatsworth in 1686 he had already designed a vast house at Thoresby in Nottinghamshire (destroyed by fire in 1745), and was engaged on Uppark. These achievements no doubt sufficed to recommend him to Cavendish, whose main desire was

138
136, 137

138 The grandest front of Chatsworth, to the west.

XIII Opposite: the State Drawing-room at Chatsworth, decorated between 1689 and 1699, with a painted ceiling by Laguerre and elaborate woodwork that combines sculpture and marquetry. The Mortlake tapestries from Raphael's celebrated cartoons of the Acts of the Apostles were woven in about 1630.

to employ an architect willing to comply with his own ideas. In 1689, however, when he was still working at Chatsworth, Talman was appointed to the highest architectural post in the country: the Comptrollership of the Royal Works.

Talman's south front consists of two storeys rising above a rusticated basement. 137 Unlike the west front it projects in three pilastered bays at either end; these contrast with the plainly treated central bays, to which a central emphasis is imparted by flights of balustraded steps making sharp angular turns and rising with quickening rhythm on either side of a broad basement projection. The effect is palatial and Italianate, and it is difficult to believe it emanated from the same source as Uppark. The east front is conceived in the same spirit, but the projecting end bays, again 136 articulated by big pilasters, are much narrower. Survivals from the earlier house dictated their proportions, for they enclose Elizabethan spiral staircases.

The north front is almost certainly the work of Thomas Archer. Archer had spent four years in Italy and his imagination was fired by Roman Baroque architecture, the principal influence in his powerfully romantic buildings. The great dramatic bulk of St John's, Smith Square, in London, is his invention and so is the splendid house of Chicheley in Buckinghamshire, where restless Baroque rhythms are 139 embodied in unpretentious brick.

At Chicheley gigantic stone pilasters adorn the main front; the boldest of them, those flanking the forward-thrusting centrepiece, are set on double bases, one on top of the other, and thus send the whole projection shooting up above the rest of the façade. A rich frieze resting on the capitals scarcely interrupts the dynamic ascent, for the frieze is but the base of further pilasters sweeping up to the parapet. The windows, which vary in design, all aspire, either through strong keystones in square, arched or

shouldered heads or through curiously stepped arches repeating in reverse the design of the broad brick aprons below the first-floor openings. Chicheley, like Chatsworth, is seen in relation to water – here in the form of wide canals enclosing the great lawn on three sides and providing, with their clear, still geometry, a perfect foil to the movement of the house. At Chatsworth Archer's façade imparts a curving, smoother and more ample movement to the character of the house as a whole. It swells in a shallow bow which rises well above the rest of the front. This greater height, in conjunction with the later eared attic windows set in the same frame as the tall windows beneath them, between the huge capitals of pilasters, conspires to create the surprising impression that this colossal bow has a perceptible entasis and thus a slight, vertiginous backward inclination.

XIII   The interiors of Chatsworth match the exterior in their sparkling vitality. The Duke engaged some of the best-known artists of the period for the profuse decoration – the ironworker Tijou, the sculptor Cibber, the painters Laguerre and Verrio. He also employed a local woodcarver, Samuel Watson from Heanor near the Nottinghamshire border. His work, though 'gaz'd at and admir'd by all' according to his epitaph, never attains the buoyancy of the exquisitely meticulous three-dimensional naturalism of Grinling Gibbons's carvings, but the lively rhythm of the wreathed and festooned overmantels, window-heads and overdoors, architraves and cornices dictates the restless mood of the sumptuous rooms with more *brio* than the painted ceilings with their mythological flurries. Watson's use of twisted, bunched and looped drapery among his wind-blown leaves, dead game, flowers and musical instruments is immensely effective in stimulating the movement of his imagery, while his idiosyncratic overmantel designs oppose the figurative with abstract, spatial, kinetic conceits: realistic birds, foliage, flowers and hangings surround elaborately moulded panels of geometric shape in which a small oval or circular portrait is set in a field of marquetry where triangles, lozenges and squares create strange optical illusions of shifting patterns and recessions.

139 Chicheley House, Buckinghamshire, built by Thomas Archer about 1690 for Sir John Chester.

XIV Opposite: the chapel at Chatsworth, with its paintings and theatrical reredos adorned with allegorical statues by Cibber, could almost be taken for a fervent Baroque work of the Continent.

The Baroque temper of Chatsworth reaches a climax in the chapel. It rises XIV through two storeys, and ascends yet further within the painted oval of the ceiling, where an angel host flies among soft cumulus clouds. On the walls, above Samuel Watson's garlanded panels, the room moves outwards through the columns of a painted colonnade and beyond vehement Biblical figures to merge into Italianate architectural fantasies. The focal point of all the exuberance is the reredos, of local alabaster, dazzlingly pale against the wall panelling and the cerulean blue of the painted skies behind it. The open pediments, the flaming urns, the looped draperies suspended on either side of a darkly glowing picture, *Doubting Thomas* by Verrio, the allegorical figures swaying beside prodigious volutes, the central niche adorned with angels and roses and theatrically advancing – all these moving forms derive enhanced vitality from the gentle opalescence of the material, so much more tractable than the marble of their Continental counterparts.

The connection between William Talman's work at Chatsworth and the east front he designed for Dyrham House in Gloucestershire is clear. Although the scale X is smaller, Dyrham has the same resplendent air. It again shows a recessed central block with shallow projections at each end, but here a central emphasis is provided by a pillared entrance and an enormous eagle spreading its wings from a small pediment on the parapet above. The house is set across the bottom of a deep, tree-planted valley and to the charm of its situation is added the charm of the contrast between the classical mansion and the Perpendicular church adjoining it, both built of pale gold limestone, and the charm of the visual allusion to the traditional relationship of manor house and church. For the present house stands on the site of an Early Tudor manor.

William Blathwayt, Secretary of State to William III, married the Dyrham heiress in 1686 and at once set about rebuilding the old house. He first commissioned a French Huguenot called Samuel Hauduroy to build a western block, and then, a few years later, added an eastern range, this time by Talman. Dyrham is thus like two houses set back to back. Hauduroy's front looks towards the garden. It has 140 only two storeys, but the broad high terrace on which it stands, approached by a double stair, and the tall balustraded parapet, animated by urns and a sprightly lead figure of Mercury, counteract the horizontal emphasis of the composition. Wings at either end add a forward movement, which is reinforced by square pavilions jutting from each end of the terrace, and a central balcony on outsize scroll-brackets gives a touch of deeper chiaroscuro.

The room behind this balcony sustains the Baroque feeling. It is perhaps the most arresting of the interiors, which with their several leather-hung walls, their blue and white Delft ware, bird and perspective paintings evoke the atmosphere of the period as vividly and more genially than those at Ham. The Balcony Room looked more opulent when its decoration was first finished, for the gilded panelling, now dark with age, was then richly marbled. Hauduroy had himself done the work. The furniture includes two striking torchères in the form of sinuous blackamoors balancing scallop shells on their heads. William Blathwayt inherited them from his uncle Thomas Povey, a great collector and friend of the diarist Samuel Pepys.

While Chatsworth, Chicheley and Dyrham exhibit unmistakable elements of the Baroque, they cannot, except for the Chatsworth chapel, be compared for vigour of execution and for extremes of contrast and chiaroscuro with great Continental houses such as Stupinigi or Pommersfelden. But there were two architects working in England at the close of the period whose work does admit of such

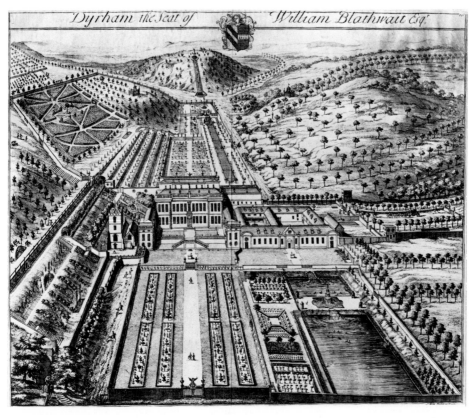

141–
143
a comparison, even while they remain wholly individual. At Easton Neston in Northamptonshire Nicholas Hawksmoor unites traditional features and the noblest classical manner with magnificent Baroque bravado. Unlike many builders of that time he had devoted himself solely to his art from the beginning, first as an office boy, then as a close collaborator of Wren. The association never submerged him: it served only to develop his own great and idiosyncratic talent. His architecture is an architecture of movement, it is superbly pictorial and it magnificently celebrates the triumph of art over utility.

Easton Neston was built for Sir William Fermor, later Lord Lempster, at the time of his marriage to Sophia Osborne, daughter of the Earl of Danby. The commission probably came through Wren who was related to Fermor by marriage. The rectangular block of the house is strikingly tall, even by comparison with

138 Chatsworth, and it would have been taller still if Hawksmoor's projected cupola, a lofty pepperpot encircled by a colonnade and tremulous flame-filled urns, pictured in *Vitruvius Britannicus*, had ever been added. Giant Corinthian pilasters set rather close and supporting a ponderous frieze accentuate the height of the building on every façade, but no two façades are alike. The seven central bays of the east and west fronts advance, and the entrance bays project yet further in both cases. That on

142 the west façade is flanked by huge columns, as massive to the eye as those of Bernini's colonnade in Rome, surmounted above the frieze by a curving pediment and coat of arms which interrupt the parapet with its urns and lions. On the east side the

141, columns yield to pilasters. On the south front the two tall storeys of the entrance
142 and garden elevations suddenly become three storeys, the frieze has vanished, and

140 Dyrham Park, Gloucestershire, from the west. Kip's view, published in 1712, shows the original relation of the house and church (at the left) to the hilly landscape. George London's splendid gardens, now vanished, included a cascade rivalling that of Chatsworth and a long canal, both visible beyond the house.

141

attenuated prolongations of the immensely tall pilasters of the narrow central bay scarcely suffice to hold down the open pediment poised above them. The same strange floating movement characterizes the north front, and here it is accompanied by a totally unexpected disposition of the windows. A two-storey elevation in the centre and at either end of the composition is combined with four storeys. Although the internal arrangements correspond to this fantastic design, an added reason for it was surely the artist's delight in variety.

The interior of the house is striking. It is amazing to discover in a building so apparently remote from the old H-plan that the hall (now the dining-room) is in its traditional place, parallel to the façade. Originally there was even a screens passage. But the noble room has been divided, and the end which contained the screens passage has been merged with an adjacent apartment to make an entrance hall. Hawksmoor designed the grand, lofty stone-vaulted room to house the Arundel collection of marbles – assembled by the 2nd Earl of Arundel, Inigo Jones's travelling companion in Italy – which Fermor had acquired.

The staircase which lies beyond the hall to the left is as instantly impressive as the hall. It is uniquely situated in a long, narrow space which rises to the full height of the tall house and runs from north to south like the hall. A richly plastered barrel-vault gives increased height to the space and accentuates the drama of the two great flights, so arranged that the stairfoot is immediately beneath the upper landing and the broad shallow steps mount first towards the high arched window of the north front then, with a startling change of chiaroscuro, turn their back on the source of light and advance to the top floor past monochrome paintings of classical themes and beckoning statues in shell-headed niches. The rather slow rhythm of the ascent is punctuated by two half-landings and is countered by the bright staccato of the wrought-iron arabesques of the balustrade.

143

141–143 Easton Neston,
Northamptonshire, of about 1700,
by Nicholas Hawksmoor.

Opposite: the east, or garden front,
emphasized by giant pilasters. A
contemporary called its Helmdon
limestone 'the finest building stone I
have seen in England'.
Above: the startling change from the
two-floor, big-scale design of the
entrance front, on the left, to a three-
storeyed elevation on the south side.
Right: the staircase, perhaps designed
in collaboration with Sir Christopher
Wren.

144 Above: Sir John Vanbrugh, painted by Kneller in about 1704–10.

145 Above, right: the Satyr Gate at Castle Howard, Yorkshire.

At about the time when Easton Neston was going up, in the last year of the seventeenth century, Hawksmoor was involved in another house, which surpassed it as an expression of Titan energy – Castle Howard in Yorkshire, one of the master-pieces of the Baroque style. Hawksmoor appears to have been in charge of the building operations, but the designer was Sir John Vanbrugh. This astonishing house was his first work of architecture. He was then thirty-five years of age, and had been a professional soldier. In 1692 he had emerged from two years in French prisons (where he had been held under suspicion of being an enemy agent) as a writer of rollicking comedies. Vanbrugh's entrance into architecture was again sudden. It was occasioned by the remarkable opportunity given him by his friend Charles Howard, 3rd Earl of Carlisle, after a quarrel with Talman whom he had originally chosen to rebuild his castle, recently destroyed by fire. Even though the age favoured gifted amateurs, Vanbrugh's appointment provoked surprise. Swift wrote,

> Van's Genius without Thought or Lecture
> Is hugely turned to Architecture

But architecture was clearly the right medium for his powerfully visual and scenic imagination and the only one which could satisfy his obsession with the monu-mental. His grandiose art is born of the same spirit as that of the author of Bolsover. A glance at the monstrous details of the Satyr Gate suffices to declare the affinity, which is confirmed beyond dispute by the presence in the park of obelisks, pyramids and the Gothic-derived castellated wall with its fantastic bastions, all gargantuan.

145–
151
144

145

149   The plan of Castle Howard is distinguished by a remarkable and novel feature –
long, one-storeyed wings stretching out on either side of the main block, counter-
balancing with their horizontality the soaring motion of giant orders, pediments,
lively figures and urns dizzily poised against the sky, and a tall dome as restlessly
gyrating and ornate as that of the Salute church in Venice, and of a size to kindle a
sense of disproportion and consequently surprise at its being thus upheld in mid-air.
As at Easton Neston and Chatsworth the façades are variously designed: that on
the garden side is animated by regularly spaced elephantine Corinthian pilasters
set up on a rusticated basement with two floors of round-headed windows between
146 them, while the forceful entrance front moves to an uneven, heavy rhythm accentuated by four pairs of Doric pilasters rising smoothly against a background
of banded rustication. Between the coupled pilasters niches take the place of windows
and within them stand draped statues and colossal vases. A broad frieze carved with
trophies of arms intensifies the sombre mood of the composition, which is that
148 also of the remarkable garden and of the great two-storeyed stone hall (restored after
a fire in 1940) and the dramatic tunnel of the corridor which runs right through the
centre of the house and the low wings. So monumental a hall, inviting comparison
with the relics of Roman antiquity rather than with any seventeenth-century palace,
had never yet been seen in England. The shape is a Greek cross; immensely high
arches springing from mighty fluted piers open into the short arms and mount up
towards the painted dome which hangs over the apartment like a cloudburst.
Marble statues, human beings and their appurtenances shrink to insignificance in
these huge and magniloquent perspectives.

146 This near view of
the entrance front of
Castle Howard, built
between 1699 and 1712,
at once proclaims the
dramatic character of
Vanbrugh's heroic
architecture.

145

147 Above: the Temple of the Four Winds at Castle Howard, completed by Hawksmoor after Vanbrugh's death in 1726. Just visible in the distance on the right is the Mausoleum (see ills. 150, 151).

148 Right: Vanbrugh's hand is unmistakable in the strange chimney-piece and giant proportions of the hall at Castle Howard.

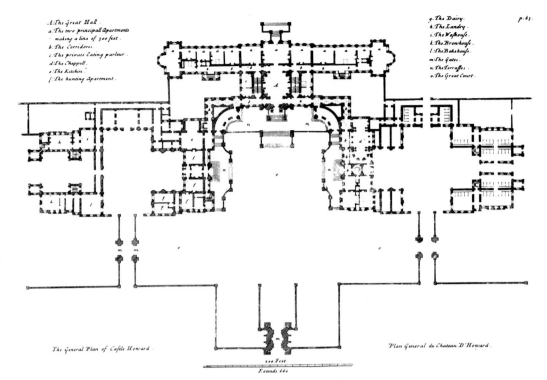

A: The Great Hall.
a: The two principall Apartments making a line of 300 feet.
b: The Corridores.
c: The private Eating parlour.
d: The Chappell.
e: The Kitchin.
f: The hunting Apartment.

q: The Dairy.
h: The Landry.
i: The Washouse.
k: The Brewhouse.
l: The Bakshouse.
m: The Gates.
n: The Terrasses.
o: The Great Court.

The General Plan of Castle Howard.

Plan General du Chateau D'Howard.

200 Feet
Extends 660

The word 'picturesque' has been used earlier in these pages to describe a trait which appeared in English architecture long before the so-called 'Picturesque movement'. The word still waited to be coined when Vanbrugh designed the setting for Castle Howard, but his immense vistas, his groves and ornamental waters enlivened by temples and follies can only be described as picturesque in the special eighteenth-century sense of a pictorially conceived landscape. It was Vanbrugh rather than Kent or Bridgeman who first translated the pictorial vision of a classical landscape into three-dimensional reality, even though his temper was that of ancient Rome itself rather than that of Claude. The trend of Vanbrugh's imagination is clear from the advice he gave when he was consulted later about the layout of the park at Blenheim: 'You must send for a landscape painter', he said. He had not altogether cast aside the seventeenth-century formal concept of the garden at Castle Howard; for although he thought of the vast house and its surroundings as one pictorial design, the layout in the immediate vicinity of the mansion as shown in the perspective views in *Vitruvius Britannicus* was intended to echo the curves and spatial complexities of the house, thus stressing its Baroque rhythm and movement.

147 The Temple of the Four Winds is based on the same plan as Palladio's Villa Capra, but it is no more Palladian in atmosphere than the prospect in which it stands is a nostalgic reconstruction of a vanished Golden Age in the manner of later landscape gardens such as Stourhead. The verticality of the Temple is pronounced and, curiously, its mood is more severely Roman than that of Palladio himself. It prepares
150, the mind for the sombre nobility of the Mausoleum, built by Hawksmoor after
151 Vanbrugh's death. This majestic, circular, colonnaded building with its high drum and shallow dome, poised aloft on its rugged base of projecting rectangular blocks and great bastions, is no mere ornament: it concentrates the solemn, elegiac character of this whole terrain, for it is an actual tomb. It encloses the remains of Vanbrugh's friend and patron, Lord Carlisle.

149 Vanbrugh's plan for Castle Howard, from *Vitruvius Britannicus*. To the left of the entrance front is the kitchen court, for domestic services, to the right the stable court, which was never built.

147

150, 151 The sombre, brooding Mausoleum at Castle Howard, designed by Hawksmoor in 1729 but not finished until 1742, six years after his death.

Vanbrugh's next commission was one for which he was supremely suited. It was
152, to design the residence of a public hero, Blenheim Palace, the nation's gift to John
54– Churchill, Duke of Marlborough in commemoration of his victory over Louis XIV.
157 It is not certain how Vanbrugh came to be chosen rather than Wren. The decision
would seem to have been the Duke's: Vanbrugh had been a soldier like himself and
he understood the clash of battle as well as the drama and bravura of magnificence;
he more than any other artist knew how to celebrate military glory in stone. The
history of the actual construction was stormy, affording a parallel to the character
of the great house itself with its complex, changing masses and rhythms and the
grand rhetoric of its roofscape and landscape: Vanbrugh encountered endless
153 vexation and difficulties through the interference of the Duchess, Sarah Churchill,
which at last resulted in such a quarrel that he was refused admittance to his own
building, though he did once manage to look over a wall. What is important is that
this marvellous monument to an unexampled achievement was in the end, with the
assistance of Hawksmoor, completed.

Blenheim is unique in England not only because of an immensity which rivals
that of Versailles – as one stands in the middle of the grand saloon one is on the
centre of an axis stretching for more than two miles from Bladon's church tower
through the house and the great Kitchen Court and across the bridge to the statue of
Marlborough standing on his victory column – but because it is firstly a monument
and only secondly a house. To the Duchess it was that 'wild, unmerciful house'
which not even 'a vast number of feather beds and quilts . . . all good and sweet
feathers, even for the servants', and the bookcases she stood along the intimidating
157 walls of the long gallery could domesticate. For this grandiose, declamatory pile,
more like a mountainous work of sculpture than architecture, was intended to
honour Marlborough through art and not function. It is supremely successful as a
Baroque composition of movement, of intricate retreating and advancing planes, of
light and shade, of contrasted smooth and rusticated surfaces. And despite arched
windows, the segmental colonnade of the main front and the interplay of convex

152 The entrance front of
Blenheim Palace,
Oxfordshire, seen from
the great court, embodies
Vanbrugh's superb
feeling for the complex
grouping of masses at its
noblest. The vast house
took nearly twenty years
to build, from 1705 to
1724.

153 Sarah Churchill, Duchess of Marlborough, from a portrait after Kneller. Vanbrugh spoke of her as 'spoiling Blenheim in her own way'.

and concave forms, the movement is in general, like that of Elizabethan buildings and unlike that of Continental Baroque architecture, predominantly angular. The movement of the main block is all contained within the space defined by the four 152 identical angle towers, and controlled also by their weight, even though their corner pinnacles – which take the appropriate though improbable shape of coroneted grenades – flare aloft. The towers above all balance the tremendous vertical thrust of the main portico, which is as strikingly individual and unorthodox in character as any sixteenth-century conceit. It moves massively forward and then, in a surprising, quite unprecedented way, projects the paired piers of its elevation upwards beyond the pediment they support to carry a second, broken pediment with yet another seeming pediment behind it, though in reality this is the gable-end of the hall roof.

The Corinthian order of the portico penetrates the house itself and determines the character of the square hall with its two tiers of arches and its tall angle columns, 154 dominates the painted colonnade in the saloon, and reappears in another portico on 155 the garden front. Here there is no pediment but an inscribed attic surmounted by a marble bust of Louis XIV, part of the spoils of Tournai.

The intensely emotional and gargantuan quality of the exterior is so entirely maintained within that it is the masonry and its articulation and the spatial design which are remembered rather than any of the furnishings – apart from Rysbrack's statue of Queen Anne in the Long Library, put there by Sarah after her husband's death, and the organ facing her. That was only installed in 1890, but the sweeping 157 corrugations of the pipes amplify the flutes of the rhythmically spaced piers in a

154 Above: the immense hall at Blenheim. Its theatrical atmosphere is determined by the proscenium-like arch at the end framing the door into the saloon, and by the giant arcading.

155 Left: the saloon at Blenheim. Laguerre's paintings suggest a gallery open to a turbulent sky; between the giant columns are groups of people, some of whom seem to be gazing over the marble parapet into the room itself.

dramatic and satisfying way. This room, 180 feet long and occupying the whole of the west front, is a remarkable visual experience, especially seen from the gallery 157 above the marble Queen, for there the eye, excited by the proximity of the enormous capitals of coupled Doric piers carrying a great arch, grasps the giant proportions of the room and perceives it as a sequence of different but related spaces.

The magnificent house rises amid two thousand acres of land on a site selected by Vanbrugh. It was an inspired choice – not the site of the original manor house of Woodstock (ruined in the Civil War) which was confined by steep slopes, but a vast expanse of level ground falling sharply away to the left to command splendid prospects. The present park, the chief adornment of which is Vanbrugh's mighty 156 bridge, was later 'improved' by Capability Brown. The parterre the architect designed on a mammoth scale to match the movement of the garden front of the palace was replaced by turf, and this was a loss, but the lake, on the other hand, which took the place of Vanbrugh's 'ditch', enhances the massive character of the bridge and adds another dimension to the changing, tree-framed views of the rolling terrain and the bold projections and irregular roofline of the building. As at Castle Howard the landscape is on the same stupendous scale as the house, and the gravity of its mood sets it apart from later Picturesque layouts.

Vanbrugh's genius for creating a synthesis in the Elizabethan tradition is most perfectly expressed in his last great house, the ruined Seaton Delaval in North- 158 umberland. This smoke-blackened, dark stone image haunts the memory as 161 unfadingly, as Hardwick and presents a similarly novel and transporting combination of the traditional and the classical, the vertical and the horizontal. The architect's powers were as appropriately employed here as at Blenheim, for there was an

156 The bridge at Blenheim, here reflected in Capability Brown's lake. To Sir Joshua Reynolds it seemed intended for the tramp of Roman legions.

157 Opposite: the long library at Blenheim, fitted out when the Duchess inherited the library of her son-in-law Lord Harley who died in 1722. The decorative details are by Hawksmoor, who finished the room after Vanbrugh's death.

158 The north front of Seaton Delaval, Northumberland, begun by Vanbrugh in 1718.

xv Opposite: the south ante-room at Syon House, Middlesex, designed by Robert Adam, of 1762–3 (see p. 190).

atmosphere of drama and wildness both about the site in its bleak landscape above the sea and about the lives of the Delavals which accorded with Vanbrugh's own temperament. All the family were spirited, gifted and debauched. Admiral George Delaval, Vanbrugh's patron, died suddenly while the house was in course of construction and the architect himself was dead before it was finished. The composition is more inevitable than that of either Blenheim or Castle Howard, for every stone of the cyclopean masonry plays its part in the heroic drama of the house. In its picturesque monumentality it is more like the engraved ruins of Piranesi than any actual work of architecture, though Piranesi was not born until two years after the building of Seaton Delaval had begun.

The central structure, facing north, rises abruptly above its two-storeyed wings 158 which, linked to it by low arcades, lie at right angles to it, thus embracing it in a prodigiously long forecourt. An ample flight of steps climbs to the arched door which is flanked by angular groups of giant ringed Doric columns and surmounted by a huge semicircular window. Both door and window exhibit keystones of nightmarish proportions, the upper of the two extending indeed to the deep metope frieze of the entrance bay. Immediately above the frieze and of the same width as the entrance bay rises a tall attic storey pierced by three lofty windows and crowned by a pediment filled with weather-scarred sculpture. This highly personal yet thoroughly classical façade is surprisingly flanked by octagonal turrets which instantly recall the sixteenth century, while behind them, on the east and west fronts, stand strange square towers ornamented with heavy banded rustication. Vanbrugh's Baroque shows itself most clearly here as a development of the Elizabethan version of the style, a development which is bolder and more severe, more massive and at the same time more spectacular in its use of light and shade.

154

159 The ruined hall at Seaton Delaval.

The same spirit pervades the interior, the main part of which was gutted by a fire
159, in 1822 (caused by jackdaws' nests in the chimneys). The bareness of the deserted
160 stone hall augments its sombre yet deeply romantic castle air. The high walls are
articulated by gigantic blank arcading and arched niches from the recesses of which
expressive broken statues survey the intruder. The atmosphere is that of Webster's
two violent Italian tragedies for which this hall would provide a perfect setting.
161 Even the stables are grandiose.

There was a specifically English quality in Vanbrugh's genius which was later to
recommend him to architects, among them Robert Adam, who valued the sublime, the colossal, the irregular and all the properties of the 'picturesque'. He
supplied the link between them and the Elizabethans. But in his own time he was
neither understood nor appreciated, and he had no immediate followers: as soon as
the Palladian rule was established his art was condemned as too rhetorical, too
theatrical and too unrestrained.

XVI Opposite, above:
the 'Gothick' library at
Milton Manor, Berkshire,
added by Stephen Wright
in 1776 (see pp. 195–6).

XVII Opposite, below:
the long gallery at
Strawberry Hill,
Middlesex, designed by
Thomas Pitt and
completed in 1763 (see
p. 197). The door was
copied from the north
door of St Alban's
Cathedral, the vault
from Henry VII's Chapel
in Westminster Abbey.

160 Looking up the staircase in the main block at Seaton Delaval.

161 The stables at Seaton Delaval. Great broad transverse arches contrast with the lesser simple arches of the niches where the horses ate their hay in unparalleled style.

5 A GOLDEN AGE

the eighteenth century

HISTORY PRESENTS US WITH the spectacle of human society pursuing now this, now that quite contrary objective, never achieving the perfection it seeks but emphasizing continually changing aspects of its goal. To those who view the preoccupation of our own century with material well-being and social equality as a form of progress, the Georgian period must seem painfully remote from the perfection implied by the title of this chapter. They will point to the appalling infant mortality among the poor, to the illogical harshness of the law; they will recall Dr Johnson's calculation that malnutrition killed off more than twenty people a week in London alone; they will refer to Hogarth's famous delineation of 'Gin Lane'; they may allude to Wesley's heart-rending description of a family he visited at Bethnal Green in 1777 – 'one poor man was just creeping out of his sick bed to his ragged wife and the little children who were half naked, and the very picture of famine, when, one bringing in a loaf of bread, they all ran, seized upon it and tore it to pieces in an instant'. There are some others, however, to whom the price paid for the remedy of these ills, the sacrifice of a highly civilized, sophisticated governing class and with it of aesthetic standards and of conditions supremely favourable to the creation of great works of art, may seem too high. It is significant that the order of society which we have destroyed produced a greater number of original minds than our own age – despite a much smaller population and far from universal education. Any other criterion undervalues the unique characteristic of the human being, the power to create.

It is the recognition of the transcendent importance of this human ability by the leaders of society which sets the period now to be considered apart from all others, and which constitutes its chief claim to be called a Golden Age. The main concern of the possessors of power and wealth was with the arts: it is due to this astonishing fact that the disrupting influences which had been active in society at least since the reign of Elizabeth I were held at bay for nearly another hundred years. The eighteenth-century landowners were responsible for the establishment of a situation in which a high level of taste and production was unquestioningly accepted throughout society, and in which even an uninspired designer could achieve a measure of distinction. They were dominated by a noble zeal for building, for laying out gardens, planting avenues and improving their land and (in striking contrast to ourselves) enhanced instead of destroying natural beauty, achieving a deeply satisfying equilibrium between man and his environment. They patronized living writers, musicians, painters, sculptors and architects, whose art was then part of a process of supply and demand and not the fringe activity it has since become; and even though some of their antique marbles and old masters are of doubtful authenticity, their collections, even the humblest of them, are informed by such ardent devotion to the classical ideal that, despite our superior factual knowledge, we cannot look at them unmoved or without awareness of our own uncertainty of purpose.

The standards of taste set by the great landowners such as Lord Burlington, Lord Bathurst, the Earls of Pembroke and Leicester, and many others, were maintained not only by their own example but by their sponsorship of the publication of such works as Colen Campbell's *Vitruvius Britannicus* (1715–25), Kip and Knyff's *Noblemen's Seats* (1709), Kent's *Inigo Jones*, Batty Langley's *Treasury of Designs* (1740) and James Paine's *Plans and Elevations of Noblemen's Houses* (1783). These books provided models for country builders as well as for professional architects, and they induced a great many laymen to become intelligently interested in architecture. A new and keen enthusiasm for the principles of critical discrimination, originally prompted by Lord Shaftesbury, also played its part in establishing general agreement as to what constituted good taste.

The wholly classical character of the period, of course, and the fantastic improbability of this triumph of the classical orders among a northern and essentially romantic people are themselves suggestive of a Golden Age. It was a time of rare harmony, not the harmony of a taut balance between opposites, but of a current flowing in one unobstructed direction. It was an interval of tranquillity between the discord and fanaticism of the seventeenth century and the evils of industrialization and class conflict which were soon to fragment and dominate society. Marlborough's great victories at Blenheim, Ramillies, Oudenarde and Malplaquet, in making Britain one of the leading nations of the world, had fostered a sense of security and, above all, of permanence. Perhaps the most impressive manifestations of this were the way in which gardens and trees were planted for the enjoyment of grandchildren not yet conceived, and the system whereby an heir was in fact only the life tenant of his property when he succeeded and could only sell his inheritance by means of the expensive process of a private Act of Parliament. Again, the scientific habit of mind which had earlier seemed to threaten religion was now miraculously and briefly brought into accord with it through the glorification of Nature. *Nature* was the key-word of the eighteenth century: it stood for order and proportion, authority, clarity and concord, and no hint of its possible ambiguity disturbed the conviction that the laws of Nature were the laws of reason and that the works of Nature, as Locke proclaimed, 'everywhere sufficiently evidence a Deity'. A mysterious and menacing universe had been transformed into a vast but comprehensible, all-embracing structure of mathematical precision and beautiful simplicity.

The men of this new Golden Age were conscious of kinship with those of the vanished Golden Age of antiquity: each, it seemed to them, inhabited an eminence of light, between which lay the murky gulf of medieval superstition, barbarism and ignorance. It was as natural that classical scholarship should be regarded as proper to the character of a gentleman as that he should live in a house where not only the portico but the proportions, the fireplace designs and the ornaments were derived from the classical temple. This was the era when the sculptor portrayed British statesmen draped in the toga of the ancients. We may think it a little ridiculous that Charles James Fox in Bloomsbury Square in London should be dressed as a Roman orator, but to his contemporaries the robes befitted the denizen of an acknowledged idyllic period of enlightenment. Those who are the concern of these pages, the owners of country seats, the wealthy and the educated, must indeed have enjoyed a state of felicity rarely known on earth. Fox himself testified to it with his last breath, for this most unsuccessful of politicians said on his deathbed that he had 'lived happy'.

The sense of 'living happy', of being part of an evenly lit and serene world, can be recaptured even now in the surviving parks and houses of the eighteenth-century ruling class. We are enveloped by it as soon as we step into the three-dimensional picture of Stourhead where ravishing variations on the Arcadian theme follow one another in poetic sequence as we pursue the irregular contours of the lake; we partake of it as we wander enraptured among the statues of pagan gods in the lovely groves of Rousham; we experience it with sharp nostalgia when we enter the rose and amethyst sculpture gallery at Newby reeking of that pungent musty damp smell of the past, compellingly expressive of the taste and enthusiasm of the man for whom it was built, William Weddell. He was a wealthy collector and one of many grown rich in government office, in law or commerce who, as in previous ages, had acquired land from the gentry, in this case Sir John Blackett. But whereas in the seventeenth century land transfers had caused grave social as well as political dislocation, in the eighteenth century they made for stability because the estates invariably went to the most conservative section of the community.

186–188

As in earlier periods, society was characterized by mobility and the possibility of rising: the gentry were not a class apart: Defoe commented,

> Fate has but little distinction set
> Betwixt the Counter and the Coronet.

Younger sons were sent to make their fortunes at the Bar, in the army, in industry or commerce and it was not obligatory for a country gentleman to send his sons to exclusively patrician schools. If they were not taught at home by a neighbouring parson, his children might attend the nearest local grammar school alongside those of the yeomen and shopkeepers who had been selected for a classical education. Marriages between members of different classes were not uncommon: Lady Caroline Keppel's husband was a surgeon, Lady Elizabeth Bertie – herself the descendant of a mixed marriage – was united to her dancing master, while the 5th Earl of Berkeley married the daughter of a butcher. It is typical of the easygoing relations between the classes that in the celebrated cricket match in 1746 when Kent beat all England by 111 runs to 110 in the presence of the Prince of Wales, Lord John Sackville of Knole played in the winning eleven under the captaincy of Rumney his head gardener.

The eighteenth-century landowner spent part of his year in London. Politics were supposedly his special concern, but the round of social engagements which began each day before breakfast was of almost equal importance, as upon it depended the matrimonial hopes which were a major reason for the migration. Some aristocrats like the Bedfords owned a grand town house to which they decamped when the Parliamentary session began; but in general it was the custom to buy or rent a relatively modest house for the Season in one of the terraces and squares which were going up in Bloomsbury. The Season was over by early June and the landowner lost no time in hastening to his country seat. Arthur Young noticed this English peculiarity: 'Banishment alone will force the French to execute what the English do from pleasure – reside upon and adorn their estates.' If he was not rebuilding his house or transforming its setting the landowner would be improving his methods of cultivation, often devoting to agriculture money derived from cotton,

162 Thomas Coke, the
pioneer agriculturist,
painted by Thomas
Weaver about 1800.
The picture celebrates
both his fine Southdown
sheep and his great
house, Holkham Hall
in Norfolk, seen in the
distance (compare ill.
175). Coke's
'sheepshearings' were
attended by agricultural
experts from all over
Europe.

coal or commerce. The age saw the introduction of new ways of sowing, manuring, draining, breeding and feeding cattle and the growing of new crops. Lord Townshend of Raynham Hall and Thomas William Coke of Holkham (whose father had 162 inherited the Palladian house and its estates after the death of the Earl of Leicester in 1759) set the example and made their formerly backward county of Norfolk the foremost in English agriculture. Among their innovations was the raising of root crops to feed cattle and sheep through the winter. Thus for the first time in history there was no need for the wholesale slaughter of stock at the end of autumn. The consequences for diet were considerable: the enormous consumption of beef and mutton is one of the first things likely to strike the reader of an eighteenth-century gourmet's diary, such as that of Parson Woodforde. 'Sirloin of Beef roasted, a leg of mutton boiled', were repeatedly served during a single dinner in Woodforde's establishment.

Dinner was eaten at about 5 o'clock in the latter half of the century when Woodforde was writing. It was formerly served at 2 or 3 o'clock and became progressively later: 'I am so antiquated', wrote Horace Walpole in 1789, 'as still to dine at four.' It is interesting to note that Walpole often did not put on his 'dress of ceremony', which might now be called evening dress, until *after* dinner. Breakfast, sometimes taken as late as 12 o'clock, was preceded by social engagements and consisted of no more than bread and butter and tea – which had become a national drink, rivalling the prodigious consumption of beer and spirits, by the beginning of the reign of George III. Supper might be served at any time between 9 p.m. and 2 a.m. It was a lighter meal than dinner, yet a supper served at Blenheim Palace by George, 4th Duke of Marlborough, to celebrate the birth of a son, included roast beef, mutton

and pork; loin and fillet of veal; pork and mutton pies; roast chickens, ducks and geese; boiled tongues, hogs' heads and two dishes of souse; two plum puddings and an apple pie. Table manners and the implements used at table differed from ours: peas were eaten with a knife, forks had only three prongs and there were no dessert-spoons.

Country-house entertaining was on a lavish scale; large parties of visitors would stay for weeks or even months. The organization of the large household was assisted by a retinue of servants of diverse and strictly maintained rank and degree. The most important was the steward; then, in descending order, came the clerk of the stables, the clerk of the kitchen, the cook, the confectioner, the baker, the bailiff, the valet, the butler, the gardener and the groom of the chambers; below them came the liveried servants: the coachman, the footman, the running footman and the groom, the under-butler and the under-coachman, the park-keeper, the game-keeper, the porter, the postillion, the yard-boy, the provisions boy and finally the page. The female staff were ordered according to a similar hierarchy. The lady's maid, the housekeeper and the cook belonged to the highest rank; below them were the chambermaid, the housemaid, the maid of all work, the laundry-maid and the dairymaid, while lowest of all came the scullery-maid.

Guests in a great country house lived life at its fullest, for all the means for satisfying the most varied interests were to hand. There were outdoor pursuits: field-sports, of which fox-hunting was now the most popular, games, such as cricket and bowling, and probably antiquarian or archaeological expeditions. The opening of barrows was a recent enthusiasm, encouraged by the Earl of Pembroke who had founded the Society of Roman Knights to promote the study of Roman Britain. Among the

163 In September 1660 Pepys wrote in his diary: 'I did send for a cup of tee (a China drink) of which I never had drunk before.' Tea, kept carefully locked in caddies like the one standing here on the carpet, was still a drink for the élite when Van Aken painted this family group in 1720.

members of this Society, who were united in their disdain of the Gothic, was William Stukeley, the first scholar to take accurate measurements of the monoliths at Stonehenge. Indoors there was betting and gambling with cards (on which the kings, queens and knaves had feet). Gambling all too often became an obsession which brought ruin on host or guest. The extravagance with which it was indulged is illustrated by a picture at Clandon of a member of the Onslow family playing chess 164 with Lord Fitzwilliam while Lord Pembroke looks on. The stake is a Negro servant, who is seen in the background of the painting. The game resulted in a terrible quarrel and the two players never spoke to each other again. But in addition to such dubious pastimes, there was talk, endless, some of the best that has ever been talked; and there was music and literature. It was not uncommon for a whole orchestra to be lodged in a country house. Lord Chandos kept an orchestra of twenty-seven players; and Handel's operas *Silla* and *Armadigi* were first performed in the house of his lifelong supporter, Lord Burlington. Hardly a country house was now without its library, leather-bound volumes of the English, Latin and Italian classics, splendidly illustrated tomes of history and travel and books of engravings. Then there was the host's collection of paintings and marbles, medals and antiquities to enjoy and admire, most of them brought back from the grand tour of France and Italy upon which all the wealthy embarked to complete their education.

Among the first of those who made the grand tour was Richard Boyle, 3rd Earl of 165 Burlington, 4th Earl of Cork and 4th Baron Clifford of Lanesborough: as the greatest patron of the arts and learning in the Early Georgian period and as a distinguished architect in his own right, he more than any other individual was responsible for the establishment of a fixed canon of taste and for the revival of Inigo Jones's Palladianism.

Both the Baroque and the traditional were despised by the Palladians; yet although Vanbrugh's grandiose achievement was dismissed as too extravagantly theatrical, the dramatic element in his work corresponded too closely to a natural bias in the English genius to be wholly suppressed; and tradition lived on as a strong undercurrent of inherited craftsmanship, imparting a distinctive, vital, national character to the classical style of smaller houses of the period. For, though the horizontal mode was a perfect equivalent of the habit of mind and of the scientific and historical background of the age, it denied the feeling for exaggeration and fantasy which had played their part in English domestic architecture ever since it developed beyond the primitive stage of mere function. And just as the exquisite surface of the literature of the eighteenth century, the poetry which polished up into pleasing form 'what oft was thought but ne'er so well expressed', the puns, epigrams, the easy flow of language, are shadowed by Swift's savage disgust at man's failure to realize his potentialities, by Johnson's abject fear of death and Cowper's dreadful conviction that he was marked for eternal damnation; just as the intellectual approach of the period to religion was eventually undermined by the Evangelical Revival, which, as Wesley said, was 'a disposition of the heart, not a train of ideas in the head', so an architecture based on the reasoned application of the classical orders was modified by strong emotions and sensibilities and finally by a predilection for verticality and idiosyncrasy which would not be stifled.

Lord Burlington, without whom Palladianism might never have flourished on 165 English soil, was immensely wealthy and owned vast territories in Ireland and Yorkshire, in Chiswick and in London on the north side of Piccadilly (the streets in this area, some of which still bear his name, were developed under his supervision

and those fragments which have survived the mutilation and demolition of the present century testify to his feeling for urban design). He was a serious, precocious young man who became a Privy Councillor before he was of age, and only a year later was made Vice-Admiral of the County of York and Lord-Lieutenant of the East and West Ridings. Burlington was still under thirty when he was elected Fellow of the Royal Society and Fellow of the Society of Antiquaries. Despite all these and other honours and unlike some other landowners encountered in these pages, Lord Burlington was altogether without worldly ambition and without real interest in mundane affairs. By 1733 he had relinquished his various offices to devote himself to his absorbing passion, the arts. On his first visit to the Continent, his grand tour of 1714, he does not seem to have attached any special importance to Palladio's architecture, for he passed through Vicenza without even staying the night. Pictures attracted him more than buildings.

In 1715 there appeared the first volume of Colen Campbell's *Vitruvius Britannicus*, a collection of engravings of country houses by contemporary architects including Campbell himself. His intention was to launch a revival of what he called 'the antique simplicity' which had been inaugurated by Inigo Jones. In the same year a folio entitled *The Architecture of A. Palladio in four Books, Revis'd, Design'd and Published by Giacomo Leoni* was circulated in a translation by a Huguenot refugee, Nicholas Dubois. Lord Burlington's mother had subscribed to this publication and he himself sponsored the second edition of 1720. These two publications were a revelation to Lord Burlington: he realized at once that enthusiastic intelligent leadership was needed to start the movement of which the preface of Campbell's book might be regarded as the manifesto, and he decided to take on the role of chief patron of the new style. He financed the publication of the second volume of *Vitruvius Britannicus* in 1717 and embarked on his first architectural venture, the entire remodelling of Burlington House in Piccadilly. He took the design from

164 Above, left: a pastel by Daniel Gardner at Clandon Park, Surrey, showing Edward Onslow (right) and Lord Fitzwilliam playing chess to win a Negro servant.

165 Above: Lord Burlington chose to be painted with one of his 'geniuses', Inigo Jones, whose bust stands in the background. The book on which he casually rests his hand is probably the *Designs of Inigo Jones* (1727), which Lord Burlington had commissioned William Kent to edit. The portrait, by Knapton, is at Chatsworth.

166 William Kent by Benedetto Luti, a portrait at Chatsworth.

167 Above, right: Houghton Hall, Norfolk, of 1721, by Colen Campbell and Thomas Ripley, given a Baroque skyline by James Gibbs.

Leoni's book and asked Colen Campbell to execute it. The work was left in Campbell's hands when in 1719 Lord Burlington set off to Italy for the second time. His goal now was Vicenza and the Veneto, where, after buying a copy of Palladio's *Quattro libri*, he began to look at the master's works and scribble notes in the margins.

On his previous visit to Italy Burlington had met William Kent, who was 166 painting and acting as a guide to English visitors in Rome: he now brought him back to London. They became lifelong friends and collaborators, and Kent remained under Lord Burlington's roof for the rest of his life. His uninhibited, ill-spelt letters reveal a person of immense charm, good nature and high spirits. He was always nostalgic for Italy, went twice a week to the opera 'to think myself out of this Gothick country' and was generally known as 'the Signior'. His part in the creation of the new movement was as important as those of Lord Burlington and Campbell. He was of humble origin and had been trained as a coach-painter in Hull, but had early found his way to Italy through the generosity of a Yorkshire patron. Kent was immensely versatile: he distinguished himself as an architect and a landscape-gardener and was one of the few very great interior decorators and furniture-designers. He had studied Italian furniture in Rome, but his exuberant imagination, quite the reverse of Lord Burlington's cool, controlled talent, transformed Italian motifs into something as magnificent but quite new and personal.

Kent's superb golden furniture at Houghton, Wilton and Holkham ranks among XI, the finest English works of art, and its dynamic zest gives life and sparkle to the 177 Palladian shell in every case. At Houghton Kent designed the splendid chimney-pieces of the Stone Hall and the dining-room, each with overmantel reliefs by Rysbrack. Caryatids bearing baskets of flowers on their heads flank the Stone Hall fireplace; the cornice, boldly projecting in three stages, is interrupted by a central bust and the Rysbrack relief is broadly framed and surmounted by a broken pediment. In the dining-room massive volutes at right angles to each other take the place of the caryatids and fabulous creatures feed from a bowl of grapes (considered

a suitable motif for dining-rooms) where the pediment bursts open. The furniture
177 at Holkham reveals Kent as the master of the scroll and the shell combined with
 XI cherubs, female masks and incredibly vital foliage, while at Wilton volutes take the
place of legs and sphinxes with mermaid tails undulate along the fronts of sofas.

167   Houghton Hall in Norfolk, built in 1721, was among the earliest Palladian houses,
though it no longer resembles Campbell's design as illustrated in *Vitruvius Britannicus*.
It was completed to Campbell's plans by Thomas Ripley, the architect of near-by
Wolterton Hall, a Norfolk man who had been trained as a carpenter. At first sight
Houghton recalls German rural palaces such as Brühl and Benrath, for its shallow
corner projections are surmounted by opulent domes lit by round-headed windows,
and urns and statues animate the ornate skyline. These domes replaced the severe
pediments of Campbell's elevations. They were the work of James Gibbs, a Palladian
with strong Baroque inclinations, and may in fact have been suggested by an
illustration in a German book in Gibbs's possession, Decker's *Fürstlicher Baumeister*.
The house is of York stone and is thus as remote in its material as in its style from
local Norfolk tradition. With its oblong plan, rusticated ground floor and service
blocks connected to the main structure by colonnades it closely follows Palladio's
formula for villas.

168   Campbell's next house, Mereworth Castle in Kent (1723), is an adaptation of a
particular work by Palladio, the famous Villa Capra or Villa Rotonda on the
outskirts of Vicenza. It was built for John Fane, later Earl of Westmorland, who was
related by marriage to the Cavendishes. He thought of Mereworth as a scholar's
retreat rather than a permanent residence, which was also the purpose of the Villa
Capra. So there are not many rooms. Both buildings are square with a central
circular hall and a huge hexastyle portico on each façade, but two of Campbell's
porticoes are merely decorative: only those on the entrance and garden fronts have
steps for access. The most obvious difference between the two houses externally
is that the dome at Mereworth is much more prominent than Palladio's shallow

168 Mereworth Castle,
Kent, built by Colen
Campbell in 1723.
Campbell avoided
a broken skyline by
funnelling the chimney
flues up through the
dome.

169 The circular salon at Mereworth, decorated with sumptuous, jewel-like plasterwork.

cupola and gives a distinctly upward thrust to the design. It is a large, boldly ribbed melon-shape crowned by a lantern. This lantern, topped by a copper calotte, allowed the smoke to escape from twenty-four flues which were ingeniously carried up between the two shells of the dome. Campbell thus avoided the incongruous presence of chimneys.

The romantic sentiment underlying the classical proportions of Palladian architecture, a sentiment that was in the end to prove incompatible with a wholly horizontal mode, is strongly in evidence at Mereworth. Palladio's Villa Capra, based as it is on the design of a Roman temple and conceived as it is in a mood of nostalgia for antiquity, is itself a romantic work. Mereworth in its northern setting looks back with longing not only to ancient Rome but to sixteenth-century Vicenza. At the same time this classical structure bears the evocative name of Mereworth *Castle*. In accordance with its name, Campbell planned it as a moated house, so that when it was first built the dark cedars which so perfectly contrast with its pale walls framed a double image. The façades preserve the proportions of a classical column, the base of which is the equivalent of the ground floor, given up to the kitchen and offices, while the principal storey with its cornice represents the shaft of the column and the attic floor the entablature.

The arrangement of the interior diverged from that of Palladio to suit Mr Fane's needs. The main apartments comprise the circular hall and a gallery, an unexpected allusion in its dimensions if not in its position to the traditional long gallery. On the north front there are two identical rooms, one on each side of a narrow entrance passage, and the east and west fronts are each taken up by a state bedroom and antechamber. The decoration of the domed hall, or 'salon' as it was called by the 169 architect, and the gallery comes as a surprise to the reader of *Vitruvius Britannicus*, whose author was so averse to architectural drama that even Wren is represented by no more than two plates: the effect is sumptuous, and includes a magnificent example of the art of illusion in the ceiling of the gallery. The motifs of the plaster reliefs in the circular salon, executed by the Italian Bagutti, are based on designs in the third volume of *Vitruvius Britannicus* (1725), but much elaborated. Brilliantly white portrait busts, medallions, foliage pendants, putti, shells and female figures holding emblems of the arts and sciences gleam like giant cameos on an apricot ground.

Poetic though Mereworth Castle is, it is surpassed as an architectural conceit by
170 Lord Burlington's house at Chiswick, which is a more intellectual and subtle version
of the Villa Capra. Lord Burlington called his house a 'villa', following the Romans
and Palladio, thus reintroducing into our language a word well known in Roman
Britain and later to undergo various debasing metamorphoses of meaning until it
came to signify a peculiarly English type of suburban house. At Chiswick Burlington
followed the Vitruvian rules meticulously throughout; but, because he had seen
the remains of ancient Rome as well as Palladio's work, which Campbell had not,
his building directly echoes Roman motifs as well as reinterpreting Palladio's Villa
Capra design. Burlington boldly decided that chimneys were essential to an English
house, but he brought them into harmony with the classical ideal by giving them
the form of short obelisks, four on the west, four on the east side. The central dome is
octagonal rather than circular, raised on a drum pierced by large semicircular
windows to let in more light than was needed in Vicenza. Then, unlike the Villa
Capra, which is absolutely symmetrical, but like the typical large Georgian
mansion, for which Chiswick Villa set the standard, the entrance front of Lord
Burlington's house is the most important elevation and differs from all the rest. A

170 The entrance front of
Lord Burlington's Villa
at Chiswick, Middlesex,
of the 1720s.

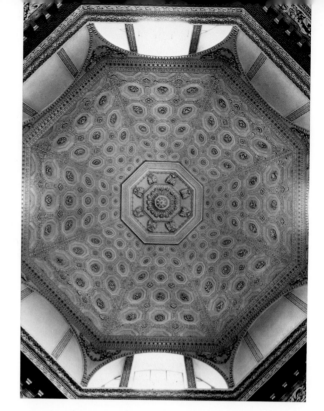

171 A vista along the garden side of Chiswick House, from the octagonal eastern room, through the apsed gallery, to the circular room at the west with its bold chimney-piece and mirror overmantel.

172 Above, right: the dome of the octagonal central hall at Chiswick House.

grand double sweep of stairs – instead of Palladio's simple straight flights – mounts to a noble Corinthian portico. Two statues with agitated draperies and dramatic gestures, one on either side of the façade, seem to set the complex rhythm of the steps in motion and emphasize the Baroque element which has crept into this austere work despite its designer's prejudices. The figures are the work of Scheemakers and represent the presiding genii of the house, Palladio and Inigo Jones. On the garden side similar double flights of stairs meet in front of a Palladian or Venetian window, with a round-arched central light flanked by rectangular side lights framed by columns. Such windows became a feature of Palladian houses.

The interior of Chiswick is remarkable for the variety of room-shapes achieved within such a relatively small space. On the garden side, for instance, a gallery with apsidal ends opens from the central domed octagonal hall, and is flanked by two small chambers, one circular, the other octagonal. This idea of variety as well as the notion of arched openings yielding glimpses into adjoining rooms was suggested to Lord Burlington by the ruins of the great Roman baths and by drawings of them by Palladio which he had acquired and published and which are now exhibited on the ground floor of the villa.

Kent's decorations enhance the grandeur of his patron's conception. He had just been editing Inigo Jones's architectural drawings for Lord Burlington and his work at Chiswick is informed with the same richness and vitality as Jones's designs for the Double Cube Room at Wilton. Broken pediments supported on vigorously swelling brackets surmount the doorways, voluptuous fish-tailed amorini rise from swirling foliage to uphold framed circular paintings, robust friezes of masks and garlands adorn the chimney-pieces, gilded scrolls and swags festoon the overmantels and broad, elaborately ornamented ribs divide the ceilings into rectangular compartments, while the central dome, inspired by that of the Pantheon in Rome, is covered with deeply moulded, profusely decorated octagonal panels decreasing in size towards the crown.

171, 172

XI

172

170

173   If Chiswick Villa marks a new epoch in country-house design, its garden (now being restored after long neglect) is of equal importance, for it develops Vanbrugh's concept of the house and its setting as a three-dimensional interpretation of a painter's vision, relating it more closely to the compositions of Claude and Poussin and an imagined yearned-for Arcadia. It is the forerunner of the romantic landscapes 186 of Stourhead, Pains Hill, Hagley and its almost legendary neighbour, The Leasowes, laid out by the poet Shenstone (now, alas, a golf course) and many another fabulous park with its pillared mansion, temples and grottoes. Shenstone described the ideal behind all these gardens: 'Landscape should contain variety enough to form a picture upon canvas; and this is no bad test as I think that the Landscape Painter is the gardener's best designer.' James Thomson enlarged on the theme, writing of

173 A drawing by William Kent for a great walk and exedra at Chiswick, made after 1724, shows to the left beyond the trees the Ionic temple and obelisk already built by Lord Burlington. The exedra at Chiswick eventually took the form of a curved evergreen hedge, and Kent used the idea seen here for the Temple of British Worthies at Stowe.

> Glimmering shades and sympathetic glooms,
> Where the dim umbrage o'er the falling stream
> Romantic hangs . . .
>
> These are haunts of meditation, there
> The scenes where ancient bards th'inspiring breath
> Ecstatic felt.

Thus the formal classical house was from the start conjoined to an informal picturesque setting which encouraged principles opposed to Palladianism and in the end destructive of it.

    There is still a certain formality at Chiswick, the formality of ordered vistas and of an avenue of sphinxes and great urns leading to statues of Julius Caesar, Pompey and Cicero set in evergreen niches, but this is counteracted by the meandering of an artificial stream, precursor of the irregular sheets of water and winding rivulets which were later to grace every country seat, by a wilderness threaded by mazy footpaths and by the unexpectedly asymmetrical placing of a Claude-like Ionic 173 temple on the bank of a pool with an obelisk coming up from the midst of the water.

174 Thomas Coke, 1st Earl of Leicester, builder of Holkham Hall: a bust by Roubiliac on his tomb in the church at Tittleshall, Norfolk.

Like Chiswick, Holkham Hall, one of the most monumental and exquisitely 175–balanced of all English country houses, is a work of collaboration – between Kent, 177 Lord Leicester and Lord Burlington, with Matthew Brettingham, a Norwich architect, as Clerk of the Works. Thomas Coke, who was to become Lord Leicester 174 in 1744, had met Kent in Naples during his first Continental tour, upon which he had embarked at the early age of fifteen; and Kent had accompanied him to Rome and northern Italy. It was probably just after Coke's return from this journey, which lasted for nearly six years, from 1712 to 1718, that he and Lord Burlington became acquainted. From May 1721 he was a frequent visitor to Chiswick, where he renewed his friendship with Kent. Coke, though very different in character from the austere and intellectual Burlington – he was as earthy as Henry Fielding's 165 Squire Weston – shared his passion for architecture, had taken lessons from a Signor Giacomo (could it have been Leoni?) and had amassed an even greater library of publications on this subject than his friend, as well as collecting rare books and manuscripts: he was the owner of Leonardo da Vinci's notebooks and of a large number of Greek manuscripts.

Lord Leicester and Lord Burlington had worked together on alterations to Coleshill House (shamefully and needlessly demolished in 1952 after a fire). To judge from their correspondence, they discussed together and with Kent all the details of the mansion Coke wished to build in place of his ancestral home at Holkham, to house the quantities of treasures he had brought back from his travels. Some of those treasures are still among the delights of Holkham – the marvellous Claudes, including the magical moonlight sea-shore scene with Perseus and the head of the Medusa, which once adorned Cardinal Albani's bedroom; Rubens's *Flight into Egypt*; the bust of Thucydides; and the head of Aphrodite from the Parthenon. The eventual design of the great house was Kent's and, although it was later altered by Repton, the park, one of the grandest and least known of landscape gardens, owes its noble poetry in part at least to Kent. Nevertheless both Lord

Burlington and Lord Leicester have left their imprint on the building. Lord Burlington gave advice and inspiration as the work progressed. Lord Hervey saw the designs in 1731 of what he called a 'Burlington house with four pavilions': the idea of the four pavilions originated in Lord Burlington's alterations and additions to the house of his brother-in-law, Lord Bruce, at Tottenham Park in Savernake Forest. Lord Leicester's own peculiar combination of scholarship and hedonism, grossness and fastidiousness, transmitted through the medium of Kent's flamboyant genius, determined the whole pagan, ponderous yet exhilarating character of the house and its ambience.

The house is built of greenish-cream bricks the colour of the sand of Holkham Bay, which lies a mile from the edge of the park. They were made at Burnham Norton on the estate, though Lord Leicester's choice of material was not decided by any partiality for regional products: he was merely following the example of Palladio and the white Villa Capra; but the colour of the great house and the texture of its fabric suits the bleak yet buoyant Norfolk coastal landscape and the drama of its brilliant light just as much as those other special materials of the district, carstone and flint, and far better than the alien ashlar of Houghton. The house, a main block with turreted corners and with four pedimented wings, each with a raised centre, is not at first sight attractive; on the contrary many people find it dismaying. The perfection of the composition and proportions, the exactitude and regularity of the design, which yet never becomes tedious, only gradually reveal themselves. This is partly on account of the insensitive removal of the glazing-bars from the windows in the last century, a seemingly minor change but one which has upset the pattern of the elevations. These glazing-bars were originally gilded, a not unusual practice in the Early Georgian period, and must have imparted an exotic lustre to the stern façades. When it was first built and the park trees were only nurslings Holkham could be seen from the sea, an astounding sight in that remote countryside.

167
175

175 Holkham Hall, Norfolk, begun by William Kent in 1734. In this view from the west lake reflections soften the austerity of its grand design.

176, 177 Two of the great rooms at Holkham: the Marble Hall (above), reflecting William Kent's fresh delight in the antique, and the saloon, in the Italian manner.

The contrast between the exterior of Lord Leicester's house and the magnificent pomp of the interior is one of the great country-house experiences. The entrance is through a most inconspicuous front door in the rusticated basement: this makes the first glimpse of the huge, immensely lofty, richly complex Marble Hall all the 176 more overwhelming. It is quite unlike any of the halls so far described or illustrated, for the design is dominated by the idea of a change of level from the ground floor to the saloon which opens out of the hall on the *piano nobile*. A flight of steps rises beneath a great coffered apse to a high base on which is set a colonnade of fluted Ionic columns of variegated alabaster ranging in colour from deep red to pale green. They were carved by a Norfolk mason, Joseph Pickford. The two innermost columns at the top of the stairs frame a further coffered apse in which is set the door into the saloon. The columns support a grandiose frieze of swags suspended between putti and rams' skulls: this frieze and the coffered panels of the apses were copied from Roman models, via Desgodetz's *Edifices antiques de Rome* of 1682. The thick, deep ribs of the ceiling, moulded with flowers and foliage, were inspired by a drawing by Inigo Jones in Lord Burlington's possession. The columns and the apsidal end recall, and were meant to recall, the design of the antique basilica, while the idea of a vista through a colonnade was suggested by Burlington, who wrote of Palladio's church of San Giorgio Maggiore in Venice, 'An open intercolumnation discovers the choir: it ends in a semicircle – most beautiful.' The precepts of Vitruvius, Palladio and Inigo Jones, the revered trio of the Palladians, are thus all combined in this marvellous hall. It was what Pope in the fourth of his *Moral Essays*, dedicated to Lord Burlington, had recommended:

Erect new wonders and the old repair;
Jones and Palladio to themselves restore
And be whate'er Vitruvius was before.

177   To step from this marble splendour into the gorgeously coloured saloon is to enjoy a contrast as stimulating as that between the exterior of the house and the hall. The doorways, the coving of the ceiling, showing diminishing octagonal panels of rosettes, and the luxuriant entablature with its foliage frieze, are all white and gold, while the walls are hung with crimson Genoese velvet. Kent's superb furniture is upholstered in green Genoese velvet. The twin fireplaces of Sicilian pink and white marble flank the central door above which a bust of Athene starts from a broken pediment.

The great park of Holkham was made from barren marsh and heathland which Leicester had reclaimed in 1722. The idea for it may have been inspired by Lord Bathurst's glorious creation at Cirencester, where Kent had worked. At Cirencester immense masses of trees had been planted with (for the first time in gardening history) great emphasis on varieties of colour, and then, out of the dense growth, Lord Bathurst had cut vast straight rides and glades embellished with classical temples and two Gothick follies. At Holkham the focal point of the layout is a huge obelisk, eighty feet high, designed in 1729 by Kent. From it eight vistas opened in different directions, one due north to the house, a second due south to the Triumphal Arch, a third north-west towards the parish church on its steep wooded hill, a fourth south-west to the Temple, a fifth east to Wells-next-the-Sea, and the sixth, seventh and eighth to distant plantations. Even though the formality of the eight vistas has been disturbed by later landscaping the tremendous stretch looking south from the Triumphal Arch is unforgettable. The mood of this expanse is much nearer to that of Castle Howard than to the later gardens of the Golden Age. Kent's
178 heavy arch is splendidly Roman in its solemnity, a great high central pedimented opening topped by balls and with saplings springing from its crannies, flanked by two pedimented arches which should have been completed by pyramids. The artist's lively invention is brilliantly displayed here in his use of local flint for the bold rustication which completely covers the structure. The Temple is based on Palladio's San Francesco della Vigna in Venice, a composition of half-pediments on either side of a towering complete pediment, while its octagonal dome resembles that of Chiswick. The Doric portico derives from an antique fragment found at Albano. Kent's sketches for other ornamental buildings at Holkham, which have since been destroyed, show that they were conceived in the same spirit of gravity.

178 Kent's drawing for the Triumphal Arch at Holkham shows pyramids on the flanking arches, a Vanbrugh-like conceit which was never built. Perhaps as an afterthought, he has sketched in an animal (a donkey?) to give scale.

179, 180 The Palladian
Bridges at Wilton House,
Wiltshire (above),
designed in about 1737
by the Earl of Pembroke,
and Stowe (opposite),
built by William Kent
before 1745. Kent's
bridge, intended for
carriages, has a less steep
approach, and is
characteristically
enriched by masks on the
lower keystones.

The gardens Kent designed later at Rousham in Oxfordshire and Stowe in 180
Buckinghamshire are less monumental in scale and pursue the picturesque qualities
of intimacy, informality and irregularity first embodied at Chiswick. Rousham, 173
which belonged to General Dormer, was first laid out by Charles Bridgeman, an
early practitioner of pictorial gardening in the manner of Vanbrugh, but the
General was displeased with his work and Kent was called in to create a domain
which, apart from Stourhead, is the most ravishing of all surviving eighteenth- 186
century garden conceits. The territory is naturally picturesque for it slopes and is
watered by the little River Cherwell which takes a naturally serpentine course
through the grounds. Kent exaggerated and hollowed the descent from the house
to the river, planting it with trees to make a falling leafy vista. The visitor enters the
wood to the left of this vista and is instantly caught up in a series of changing poetic
scenes formed by pools, winding paths, the deep shade of yews cheered by Van
Nost's incomparable lead figures of satyrs and pagan deities, a Glade of Venus with
urns, a damp Palladian colonnade, a statue of the goddess above a tiny grotto on
either side of which a cherub wrestles with a swan, and a sinuous rill, artificially
contrived with a narrow masonry channel, a perfect translation into three-dimensional terms of the S-shaped curve which Hogarth had declared in his *Analysis* to be
the basis of true beauty. Then, suddenly, in contrast to all the moist gloom and
intimacy, a prospect opens towards a far-distant stone screen, and a sensational
group by Scheemakers of a lion attacking a horse marks the point where the garden
melts imperceptibly into the surrounding countryside. This effect was contrived by
means of a sunken fence, a device invented by Bridgeman, though Kent was
the first to use it to unite a garden and the enveloping landscape in a single
composition.

At Stowe the garden was again begun by Bridgeman and transformed by Kent.
He added to the number of temples for which Stowe was already famous, spurred on
perhaps by his patron's family motto *Templa Quam Dilecta* (How delightful are thy
temples); he planned the wholly picturesque Elysian Fields and Grecian Valley

181 Lancelot 'Capability' Brown, painted by Nathaniel Dance.

where cornice, column and pediment rise from dishevelled glades, and he gave a more irregular look to Bridgeman's lake. Among the most Arcadian of his garden 180 ornaments is the Palladian Bridge: here, for the second time, English builders gave reality to a project which Palladio had imagined and set down in a stilted woodcut in his Third Book but never executed – the idea of a double colonnade between a pair of porticoes resting on the three arches of a bridge. Helped by the verdant English setting, the pellucid water and luxuriant trees, Kent has changed that woodcut into a wonderfully pastoral and pensive image. But his bridge is a close copy of an earlier and even more ideal version of Palladio's invention, Lord Pembroke's bridge at 179 Wilton. The quality of the stone gives Lord Pembroke's masterpiece an air of time- lessness which enhances its nobility. With John Devall as his mason and Roger Morris as his Clerk of Works, the Earl spent two years on his creation, and if this were his only work it would justify the name by which he was known to his contemporaries – the Architect Earl. The Wilton Bridge prompted another copy besides Kent's, the Palladian Bridge at Prior Park, built by John Wood the Elder for Ralph Allen, the Bath Postmaster. Wood, who was probably closer in temperament to Palladio than any of his English followers, has imbued his bridge with such classical feeling that there is hardly a trace of nostalgia in the objective pleasures it gives.

The Stowe gardens were altered yet again when the house was enlarged by Robert Adam and Giovanni Battista Borra later in the century, taking on its present character of accentuated horizontality with its long colonnaded wings and pavilions. 181 Capability Brown, who in his youth had been employed at Stowe as an under- gardener, planted the banks of trees on either side of the south front which give the house and its reflection in the smooth lake so moving a resemblance to an idyllic scene painted by Claude or Poussin. Brown, who became known as 'Capability' instead of Lancelot because of his habit of speaking of the 'capabilities' he divined in the chaos of nature or the work of his predecessors, originated the idea of the broad, sweeping landscape garden with rolling belts of woodland, irregular sheets of 65 water, circular clumps of trees and of turf undulating right up to the house.

182, 183 Clandon Park, Surrey, completed by Giacomo Leoni in 1729: the house seen from the south-east (above), and the Stone Hall.

The architectural principles exemplified at Chiswick and Holkham were soon controlling many another fine, temple-like mansion. In general these new houses took the form of a single symmetrical block, like Giacomo Leoni's Clandon Park in 182, Surrey, or of a central building with wings like Stourhead and Stowe. Although 183, Lord Burlington had subscribed to the second edition of Leoni's folios of Palladio's 198 architectural designs and had based Burlington House on a plate in this book, he never employed the Venetian architect or collaborated with him. But the imposing Palladian interior of Clandon, so much more harmonious than the exterior, has been ascribed to Lord Burlington's influence. The Onslows of Clandon were a Whig family who provided no less than three Speakers to the House of Commons, the first of whom had served under Queen Elizabeth I. The present house, on the site of a Jacobean mansion, was begun for the second Speaker, Richard, 1st Lord Onslow. There was mention of plans as early as 1713 but the house was not completed until 1729. Despite Leoni's preoccupation with Palladio the outside of Clandon fails to conform to Palladian rules; in fact it has a good deal in common with houses of Baroque flavour such as Chatsworth and Chicheley. As at Chatsworth each façade shows a different design, and like Chicheley the building is of red brick with stone dressings and with brick aprons beneath the windows. The proportions of the south front in particular, with its four outsize pilasters, irrationally massive cornice and heavy swags above the first-floor windows, would never have been tolerated by strict Burlingtonians.

The interior of Clandon, however, is typically and grandly Palladian. Its great two-storeyed pillared entrance hall at first seems too overwhelmingly and chillingly 183 white, but it has to be remembered that the pillars were once marbled. The plaster ceiling, which is excitingly complex and most precisely moulded, exhibits a strongly Baroque character in an arrangement of interlacing scrolls, C-shapes and shells, overlaid by a more forcefully modelled, broken and partly curving octagon which surrounds a central circle, itself enclosing an enchantingly delicate relief of Hercules and Omphale. The broken octagon is supported by large male figures sitting on the cornice. This energetic composition was the work of Artari. The two memorable fireplaces are decorated with reliefs by Rysbrack, one showing a sacrifice to Bacchus, the other a sacrifice to Diana. These reliefs are matchless works of art, wonderfully

recapturing the spirit of antiquity, and carved with a mastery which celebrates not only the chosen themes but the blanched-almond smoothness of the fine-grained marble. Apart from the rare pleasure of these reliefs, this hall at Clandon offers a surprising Cocteau-like experience. From the white walls jut the ebony arms of Negroes holding gilded wall-lamps. Did they belong to the Negro busts shining darkly from the broken pediments of the two main doors? Do they allude to the Jamaican heiress, one of the richest of her day, who was carried off to Clandon by Thomas Onslow, son of the second Speaker, to live there so unhappily that her ghost is said still to haunt the house?

The grounds of Clandon, like those of so many country seats, were later landscaped by Capability Brown, who became a friend of George, 1st Earl of Onslow, and to him we owe the lake and the beech wood, now known as The Wilderness; but something remains of the original layout, which combined formality with picturesque elements, for the rockwork grotto in flint and brick dates from the early eighteenth century. From it damp, rounded statues of the Three Graces, deliciously tinged with green and pleasingly smooth by comparison with the rough texture of their shelter, look towards the house. This grotto was not the first of its kind: the example at Rousham has been mentioned and Pope had already constructed one at 184 Twickenham to adorn the picturesque garden on which he was working as early as 1718. It survives, although his villa has been replaced by a neo-Tudor convent. It is a long, dark tunnel with side aisles lined with minerals given to Pope by his friends and adorned with two blotched mirrors in which the poet, with his back to the entrance, watched the world go by on the river.

Leoni designed several houses in addition to Clandon: Bold Hall near Warrington in Lancashire, Moulsham Park in Essex, the south front of Lyme Hall in Cheshire and, his largest-scale work, Moor Park in Hertfordshire. His patron at Moor Park was not an aristocrat but a merchant, Benjamin Styles, who had made a huge fortune out of the South Sea Bubble. The palatial house of Portland stone once had flanking colonnades and wings which balanced the giant four-columned Corinthian portico on the entrance front. Their loss has upset the proportions; the central block, raised up on its steps, looks as ornate and imposing and fundamentally dull as the remains of Augustus's Temple of Concord in Rome.

184 Pope sitting in his grotto at Twickenham, drawn by his friend William Kent; he dedicated the fourth book of his *Moral Essays* to Lord Burlington.

185 The splendidly successful illusionistic hall ceiling at Moor Park, Hertfordshire, painted and stuccoed by Italian artists after 1720.

The static, horizontal exterior of Moor Park gives no hint of the extravagance of the hall within. The proportions of the huge cube which takes up the whole height of the house are rigidly Palladian, but the decoration is more thoroughly Baroque than that at Clandon, with illusionist ceiling-paintings in swirling panels surrounded 185 by animated figures and trophies in high relief. The big central panel cleverly counterfeits the interior of a dome. Putti and allegorical female figures adorn pediments above the doors; on the walls, set in mouldings enlivened by garlands and cherubs, are large, vigorous paintings of the story of Io. These paintings were the work of a Venetian friend of Leoni's, Jacopo Amigoni, while the brilliant plaster work was done by Artari and Bagutti.

As the eighteenth century progressed the Baroque inclinations expressed in most of the houses so far described were either suppressed, in houses which became increasingly horizontal, or they took on new guises. Stourhead, designed by Colen Campbell in 1721–4 after he had planned Mereworth and Houghton, is in its setting both a more severe and a more poetic evocation of a mythical Golden Age than either of those houses or than any house yet mentioned in this chapter. Whereas Holkham is a great architectural experience and whereas at Mereworth and Chiswick the visitor is intrigued by the ingenuity with which the Palladian exemplar has been adapted to individual needs and an English setting, at Stourhead the architectural composition is of less moment than the general quiet enchantment and ideal quality of the image. The sense of harmony it engenders, the sense almost of translation to another plane of reality, is inexplicable in purely architectural terms.

Regarded from the standpoint of design this potent image is indeed partly the result of accident. The wings upon which its calm horizontality so much depend were not added until 1793, the projecting portico with its temple atmosphere (though it follows Campbell's design in *Vitruvius Britannicus*) was only built in 1840, the emotive statues on the parapet and pediment only took up their positions after a fire of 1902 had gutted the central part of the house, while the four beautiful urns with twin eagles perching on their rims, one on each side of the two entrances to the double flight of steps leading up to the portico, date from as late as 1915. A little of the magic of this house comes from the silvery local stone which makes it one with the cool, green Wiltshire landscape.

Though Stourhead House stands at least a mile distant from its famous garden, it seems an integral part of it, a larger shrine of antique gods presiding from its upland site over the Thracian dream of the valley. We must be eternally grateful for the preservation of this perfect picture garden, even though its very perfection sharpens the realization of what we have lost elsewhere. Pains Hill, above all, where the adorable Gothic tent and Gothic arch still stand amid the havoc wrought by our age. Like Stourhead it was the creation of its owner, the Hon. Charles Hamilton, son of the Earl of Abercorn, one of whose genial designs can still be seen at Bowood in the cascade with roaring waters, subterranean passages and tumbled rocks, constructed by Hamilton for his friend Lord Lansdowne.

Henry Hoare, who made the garden at Stourhead, was the son of the banker who had engaged Colen Campbell to build the house and who had purchased the ancestral

186– 188

186 An engraving of the garden at Stourhead in Wiltshire, drawn in 1777. The view is taken from the Pantheon towards the grotto and the stone bridge, the Bristol Cross and the village church, which from here is embraced in the picturesque layout. (For the view from the Cross back towards the Pantheon, see ill. 187.)

181

187 The Bristol Cross at Stourhead. On the far side of the lake is the Pantheon, designed by Henry Flitcroft.

188 Above, right: the Temple of Flora at Stourhead was built in about 1745 and, like the Pantheon, was designed by Flitcroft. Above the door is carved a warning from the *Æneid: Procul, o procul este, profani* – 'Hence, o hence, ye uninitiated!'

lands of the Stourtons from his brother Richard into whose hands they had come in 1714. The heart of Henry Hoare's garden is an artificial three-armed lake which he 186 contrived by building a dam at the head of the valley. At the entrance to the enchanted domain there rises a genuine medieval monument, the fourteenth-century Bristol Cross, rescued by Henry Hoare after its rejection by the citizens of Bristol 187 as a cumbersome and barbaric obstruction (an unfortunate result of the spread of the Palladian anti-Gothic taste). Turning to the right of the Cross instead of passing over a stone bridge over the lake to the left, the visitor approaches the Temple of Flora 188 with its Tuscan portico gleaming above the water and above the Paradise Well. Standing between the smooth columns he views pleasures yet to come, the domed Pantheon, a miniature of its Roman prototype, perfectly composed on the edge of 187 the lake against a wooded slope, and, to the left, high up, among dense trees, the Temple of Apollo modelled on that at Baalbek. The path to these temples ascends to The Shades, the mysterious gloom of which is most penetratingly felt in early morning mist or at sunset and at a season when the alien rhododendrons, planted in the nineteenth century, are not flowering; thence the way leads down once more to the best of all grottoes enclosing the source of the Stour. The entrance is a rock arch leading to a more formal, pedimented opening; over the springs, in a rude, arched recess to the right of the central domed chamber, with its floor of pebbles, dimly lit by an eye-like roundel overhead, echoing with the plash of water, reclines the white-painted lead statue by Rysbrack of a nymph, with a verse by Pope incised on the smooth lip of the pool at her feet:

182

Nymph of the grot, these sacred springs I keep
And to the murmur of these waters sleep.
Ah, spare my slumbers, gently tread the cave
And drink in silence and in silence lave.

Ahead, through an arch and beyond a patch of vivid light from a craggy opening on to the lake, another statue, of Neptune, starts up with raised arm from a wild, dark cavern.

Before the Pantheon is reached, not far beyond the Grotto, stands the Rustic Cottage, an irregular structure with a Gothick bow window resting on ogee arches and adorned with quatrefoils. The character of this Cottage presages that of the Convent-in-the-Wood, an isolated fairy-tale little house, some two miles distant, still approachable only by footpaths. It is two-storeyed with an oddly shaped room, a hexagon on each floor and with a one-storeyed attachment. It is constructed of overlarge, rough stones and roofed with thatch varied here and there by stone slates. The chimneys are disguised as obelisks, two crooked turrets flank the west front, while a Gothick bay window lurches against the south front. In the eighteenth century the Convent was actually inhabited by a fancy-dress prioress, just as the Hermitage at Pains Hill was actually the abode of a hermit. It was all part of the pictorial effect, the result of the same impulse which led the Earl of Dorchester to replace the original village of Milton Abbas with a new village designed to harmonize with the landscaped park, and which moved Squire White of Tattingstone in Suffolk to build a group of farm-workers' cottages in the singular form of a church so that his windows should look towards a suitable eyecatcher. The Convent-in-the-Wood, though but an incident in the setting of an exquisitely classical mansion, exhibits all the fantasy, irregularity and incongruity which were to oust the Palladian rule and revolutionize the character of the country seat.

Meanwhile there was springing up a whole series of pillared and pedimented mansions in which that rule was unquestioned. There was West Wycombe in Buckinghamshire with its great deep portico of smooth Ionic columns and its fantastic two-storeyed colonnade on the south, Tuscan below, Corinthian above, looking like the imagined architecture in a painting by Desiderio Monsù. It was built by Sir Francis Dashwood, notorious as the founder of the Hell-Fire Club, but also an influential member of the Society of Dilettanti. This group for more than a century supported every enterprise of antiquarian importance both in England and abroad in Greece and Italy, and made possible the excavations of James Stuart and Nicholas Revett, the latter of whom built the west portico of Sir Francis's house.

Another mid-century house is Hagley Hall in Worcestershire, built for Lord Lyttleton by Sanderson Miller. Miller, himself the owner of a country house, Radway Grange, which he 'improved' together with the grounds, is best known for his pretty Gothick work at Lacock Abbey and for his sham ruins, not only at Hagley but at Wimpole and Wotton. At Hagley he copied the central block of Holkham in brown stone. Then there was Wardour Castle in Wiltshire, created for Lord Arundell by James Paine, vast in scale and powerfully articulated by giant round columns and square pilasters, paired and single, and with a magnificent circular staircase hall, colonnaded like the hall at Holkham. And there was the tremendously spread out, exaggeratedly horizontal Wentworth Woodhouse by Henry Flitcroft.

But the most personal variation on the Palladian theme was that of the Scottish architect Robert Adam. Classical architecture was beginning to be seen less through the eyes of an Italian Renaissance architect and more from a direct study of the works

189

176

191

of antiquity. The change in emphasis is revealed by the publication of two books by Robert Adam, *The Ruins of Palmyra* (1753) and *The Ruins of Balbec* (1757); they were followed by the handsome folio recording Adam's visit to Spalato in Dalmatia, *The Ruins of the Palace of the Emperor Diocletian at Spalato*. Enthusiasm for the remains of the classical past was quickened also by the fascinating excavations which were going on at Pompeii and Herculaneum.

The style associated with Robert Adam's name is particularly related to these new discoveries, for the charm and gaiety of Pompeian art are reflected in the grace and delicacy which distinguishes Adam's work, both his exteriors and his interior decorations, from the monumental architecture of the early Palladians. There is no recorded mention of an inspection of Pompeii by Robert Adam, but his brother James mentions a visit to the buried city 'where they are now digging'. He speaks of a room painted with arabesques and of a pretty mosaic pavement with a Medusa's head in the centre, and remarks on the stucco-work 'of the lowest relief I ever beheld'. He might well have been describing one of Robert's famous 'Etruscan' rooms (so called because their decoration resembled that on Greek vases, then thought to be Etruscan), such as those at Osterley and Moccas Court in Herefordshire, which are remarkable for their extremely shallow, attenuated, and elegant reliefs. Such rooms were also made by other architects, for instance by James Wyatt at Heveningham in Suffolk, where the work was carried out by Biagio Rebecca in pale green, white and Pompeian red and where Wyatt designed the furniture and painted candelabra, and by Thomas Leverton at Woodhall Park in Hertfordshire, where the ceiling is fluted and the white walls show garlands and medallions in brown, red and yellow. The resemblances between these rooms and the excavated interiors of the doomed but amazingly preserved cities are sometimes so close that they cannot by explained by the English artists' fragmentary knowledge of the discoveries made

189 Below: the amazing south front of West Wycombe Park, Buckinghamshire, designed by John Donovell and built about 1760.

190 Below, right: Robert Adam's Etruscan Room at Osterley Park, Middlesex, painted about 1775-7.

191 Robert Adam at the height of his career. He is holding his great folio volume, *The Ruins of the Palace of the Emperor Diocletian at Spalato*, published in 1764 when he was thirty-six.

in their time. They had an intuitive understanding of the style which points to a natural affinity between the two societies.

There is another distinction associated with the name of Adam which suggests a significant line of cleavage in the eighteenth century. In roughly the first half of the century landowners worked on equal terms with architects who, in the tradition of the great builders of the past, were often themselves amateurs or craftsmen rather than professional men. Later in the century, architects more and more assumed the role which has been theirs ever since, that of professional men, members of a firm even, seeking clients, who frequently were in no way distinguished.

Robert Adam was the son of a successful businessman, a Scot, William Adam, who had built up a lucrative architectural practice in his native land. Together with his brothers, John, James and William, Robert set up the firm of the Adam brothers. William acted as manager and treasurer to the firm, John was primarily interested in the estate, Blair Adam, which his father had acquired, and James, though a modest architect in his own right, was for the most part Robert's loyal assistant. As a firm, the brothers were in some degree responsible for encouraging standardization and the widespread use of fake or mass-produced materials which, as we shall see, contributed to the breakdown of the Palladian rule. Adam houses were often adorned with artificial stone, and their fanlights and verandas were mass produced in cast iron. Another aspect of the metamorphosis of the artist into the businessman is reflected in Robert Adam's strange lack of personality. In an age of special intimacy, famous for gossip – and gossip is always about people – the references to Adam in letters and diaries can be counted on the fingers of one hand, and they 191 disclose nothing. The alert man in the portrait remains aloof, despite the full details of his professional career. A strong romantic bias appears in his beautiful pen and ink drawings of mountain landscapes and fantastic ruins, as well as in his architecture and in his admiration of the work of his friend Piranesi.

192 The south front of Kedleston Hall, Derbyshire, begun by about 1761. This triumphant design is the most complete embodiment of Robert Adam's concept of 'movement'.

Although Adam never abandoned Palladian proportions, he considered the Burlingtonians too rigid in their adherence to Vitruvian rules; and the brothers did not subscribe to the unquestioning reverence of Lord Burlington and his followers for the great Palladio. 'Next morning,' wrote James, when staying at Vicenza, 'walked out to see the different buildings of Palladio. His private houses are ill-adjusted both in their plans and elevations. . . . The Hôtel de Ville is abominably meagre in every respect. What pleased me most was Palladio's Villa Capra or Rotonda. . . . *there* is somewhat to make a good thing of, which is more than can be said for most of Palladio's buildings.' The architect whom, of all others, Robert admired was Vanbrugh and it was Vanbrugh's example which inspired him with the idea of 'movement' which he thought was his chief contribution to architecture. He speaks of it in the preface to the first volume of *The Works in Architecture of Robert and James Adam* which the brothers published in 1773 as an advertisement for their firm. This is his celebrated definition of his conception of movement as related to the south front of Kedleston in Derbyshire, which he added to a house already 192 begun for Sir Nathaniel Curzon, later Lord Scarsdale, by James Paine:

Movement is meant to express the rise and fall, the advance and recess with other diversity of form, in the different parts of a building, so as to add greatly to the picturesqueness of the composition, for the rising and falling, advancing and receding, with the convexity and concavity, and other forms of the great parts, have the same effect in architecture that hill and dale, foreground and distance, swelling and sinking have in landscape; that is, they serve to produce an agreeable and diversified contour that groups and contrasts like a picture, and creates a variety of light and shade which gives great spirit, beauty and effect to the composition.

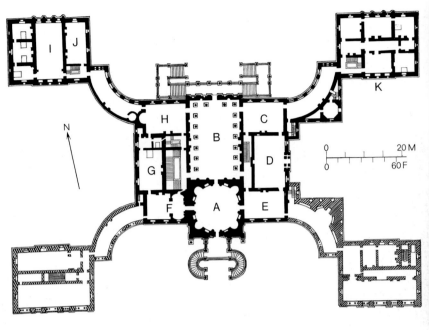

The relation of house and landscape in this passage is closer than that between any mansion and its garden yet described, for the closeness is not brought about by mood, but by the resemblance of physical shapes. This is as portentous as Adam's use of the word 'picturesque'. His whole concept, as Christopher Hussey pointed out in the book which after half a century remains the classic on the subject, heralds the invasion of architecture as well as landscape by the aesthetic ideal of the Picturesque.

The façade at Kedleston to which the passage refers is, however, remote from the irregular and asymmetrical compositions of Picturesque architecture. Palladian principles still hold firm, though the upward tendency noticeable in some early Burlingtonian houses gently asserts itself in the movement of the crab-pincer staircase and the shallow dome, which looks as though it might have floated up from the embrace of those curving arms to settle discreetly behind the strongly defined central feature, which takes the brilliantly novel form of an enchantingly elegant Roman triumphal arch applied to the façade like a rich ornament. The idea was effectively copied by the leading architect of the next generation, Sir John Soane, for the design of his own house, Pitzhanger Manor at Ealing (1803).

Adam had planned wings for Kedleston to echo the shape of the stair: these would have perfected his invention, bringing the house into deeper harmony with its hilly park, which Adam embellished with a bridge and a screen. There is in Adam's work a most sympathetic quality of grace and refinement, and such originality that we lament the fate that made him the improver of houses begun by others, for scarcely one of his larger enterprises was planned and erected by him from the foundations.

193
194

In addition to his remarks on 'movement', Adam claimed in the *Works* to have brought about an almost total change in interior decoration, 'to have adopted a beautiful variety of light mouldings, gracefully formed, delicately enriched and arranged with propriety and skill'. This claim is fully justified. And the variety consists not only in the sophisticated application of Adam's preferred motifs – garlands, vases, urns, tripods, griffins, swags, festoons of husks, palmettes, arabesques and scrolls – but in the planning of the rooms. The suite of rooms at Newby Hall, the house mentioned at the beginning of this chapter, designed and decorated for Mr Weddell, during the 1760s, already illustrates Adam's ingenious use of apses, octagonal shapes, elliptical ends and curving niches to create far greater spatial diversity than even the interior of Chiswick had shown. At Kedleston the principal 195, apartments alone, the hall and the saloon, afford astonishing contrasts in space, 199 lighting, plan and colour. The hall is the most monumental of all Adam's compositions. Intended to correspond to the atrium of Roman antiquity, it is a stupendous aisled room furnished with twenty fluted columns and a coved ceiling pierced by three small oval lanterns. The columns are of local green-veined pink alabaster, the griffin and anthemion frieze shines gold on a blue ground and upon the floor of Hopton marble a design of S-scrolls radiates within a great oval in shades of grey. The ceiling displays delicate plaster arabesques by Joseph Rose, a great stuccoist and one of Adam's most constant collaborators. Plaster statues stand in arched recesses above plush-topped sarcophagus seats, eloquent examples of Adam's

imaginative furniture design – of which Kedleston houses one of the most fantastic
196 pieces, the state bed with posts in the form of branching palm trees.

197   If the twin fireplaces in the hall at Kedleston are compared with the chimney-
198 pieces at Clandon or Moor Park the freedom and individuality of Adam's treatment
will be at once apparent. The ornament of wheat-ear drops, palmettes, honeysuckle
and candlestick are lighter than anything so far seen, but the originality of the design
lies in the substitution of statuary for the usual pedimented overmantel. The classical
female figures supporting a circular painting festooned with a light chain of husks
are of plaster and were modelled by Rose, while the fireplaces themselves were carved
by Michael Henry Spang, another of the many craftsmen who, like the members of
an orchestra under a great conductor, were enrolled by Adam to carry out the
schemes for which he sketched every minute detail.

199   The experience of walking from the hall into the saloon is spatially delightful, for
the much smaller room, a circle contrived within a square by means of corner niches
(a Pompeian device) is considerably and surprisingly more lofty. The pedimented
doorways are flanked by pilasters of blue scagliola, the coffered dome is of white
and gold, and cast-iron stoves, part of an ingenious hot-air system of Adam's
invention, stand like domestic altars in semi-domed alcoves, while candelabra
branch from the walls above stucco relief panels polished to resemble marble.

        Splendid though Kedleston is, it is surpassed for spatial variety, contrasts of colour
200– and atmosphere, gaiety and charm, by Syon. The work was done for Sir Hugh
202, Smithson, soon to become 1st Duke of Northumberland – a man, in Adam's
 XV words, of 'correct taste'. Architecturally it is supremely successful as an adaptation
of an earlier house, even though Adam's full scheme never materialized: he had
202 intended to enclose the central courtyard and make of it a huge rotunda. On the
exterior, crenellations refer playfully to the medieval origins of the building as a

195 Opposite, above:
Robert Adam's
monumental Roman Hall
at Kedleston.
Relief-like paintings
by Biagio Rebecca round
the walls depict sacrificial
and martial scenes.

196 Opposite, below:
the state bed at
Kedleston. Adam once
likened his favourite
order, the Corinthian,
to a palm tree and
suggested that this was its
derivation.

197, 198 Below: one of
the twin fireplaces in the
Roman Hall at Kedleston
(left), and a more
orthodox composition
by a designer of an older
generation in the State
Bedroom at Clandon
Park, Surrey. The
delicacy of Adam's
design, which extends
to the brass and steel
grate and fender,
contrasts with the
grandeur and gravity of
the room.

199 The circular
saloon at Kedleston.

200 Above, right: a
door in the crimson
drawing-room at Syon
House, Middlesex,
created by Adam about
1769.

201 Opposite, left: the
vast, cool entrance hall at
Syon displays the Roman
Doric order in its most
monumental form. A
bronze copy of the
Dying Gladiator, in the
foreground, is balanced
by the Apollo Belvedere
in the coffered apse.

nunnery. The austerity of the façades, of pale Bath stone, is intended to heighten the 201
stunning effect of the rooms inside. Stepping into the double cube of the hall the
visitor finds himself in an atmosphere colder than that of the reticent exterior, though
at the same time his gaze is riveted by the boldness of the patterning. The floor is of
dazzling black and white marble, squares set diagonally and crossed by gigantic
diapers in Greek key pattern which repeat the design of the plaster ceiling. White
Roman statues and antique busts stand against white walls on plinths designed by
Adam. In a coffered apse at one end of the room is set a copy of the Apollo Belvedere,
so well married to its setting that after a visit to Syon the sight of the original Apollo
in the Vatican comes as a sad disappointment; at the opposite end, through a Doric
screen, beyond a copy in dark bronze of the *Dying Gladiator*, steps can be seen leading
up from a tunnel-vaulted recess to the next surprising room. It is one of the most xv
opulently coloured of all interiors. The highly polished scagliola of the floor shines
as though it were made of yellow, brown and red inlaid jewels; the pale green walls
are adorned with gilded stucco reliefs of trophies of arms by Joseph Rose; and they
are further amazingly enlivened by an elaboration of the motif used on the front of
Kedleston, twelve free-standing columns of green marble with gilt Ionic capitals
and white and gold bases, each supporting a gilded classical figure. The columns,
some of which were found in Rome in the bed of the Tiber, form a screen at one end
of the room. The heavy compartment ceiling, more like the work of Kent than
Adam, perfectly suits their massive character.

The dining-room is quite different in colour and proportions, all gold and ivory,
apsidal, screened at either end and animated by statues in niches; one of them,

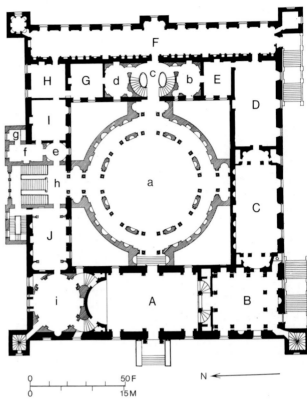

Bacchus, leans out as if toasting the guests. A flat, fluted ribbon runs along the Corinthian entablature all round the walls with long panels above it painted in chiaroscuro by Cipriani.

The crimson drawing-room with its damask hangings patterned with flowers and ribands provides another experience of vivid contrast. The ceiling is ornamented with small squares and octagons, each enclosing a panel painted by Angelica Kauffmann. The carpet of red, gold and blue was specially woven for the room. The decoration of the doors and doorcases is especially rich and remarkable. The doors are of polished mahogany with gilded mouldings, the cases, standing out against the crimson walls, are ivory-coloured with gilt wood and ormolu embellishments. The white marble fireplace gleams with ormolu ornament.

It is the gallery, running the whole length of the house and thus recalling the traditional long gallery and the long room at Mereworth, which gives the greatest pleasure at Syon. Adam himself explained the character of this room: 'It was finished in a style to afford great variety and amusement.' I know of no other famous apartment which is so steeped in an air of light-hearted joy. Its immense length has been given a sense of intimacy by a division into four units, and by the exquisite detail of the ornament, classical arabesques and reliefs of polished stucco and entertaining oval portraits. The mood of frivolity is sustained by the colouring – faded pink, green and gold – and by two delicious little closets, one at each end. One of them is square and decorated with a pattern of birds and trees; the other is circular, below a flimsy cupola from the centre of which hangs an intricate golden bird-cage containing a magical golden bird.

202 A plan of Syon as Adam intended it to be, showing in hatched lines the great central 'Pantheon' and smaller rooms which were never realized. Existing rooms: A hall, B south ante-room, C dining-room, D crimson drawing-room, E writing-room, F gallery, G bedroom, H ante-room, I dressing-room, J private dining-room.
Unbuilt rooms: a rotunda, surrounded by open areas, b powdering room, c staircase to mezzanine, d dressing-room, e ante-room, f powdering room, g closet, h main staircase, i ante-room.

203, 204 The naturalistic, flowing plasterwork of the Velvet Drawing-room ceiling at Saltram House, Devon (above), marks a reaction against Adam's stylized decoration which is so completely represented in the drawing-room of the same house (above, right).

The decorator rather than the architect Adam can be seen yet more intimately and at his richest at Saltram in Devon. The drawing-room, lit by a fine Palladian 204 window, has a coved ceiling of rose-pink and green adorned with little circular paintings on sky-blue grounds and by the most daintily moulded stucco-work, diaper-shapes in ovals, fans, palmettes and, above the frieze, griffins and winged sphinxes. The simple pilastered fireplace, with no overmantel, is of white and pink marble ornamented with a central figure relief and with small square reliefs, white on a pink ground, inset on either side of it. It is Adam's carpet, however, which draws the eye more than anything else in this room : the ground is chocolate-brown, the borders red and yellow; in the centre is a green diaper-shape enclosing a great eight-petalled flower and surrounded by voluptuous curves of ribboned flowers, while the blue corner squares are filled with open fans of pink and green. In the dining-room, where the central circle of the ceiling is decorated with paintings by Antonio Zucchi about a plaster roundel containing a web-like ornament, the carpet exactly mirrors the ceiling design, except that the paintings are replaced by precisely detailed sprays of vines.

One of the rooms at Saltram, the so-called 'Velvet Drawing-room', has a delicious 203 plaster ceiling quite unlike those of the rest of the house. Instead of being divided into compartments, flower-sprays, birds, cherubs and C-shaped scrolls are scattered loosely, as if wind-blown, across the expanse; and unlike the formalized, classical designs associated with Adam, this exuberant decoration is triumphantly naturalistic. Although it remains roughly symmetrical it breathes a different spirit from the disciplined proportions of the room. This is a minor instance of the exotic styles, which, changing with fashion, found their way into correct classical interiors during the century, giving expression to the same anti-classical instincts which motivated the taste for the Picturesque.

At Claydon in Buckinghamshire, a descendant of the Verneys, encountered in the previous chapter, decorated the enlarged family house in a manner which can only be described as electrifying. There is nothing like Claydon anywhere else in Britain, and though they are so much more modest in scale, the febrile Rococo and Chinese fantasies of this house can only be compared with those of the great stuccoists who worked at Sans Souci and Nymphenburg, though here the medium – and this is one of the marvels of Claydon – is wood. The artist's flickering, brittle intensity is so sustained that it is felt as near ecstasy. Perhaps this is why Lord Verney's architect, Sir Thomas Robinson, said he 'had no small trace of madness in his composition'. His name was Lightfoot and he was a local carpenter. That is all we know of him; but his achievement at Claydon sets him among the immortals. The room into which the visitor steps immediately on entering the house (for there is no real front door), the Pink Parlour, scarcely prepares the eye for the overwhelming effect of the North Hall. Its proportions are severely Palladian, for it is a double cube, but the virile arabesques and scrolls serpentining about the classical forms, pushing open the door pediments and almost obscuring the shape of the supporting volutes like rank vegetation, the demonic, snake-tailed birds alighting on the niches, the faintly smiling decadent heads emerging from coiling fern fronds and the statues of gorgeously dressed, hypnotic-eyed Negroes in the niches, all create an atmosphere of mystery and outlandishness wholly alien to the Vitruvian rule.

The sense of disquieting strangeness that permeates this whole house, standing so serenely in its mild river landscape, is concentrated in the extraordinary Chinese

205–207

205

205, 206 Two details of the unparalleled decoration at Claydon House, Buckinghamshire, carried out in about 1765 by the mysterious Lightfoot: a niche in the North Hall (left), and a door in the Chinese Room.

207 The Chinese tea-party, in the great alcove of the Chinese Room at Claydon. The long-spouted teapot resembles one that belonged to Dr Johnson.

Room, where the bizarre ornament, brimming with vitality, so dominates that the classical proportions are actually threatened. The two chimney-pieces, the door-heads and a recess are encrusted with brilliantly carved mingled Rococo and Chinese motifs, pagoda forms, delicate trellis-work, wildly swirling flame- and wave-shapes unexpectedly combined with absolutely naturalistic snail shells and sunflowers, which have the same mesmeric quality as the shells and sunflowers in Richard Dadd's insanely detailed painting; Chinese heads, gazing inscrutably from the tops of huge trailing leaf volutes, and suspended bells fitted with tiny carved clappers so that they actually emit a whispered tinkle. But wondrous though all this is, it is surpassed by the imagery and execution of the most staggering object in the room, an immense alcove in the form of a pagoda minutely fretted and adorned with scrolls, rocks, bells and frozen waves, which takes up the whole of the wall opposite the windows. Within it an eternal tea-party is taking place. A table covered with a fringed cloth and laid with elegant tea-things stands on a shell-encrusted rock and at it sit a Chinese man and woman arrested in the act of clapping as if to summon to the table two grotesque children who, with arms upraised in greeting, advance towards them, one on either side. Fully in the round, this formidable tableau, which has the uncanny power of remaining precisely in the memory after a lapse of many years, is the climax of the Claydon experience.

The Chinese fashion, fostered by trade with the East, was catered for in books of designs such as Sir William Chambers's *Designs of Chinese Buildings, etc.* (1757) and William Halfpenny's *New Designs for Chinese Temples* and *Rural Architecture in the Chinese Taste*, and resulted in the occasional adorning of a landscaped garden with a

206

207

structure such as Chambers's Chinese Dairy at Woburn or Kent's monument to Congreve at Stowe, crowned by a monkey which reflects the vogue for *singeries*, a development of the Chinese taste more widespread on the Continent than in England. Chinoiserie never affected the external design of a great house. Its expression generally took the form of furniture specially made to Chinese designs like the bed Chippendale fashioned for Badminton, now in the Victoria and Albert Museum, or it was manifested in the wearing of Oriental dress in the house, in the employment of Chinese boys in pointed hats and thick-soled shoes like the one painted by Reynolds at Knole, in the collection and imitation of Chinese porcelain and in the hanging of walls with pretty painted Chinese papers. Merchants and missionaries had returned from China with sheets of paper painted with gay designs as early as the end of the seventeenth century, and it gradually became fashionable to make them up into sets for the decoration of a room. The designs of Chinese wallpaper fell into three categories: landscape, birds and flowers, and scenes of domestic life. A characteristic Chinese landscape paper, with lofty peaks, pines and rivers still enlivens a room at Ramsbury Manor in Wiltshire; a paper at Saltram shows elegant groups of people; and at Milton Manor in Berkshire a charming bird and flowering tree design transforms a prosaic bedroom with the romance and poetry of a distant land. The flowers look like peonies, while among the birds the golden pheasant is conspicuous.

Another room at Milton Manor, the library, reflects a different mid-eighteenth-century fashion, the 'Gothick', which, referring directly to a native tradition in the strongest possible contrast to the classical ideal, constituted the most serious threat to Palladianism. But for the moment this was not apparent: this charming room at

208 A dressing-room used as a bathroom at Saltram House is panelled with Chinese wallpaper showing scenery and recreations.

209 The decoration of these rooms in the remodelled Lady Chapel of St Michael's Mount, Cornwall, combines the three anti-Palladian fashions, the Gothic, the Chinese and the Rococo.

Milton is less hostile to the horizontal mode than the North Hall at Claydon. The adorable arcaded frieze and the crocketed ogee arches and shafted columns of windows, doorcases, the fireplace and bookcases lend variety to the walls but in no way disturb the correct proportions of the library. The same is true of the chaste chapel, where the walls combine the square panelling of an earlier period with round- and trefoil-headed arches and the round-headed windows are set in ogival arches which are no more than adumbrated.

The Gothic style, as we have seen, had never been altogether suppressed: it had continued in use for garden embellishments and had become so much the vogue by Adam's day that this staunchest partisan of classical motifs used medieval trimmings on the exterior of Syon House and in his youth had built Culzean Castle on the Ayrshire coast with bastions and castellations, even though it was wholly classical within. Among the earliest instances of the introduction of Gothick inside the house are the drawing-room and boudoir at St Michael's Mount, Cornwall. The work 209 must have been done before 1744, for Sir John St Aubyn, for whom it was carried out, died in that year. He made the two rooms out of the Lady Chapel of the former monastery on the site; they are decked with coroneted ogee arches, trefoiled friezes, a Rococo plaster ceiling and a chimney-piece half in the Gothick, half in the Chinese taste. The new fashion must have been an irresistible choice in view of the earlier history of the building. Here at St Michael's Mount the future merging of Gothick and Picturesque into an anti-classical architectural style is dramatically foretold by the conjunction, fortuitous though it is, of this mock medieval embroidery with one of the most outrageously romantic sites in Britain, a savage, toppling, foam-lashed rock.

The famous Strawberry Hill, the house Horace Walpole bought in 1747 and
reconstructed as a fairy-tale lath-and-plaster castle, is probably the first example of
210 a Gothick country-house exterior. It was an ideal setting for the author of *The Castle
of Otranto* and the writer of catty letters. But the most significant thing about it is
that it is a conscious translation into architecture of the Picturesque principles of
eighteenth-century gardening. 'I am almost as fond of the Sharawaggi or Chinese
want of symmetry in buildings as in grounds or gardens', wrote Walpole in 1750.
XVII The grouping of his house, by the time it was finished in 1776 – with its long gallery,
Holbein Chamber with the Little Cloister below it, Tribune and Great Bedchamber,
round tower and Beauchamp Tower – was asymmetrical. Yet the Georgian period
was so averse to irregularity in house design that Strawberry Hill had no immediate
influence on the symmetry and horizontality of the country mansion. Walpole
himself did not take his fantastic house seriously or fully realize its implications: the
very words he uses for the genuine Gothic buildings in which antiquaries were
becoming interested – 'pretty', 'neat', 'venerable barbarism' – show how completely
he was in key with the prevailing attitude of his day; and he refers to the Chippendale Gothick staircase in his house as breathing 'the most venerable gloom . . .
that ever was since the days of Abelard' and at the same time as 'so pretty and so
small that I am inclined to wrap it up and send it to you in my letter'. The Strawberry Hill interior is all deliciously high-spirited and artificial, a shell of comfortable
Georgian proportions overlaid with imitations in plaster of tombs turned into
chimney-pieces, toy-like copies of medieval screens incorporating classical details,
painted-paper perspectives and gilded fan-vaults and niches tricked out with bits
of mirror glass.

210 Strawberry Hill,
Twickenham, Middlesex.
By the time Horace
Walpole finished
gothicizing his toy-house
in 1776 he had called
upon the wits of a
number of designers,
including Robert Adam,
who built the large
round tower, and James
Essex, perhaps the most
scholarly Gothic architect
of his day.

197

211, 212 Sir Roger Newdigate, painted by Romney, and the exhilarating bay window in the saloon of his house, Arbury Hall, Warwickshire, created almost certainly by Henry Keene in 1793.

Another house which exhibits the same gaiety as Walpole's sham castle and the same adherence to the classical formula beneath its fantastic ornament is Arbury 212 Hall, Warwickshire. It was originally a Tudor building on the site of an Augustinian priory, and it was only to be expected that its owner, Sir Roger Newdigate, like 211 Sir John St Aubyn of St Michael's Mount, should be attracted by the idea of gothicizing such a house. Externally, apart from its sash windows, Arbury largely preserves the character of its quadrangular predecessor with its castellations and pinnacles and even its symmetry and does indeed embody some of the fabric of the sixteenth-century structure. But the astonishing interior throws into splendid relief the different concepts of Gothic in the Tudor and Georgian periods. Both used the Perpendicular style, but whereas the earlier age absorbed classical details into the traditional theme without undermining its vertical character, in the eighteenth century the most luxuriant Gothick trimmings were applied to a classical framework without altering its basic horizontality.

The structural work at Arbury was carried out by the architect-masons William Hiorn, Henry Keene and Henry Couchman, while the matchless plaster decoration was done by William Hanwell, William Wise and G. Higham, local men. Playful allusions to fan-vaults, ribs, pendants and clustered shafts, magnified, caricature versions of their medieval stone prototypes consort with classical proportions and round arches. The groined and barrelled ceilings, the shrine-like chimney-pieces, the gold and white bosses, the chamfers and ogees, the filigree tracery and fluted pillars, with all their staccato excitement, move to the ordered rhythm of their period, a rhythm quite unlike the irregular, aspiring motion of true Gothic.

213 The Triumphal Arch at Shugborough Park, Staffordshire, designed by James 'Athenian' Stuart about 1764 in emulation of the Arch of Hadrian at Athens.

While they expressed reactions against the classical orders, the Chinese and Gothick modes, far from overthrowing those orders, at first stimulated a movement against the horror of 'barbarism', a movement in favour of greater simplicity and an inclination for Greek rather than Roman models. Interest in Greek antiquities was specially promoted by the work of James Stuart, known as 'Athenian' Stuart, and his collaborator Nicholas Revett. From 1762 onwards, after they had made the expedition to Greece mentioned earlier in this chapter, they published *The Antiquities of Athens* which as a formative influence was as important as Adam's *The Ruins of the Palace of Diocletian at Spalato*. James Stuart, who started life as a painter, gave evidence of a powerful imagination in his interior of the chapel at Greenwich Hospital and in some of the ornaments he designed for the grounds of Admiral Anson's house, Shugborough in Staffordshire – ornaments in which the Admiral was able to indulge after capturing a Spanish galleon laden with riches. The most interesting of these buildings, which include copies of the Choragic Monument of Lysikrates and the Tower of the Winds at Athens, is the Triumphal Arch, also derived from Athens. It is of two storeys; the upper takes the form of a pedimented colonnade, in which, on either side of a naval trophy by Scheemakers, stand sarcophagi surmounted by the busts of the Admiral and his wife. The arch stands near a railway cutting and soot has magnificently marbled the stone. But 'Athenian' Stuart never realized his potentialities: he was an irresolute character and ended a drunkard.

Adam's characteristic style was simplified, in accordance with the new Greek taste, by his chief and almost legendary rival James Wyatt. Wyatt strikes us as a more human character than Adam. He was born in Staffordshire and his talents came to the

213

214 The north front of Heveningham Hall, Suffolk, designed by Sir Robert Taylor about 1778. The wings are Palladian, but the monumental centre looks back more directly to ancient Rome.

notice of a local landowner, Lord Bagot, who took him to Italy when he was only sixteen. Wyatt showed promise in music and painting as well as architecture, but after two years in Venice and four in Rome he set up a practice in London. His output was enormous, but he had to struggle all his life against intemperance and an Oblomov-like indolence. Farington in his *Diary* noted that Beckford, Wyatt's client at Fonthill, 'is much dissatisfied with Wyatt who perpetually disappoints him. 225 He said if Wyatt can get near a big fire and have a bottle by him he cares for nothing else.'

At Heveningham in Suffolk, built for Mr Vanneck, a Dutch merchant settled in England and later to be made Lord Huntingfield, Wyatt took over from Sir Robert Taylor. The exterior of the house is Taylor's, but the interior decoration 214 is by Wyatt, and Wyatt also designed a charming orangery in the park. His great contribution is the hall, one of the loveliest rooms in England. The composition XVIII owes a good deal to Adam, for it is a rectangular room with a barrel-vault, divided into compartments by an open screen at either end which continues the design of the wall frieze, echoing Adam's arrangement in the library at Kenwood. But the XIX effect here is grander on account of the simplification of the ornament, which, though carried out with crisp precision, is both sparser and more ample in scale than the rich tapestry of Adam's decoration. Wyatt has varied the theme by introducing emphatic fan-vault-like penetrations in the ceiling cove, and the sumptuous colouring accentuates the fantasy of the whole invention: the stone floor of great expanse is inlaid with red and black marble, the walls are a delicate green with pure

white stucco ornament and the scagliola columns counterfeit the yellow marble of Siena. The doors of West Indian mahogany shine darkly like watered silk.

215   The fan ornament appears again in the dining-room at Crichel in Dorset, but here it is turned upside down and adorns the corners of the coving like the sections of an upheld umbrella, a surprising contrast to the painted medallions and candel-abrum motifs. The walls of this room are airily diversified by painted ovals which seem as if suspended by the lightest stucco garlands. There is a variation on this theme in the Small Hall where oval portraits are surrounded by the most graceful husk chains, above square-shouldered frames enclosing square portraits.

Another architect who was directly inspired by classical antiquity to create a plainer version of the Palladian theme was George Dance the Younger, who had spent a long period in Italy. After the exquisite colour and intimacy of Adam's linear decoration Dance's country-house work, represented chiefly by the interiors of Cranbury Park in Hampshire, built for sister-in-law, Lady Dance-Holland, seems thin and cold. Yet there is an intriguing undercurrent of romanticism in it. At Cran-

216, bury Park the ballroom is furnished with coffered apses of such delicacy that they are
217 like silver-point drawings of the Roman apses they emulate, and they are strangely associated with the suggestion of a soaring fan-vault, the fans springing from clusters of the wheat-ear motif introduced by Adam. The plain plastered walls articulated by no more than plaster panels in thin mouldings are so subordinated to the super-structure that the correct proportions of the room are subtly and disquietingly challenged.

215 A corner of the dining-room ceiling at Crichel, Dorset, decorated by James Wyatt in green and white with purple for the background of the painted medallions.

201

216, 217 The ballroom at Cranbury Park, Hampshire, by George Dance, probably designed in the 1790s. A view towards the organ recess, at one end of the ballroom, and a detail of the plaster ceiling above the doorway.

The atmosphere of Dance's work is unique, but his treatment of classical forms has affinities with that of the fashionable architect Henry Holland at Berrington Hall in Herefordshire. Holland was married to Capability Brown's daughter. It was through his father-in-law that he was commissioned by Thomas Harley, a banker and Lord Mayor of London, to build and decorate Berrington Hall, for Brown had already been employed to landscape the grounds. Holland owned an extensive library of architectural works, and made especial use of Desgodetz's *Edifices antiques de Rome* (which had inspired Kent at Holkham) and Stuart and Revett's publication on Athens. The exterior of the house strikes us as almost dull, so accustomed are we by now to the Palladian formula: here there is no adornment apart from the expected portico – tall and Ionic – and no animation. Within the house Holland's adaptation of Greek and Roman notions marks a more radical departure from Adam's festooning and patterning than Dance's quiet drama. In the entrance hall four shallow segmental arches rise from a plain Greek cornice to 219 support a simply moulded ceiling, the central oval of which is repeated in the marble floor design. Chaste trophies of arms are set in roundels above the doors. The staircase hall is less static. The staircase with its bronze railings mounts beneath a glazed 218 dome to the first-floor landing which rests on a lightly coffered arch. The composition is surprisingly monumental and in complete contrast to the attenuated ornament and pastel colouring in shades of grey, light blue, palest ochre, faded terracotta, pink and dull olive-green.

218, 219 The staircase and entrance hall at Berrington Hall, Herefordshire, designed by Henry Holland about 1778–81.

The other house for which Henry Holland is well known, Southill Park in Bedfordshire, built for Samuel Whitbread, the brewer, is more severe, more correct, for the reticent exterior consisting of the orthodox central block with side pavilions attached to it by colonnades is matched by the fastidious restraint of the interior. The ceilings are here and there gently vaulted, but in general they are perfectly plain except for narrow bands or ribs of plaster displaying Greek key patterns or fine ribbons of Greek foliage.

An even more extreme statement of this final neo-Grecian phase of the Classical Revival is made at Dinton House – or Philipps House, as it has come to be known after its last owner – in Wiltshire, built for William Wyndham, whose grandfather had acquired the estate in 1689. The architect was Jeffry Wyatt, nephew of James, who was later knighted and changed his name to Wyatville. The white Chilmark stone of which the house is built stresses the temple aspect of its gigantic plain portico, and this aspect is yet more emphasized by the idealized landscape in which it is set, carried out in the style of Capability Brown by an unknown improver. The interior is as austere as the outside, its main feature being a staircase which rises and then divides, a meagre, scarcely perceptible reminder in severely simple cast iron and wood of the grand Baroque compositions at Brühl and Pommersfelden. Dinton House, built in 1813–16, tasteful and discreet almost to extinction, is one of the last embodiments of the classical rules, and perhaps the last evocation of the gentle Arcadian dream which had haunted the imagination of the Georgian landowners.

6 OLDEN TIME MASQUERADE

the nineteenth century

THE PREVIOUS CHAPTER DESCRIBED a state in which an ideal was established, rationalized and sustained by a wealthy and intelligent oligarchy. Authority was recognized and its signposts followed. The possible threat to that ideal inherent in the conception of the Picturesque could not be realized while society continued confident. The exotic fashions of eighteenth-century interior design never became more than embroidery on the classical framework, and even Horace Walpole said of his Gothick rooms at Strawberry Hill: 'Every true Goth must perceive they are more the works of fancy than imitation.' Nevertheless the unique lack of symmetry in the Strawberry Hill exterior suggested that the Picturesque could become an architectural style, and towards the end of the century the spirit which had been expressed in the garden with its sham ruins, grottoes, hermitages, serpentine waters, cascades and temples took shape in the house itself.

XIX Opposite: the library at Kenwood House, Middlesex, completed by Robert Adam before 1770. A screen of Corinthian columns carries an entablature which ingeniously continues the frieze from which the unusual barrel vault springs. (See p. 200, and compare colour plate XVIII.)

The pictorial view of domestic architecture was canvassed by two West Country landowners, Sir Uvedale Price of Herefordshire and Richard Payne Knight of Shropshire. In his *Essay on the Picturesque* (1794) Price recommended irregularity as an alternative to symmetry, while Payne Knight, an archaeologist, anthropologist and connoisseur, explained in his *Analytical Enquiry into the Principles of Taste* (1805) that Picturesque meant 'the blending and melting of objects together with a playful and airy lightness and a sort of loose, sketchy indistinction' which, when applied to architecture, suggested a mixture of styles such as 'the fortresses of our ancestors transformed into Italianized villas and decked with the porticoes, balustrades and terraces of Inigo Jones and Palladio'. Payne Knight's own house, Downton Castle, finished as early as 1778, was externally the first real challenge to the classical mode. It was never intended seriously to counterfeit a medieval stronghold (for one thing, the interiors are still purely Neo-classical), but it rambles, it has no symmetry, it is castellated and it is provided with a bastioned gatehouse and angle towers.

But Downton in its remote county is not widely known even today. The man who did most to establish the Picturesque as an architectural style in its early stages was John Nash. He showed his mastery of Picturesque principles and his natural preference for them in his wonderfully diverse designs for the cottages and lodges he was asked to build for landowners to harmonize with their 'improved' parks. Nash's Blaise Hamlet near Bristol, laid out for the banker J. S. Harford in 1811, is probably the first realization of the romantic possibilities of exaggerating the rusticity of the traditional cottage. It inspired villages such as Great Tew in Oxfordshire, designed by J. C. Loudon – the author of a famous guide to Picturesque building

221 In his own house,
Downton Castle in
Herefordshire, finished in
1778, Richard Payne
Knight attempted to
translate into three
dimensions the
romantic piles which
appear in the
backgrounds of
seventeenth-century
paintings. (The part of
the house seen at the left
was made more
conventionally medieval
in the nineteenth
century, when a new
entrance was created on
this side.)

methods, the enormous *Encyclopædia of Cottage, Farm and Village Architecture and Furniture* (1833) – and reached monstrous proportions in estate cottages such as those which draw the attention of every passer-by at Sudbourne in Suffolk, and which were built for the tenantry of Sir Richard Wallace. It is significant that for four or five years Nash was working in an informal partnership with the landscape-gardener Humphry Repton.

Unlike Capability Brown, Repton took his cue from his subject instead of approaching Nature with a preconceived idea of what she ought to look like. His aim was to bring to perfection what already existed. His so-called Red Books, which show views drawn before and after 'improvement', illustrate his technique. He aspired to a carefully arranged *disorder* with, in contrast to Brown, a foreground of planting, and, ideally, the house itself was to be adapted to the 'true character' of the landscape. Among the joint works of Nash and Repton was Luscombe Castle in 222 Devon, built and laid out for Mr Charles Hoare, the third son of Sir Richard Hoare of Stourhead. After studying the terrain Repton pronounced that the house must be in the castle style, 'which by blending a chaste correctness of proportion with bold irregularity of outline, its deep recesses and projections producing broad masses of light and shadow, while its roof is encircled by turrets, battlements, corbels and lofty chimneys, has infinitely more picturesque effect than any other style of building'. Nash built a castellated, irregularly grouped house with a huge Gothic towered porch which admirably suits the forest background planted by Repton and now grown to splendid density. Caerhays Castle in Cornwall, which preceded Luscombe by three years, is an even more Picturesque house with its total lack of symmetry, its round and square towers of varying height, its turrets, battlements and haphazard fenestration.

Both Luscombe and Caerhays show an affinity with later nineteenth-century country houses in the seriousness with which the Picturesque conception has been carried out, for they are ponderous creations in local stone. But Nash's name is always associated with the unsubstantial fake material, stucco, and it is in his use of this material, even more than in his facile inventions in the Gothic manner, that Nash accomplished the overthrow of the classical orders: his Regent's Park terraces make play with the Grecian Ionic mode to extol the Picturesque taste. They have only the most superficial connection with the Palladian concept, for they are entirely scenic, a grandiose stage-set of statues, columns, triumphal arches, pediments and pavilions, magnified in scale, superbly visual and breathing an air of make-believe which is reinforced by shoddy execution, summary detail and mean, careless planning behind the palatial façades.

222 Humphry Repton created the wooded landscape of Luscombe, Devon; its focal point is the irregular castle built by John Nash in 1800.

223 A side view of Sezincote, Gloucestershire, built in about 1803 by S. P. Cockerell. The details, such as the wide eaves, the corner pavilions and the central onion dome, were all carefully based on actual Indian architecture, on which Cockerell was advised by the topographical painter William Daniell.

In Nash's Brighton Pavilion stucco and the bizarre fashions which had consorted 224 with classical proportions in the eighteenth century come together in what is the most sensational of earlier statements of the Picturesque domestic theme and the most whimsical. This building might stand as a symbol for the abandonment of those signposts of authority, the orders. It is no longer a country house – and indeed it never was one in the sense in which that term has been used in this book. It was rather a house in the country, a private diversion of its royal owner, the Prince Regent. The distinction is important, for it marks the beginning of the great change in the status of the country house which was to be accomplished before Queen Victoria died. Other architects had preceded Nash at the Brighton Pavilion. Henry Holland was the first, and he built a graceful mansion with a central oval saloon flanked by wings; then William Porden added stables and a rotunda adorned with 'Saracenic' detail. This Oriental ornament was wholly compatible with the Picturesque builder's hazy conception of the different styles, for this is what Payne Knight wrote of Gothic: 'The style of architecture which we call cathedral or monastic Gothic is manifestly a corruption of the sacred architecture of the Greeks and Romans, which is formed out of a combination of Egyptian, Persian and Italian.'

Humphry Repton was the next on the scene. He had been advising on the grounds of Sezincote in Gloucestershire for a retired nabob of the East India Company, Colonel John Cockerell, and his imagination was captivated by the pictures of Indian architecture which Cockerell showed him. He made suggestions for the house, realized after the Colonel's death for his brother, Sir Charles, by a third brother, 223 the architect Samuel Pepys Cockerell. Its exotic style, which inspired Porden's

stables at Brighton, seemed to Repton ideal for the transformation of the Pavilion. The Prince was delighted with his design, but the work had to be laid aside for economic reasons. It was finally entrusted to Nash, who was by that time the Regent's favourite architect. Although he complained about having to adjust his composition to what already existed, Nash never surpassed the poetry of this Indian dream palace, this irresistible mixture of Islamic domes, arches and minarets, 224 and Gothic friezes of cusped lozenges.

Meanwhile the Picturesque conception of architecture was taking shape in another house in the purely Gothic style and on a stupendous scale. In 1797 James Wyatt, who had shown himself so exquisite a master of the classical style, began to build Fonthill Abbey for William Beckford. The author of *Vathek* (written in 225 French at a single sitting of three days and three nights) was a West Indian merchant, gifted, aloof, enigmatic and fabulously wealthy. Fonthill was intended both as a great country seat and as a piece of gigantic landscape gardening, the focus of a tremendous vista across the Wiltshire Downs. The cruciform, irregular structure resembled a cathedral and rose in conscious rivalry of nearby Salisbury with a central tower 225 feet high. Twin towers of smaller proportions adorned the east end and there were two long galleries. Two armies of workmen each five hundred strong laboured day and night for eleven years, from 1797 until 1808, to realize the fantasy. No sooner was it finished than the tower fell. It was promptly rebuilt only to fall again, this time forever, in 1825. The contractor later confessed on his deathbed that the tower had been built without proper foundations; he expressed surprise that it had stood so long.

224 Above, left: the Royal Pavilion at Brighton, transformed by Nash after 1818 into the supreme expression of the Picturesque fantasy.

225 Above: Fonthill Abbey, Wiltshire, seen from the north-west: an engraving published in 1823, two years before the collapse of Wyatt's gigantic tower.

226, 227 The staircase hall at Ashridge, Hertfordshire, begun by James Wyatt in 1808, soars up to a delicate lantern where fans whirl about a gilded wind-direction indicator.

This staggering building was a forerunner of the extravagant, colossal country houses of the Victorian period; it resembled them in its Picturesque style, in the character of its owner who had no close ties with the land on which his house stood, and in the fact that the work was given to a contractor instead of being carried out by direct labour and small separate contracts, co-ordinated on the site by the architect. Another sign of the times was the appearance on the scene of the quantity surveyor, who provided the information, calculated from the architect's plans and specifications, on which different contractors based their competitive prices. The interest of the contractor was financial only and the presence of the quantity surveyor underlined the importance of the economic factor in an age which was fast becoming obsessed with profit-making regardless of quality.

Wyatt was the architect of another great house in the Picturesque taste, Ashridge in Hertfordshire, begun in 1808 for the Earl of Bridgwater. It is a spectacularly romantic composition in the Tudor style, a turreted house with oriels, bays, and a prodigious staircase tower that vies in importance with the tower and slender spire of the chapel, approached from the main building along a Perpendicular arcade. Inside the house it is the staircase hall which most clearly indicates the direction in which country-house architecture was to evolve. It gives an impression of vertigi- 226, nous height because the stairs are short and abrupt to begin with and then mount in 227 two excessively long flights to the first floor, which is surrounded by arcades with tall niches above them, powerfully overshadowed by a corbelled gallery beneath a fan-vaulted coving. The long narrow chapel at Ashridge, dramatically contrasting with the square proportions of the antechapel shooting up into the tower, exhibits a more scholarly knowledge of Gothic architecture than any house we have yet observed and is thus in tune with the later developments to which we must presently turn. The garden at Ashridge, too, already partakes of the character of the showy Victorian layout. It was the work of Repton towards the end of his life, and here Picturesque disorder has run riot. Winding paths and thick groves lead to the Sanctuary and the Holy Well, to the Pomarium and the Winter Walk and to the Monks' Garden, and on the way the explorer is diverted by an Embroidered Parterre, a Grotto, a Rosarium, a Fountain, an Arboretum of exotic trees and a Magnolia and American Garden.

Beguiling though the Regency examples of Picturesque country-house architecture are, they spring from an uneasy background. At the time when they were built England, despite the still unspoilt beauty of the greater part of the countryside, was already becoming an industrial nation. Formidable tools had come into existence for the transformation of life and very little thought was given to the directing of that transformation, partly on account of the absorption of the country's energies in the struggle against Napoleon. Already the landscape was darkened by factory regions, already forbidding slum towns had grown up to meet the needs of new types of employers and employees, and the only principle which guided these developments was that of quick money returns, a principle which condoned the exploitation of children as young as seven and eight years old. Despite a commission set up through the agitation of a young Tory, Lord Ashley (later Lord Shaftesbury), to investigate the conditions of life and labour in the factory towns, these abuses were regarded with what seems to us incredible complacency. The majority defended them as the unavoidable result of the laws of supply and demand. Every man must be left free to pursue his own interest, for that was the only way to keep pace with the rise in consumption.

So the stage was set for the tragedy of class division and for unresolved duality throughout the social fabric. The Elizabethan age was also dichotomous and, as it has often been pointed out, there were striking affinities between the sixteenth and nineteenth centuries. Both were periods of accelerating change, both were characterized by glorious vitality, invention, ebullience, preoccupation with worldly possessions and a fabulous domestic architecture. But the resemblances serve only to highlight the differences. Whereas the conflicting tendencies in Elizabethan England were brought into harmony by an unswerving sense of purpose and an underlying idealism which informed even the new spirit of commerce, the Victorian dilemma admitted of no solution because of the failure to confront the problems posed by the avalanche of change. The forces set in motion by new mechanical inventions, the opening of markets which turned industrial Britain into the workshop of the world, and the spectre raised by Malthus – now, with the frightening explosion of urban population, impossible to ignore – these were all met by a professed belief in progress, by which was meant economic growth and the accumulation of wealth. The result was a dangerous and confusing divorce from reality, which was encouraged by false piety and reverence for 'respectability'.

One visual expression of this divorce is the contrast between the yet surviving armies of mean, grey-slated, jerry-built houses in such towns as Preston and 224 Middlesbrough and the fairy-like Pavilion at Brighton or the fantastic High 242 Victorian castles of Peckforton and Cardiff. It is worth while considering for a moment the different attitudes to the past embodied in these castles and in those built by the Elizabethans, and the different habits of mind displayed by the sixteenth-

228 Queen Victoria's drawing-room at Osborne House in the Isle of Wight, crowded with photographs, souvenirs and knick-knacks, preserves the shrine-like character of the Victorian home.

and nineteenth-century revivals of the spectacle of the tournament. The men of both ages were romantically fascinated by the Middle Ages, but to the Elizabethans allegory and archaism in architecture as in literature and pageant were the means of communicating a burning patriotic enthusiasm for a newly discovered past and of manifesting a living ideal of chivalry. The castles of Victorian England were a form of escapism, and the famous Eglinton Tournament was part of an olden time masquerade which consorted ill with the dark reality of the growing industrialism of near-by Glasgow.

The duality of the Victorians is nowhere more clearly conveyed than in their glorification of the 'home'. It is at the same time a symbol of their single-minded preoccupation with material well-being and a symptom of deep anxiety. To us many of the objects with which they crammed their interiors seem enchanting – the wax fruits, feather and wool flowers and stuffed birds under glass domes, the shell and sand and seaweed pictures, the ships in bottles, the narrative paintings which the *nouveaux riches* collected instead of old masters, the pretty paperweights imprisoning coloured engravings beneath convex glasses which give them three-dimensional life, the scrap-books and albums – but in their original setting, seen in conjunction with the antimacassars, bobble-fringed drapes, sombre wallpapers, heavy mahogany and horsehair, the clocks and vases, the embroidered stools, the firescreens, the whatnots and brackets assembled by every Victorian householder, the effect of their sheer superfluity must have been stifling, and the atmosphere, despite the splendid vitality of the individual objects, as lifeless as that of a museum. Looking at Victorian photographs of rooms at Bear Wood in Berkshire, the home of the proprietor of *The Times*, at Queen Victoria's Osborne or at Alton Towers, it 228 is alarmingly apparent that they are not so much reflections of personal taste as memorials of personality; and the impression is reinforced by the collections of photographs on piano and writing-table. It is as though the home, and especially the home of the wealthy magnate playing the part of a feudal lord, were a feverishly erected bulwark to guarantee the survival of the individual against the tide of technology and the brutality of industry which were sweeping inexorably on towards the impersonality of the modern world.

The Victorian concern with profit-making was flagrantly at odds with the ostentatious piety of the age. Foreign observers were astounded by the piety of the English. The French critic Hippolyte Taine, in his *Notes on England* published in 1872, exclaims at the inscribed frieze of a great London bank, 'Lord direct our Labours', and at the Bibles chained to reading-desks at railway terminuses for the benefit of businessmen waiting for a train. Taine has also left us a vivid picture of the owner of an English country seat conducting prayers in the bosom of his family and household:

On Sunday evening he is their spiritual guide, their chaplain; they may be seen entering in a row, the women in front, the men behind, with seriousness, gravity and taking their places in the drawing room. The family and visitors are assembled. The master reads aloud a short sermon – next a prayer; then everyone kneels or bends forward, the face turned towards the wall; lastly he repeats the Lord's Prayer and clause by clause the worshippers respond. This done the servants file off, returning in the same order, silently, meditatively . . . not a muscle of their countenances moved.

Here the contrast was not just between piety and commercialism but between faith and unbelief. More churches were built in the nineteenth century than in any other period since the Middle Ages, yet all the time science was undermining organized religion. After the publication of Darwin's *The Origin of Species* in 1859 no thinking man could pay more than lip-service to the notion of the literal truth of the Bible; but the captains of industry went on subscribing to the new churches and would not openly admit that Darwin's theory of natural selection sanctified their hard-headed pursuit of wealth.

Not only were hundreds of parish churches built in the nineteenth century, but almost as many country houses were erected as in all the previous three centuries. Like the churches they rested – for all their immense solidity – on treacherous, uncertain foundations. The Reform Bill of 1832, the future evil results of which were pointed out in vain by men as diverse as Disraeli, Constable and the Duke of Wellington, began the transformation of the aristocracy into a plutocracy and the statesman and representative into the politician and delegate who, instead of leading public opinion, was to seek votes by following it. There was no immediate change, but the implications of the Bill could not be averted. The Repeal of the Corn Laws some twenty years later made inevitable the collapse of England's oldest activity and the one associated from time immemorial with the landowner, agriculture.

The older country seats came more and more to be financed with money from industry or investments, while the princely residences built by the new commercial plutocracy were houses in the country, not true country houses. Those who inhabited them acted the part of the former landed gentry, presided at annual fêtes, never missed a church service and sent their wives and daughters with jellies and broths to sick tenants but they had no roots in the country: their wealth was derived from the factory or from stocks and shares and they felt no sense of obligation towards the land. They were flaunting the trappings of manorial privilege when the reality was ceasing to exist, when the first crack had already appeared in the social edifice.

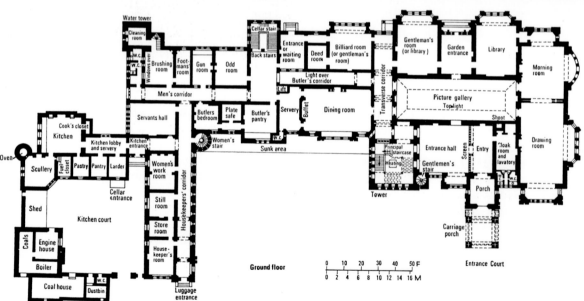

Water tower

Ground floor

Entrance Court

The great swaggering palaces of the new landowners are built of sterner stuff than Nash's stucco, and some writers therefore see a line of demarcation between them and the Picturesque architecture of Nash and his contemporaries; but they continue and caricature all the features of the Picturesque – the sense of scenic drama, the eclecticism and disregard of the appropriate, and especially the colossal size and the irregularity in composition. The latter surely reaches its architectural climax in the fashion for setting rows of windows of differing heights diagonally, as at Bear 229 Wood and at Carlton Towers in Yorkshire. The distinction between the two phases of the Picturesque is that the enjoyed frivolity of the first gave way to an earnest, pedantic and pretentious make-believe undertaken with iron determination to convince.

229, 230 Opposite: Bear Wood, Berkshire, built by Robert Kerr in 1865–74 for John Walter, chief proprietor of *The Times*. Like Holkham (p. 173) it is constructed of materials from its own estate. The plan shows the warren-like proliferation of rooms for the specialist activities of both servants and masters which was typical of the Victorian country house.

231 The Marble Hall at Elveden, Suffolk.

A comparison of two houses built in the same fantastic Oriental style but divided by half a century, the Brighton Pavilion and Elveden Hall in Suffolk, illustrates the difference. The sham materials of the former have been replaced in the Marble Hall at Elveden by stone of undeniable authenticity and solidity, yet equally removed from the tradition of English building construction – white Carrara marble. In each case Oriental motifs mingle with Gothic, but at Elveden the superabundance of curiously lifeless ornament filling every surface, walls, pillars, arches and onion dome dismays rather than delights the observer, for the pretty conceit of an Indian pleasure palace which is so ravishingly realized at Brighton has assumed crushingly elephantine proportions. The extraordinary cusping of the giant ogee arches supporting the dome of the hall is prodigiously out of scale and profoundly disquieting. Elveden, like Nash's Pavilion, was an existing house rebuilt for a prince, and here the excuse for the style was that the prince was Indian: he was the Maharajah Duleep Singh, who had been exiled to England just before the Indian Mutiny in 1857. His architect was John Norton, a pupil of Benjamin Ferrey with a successful practice which brought him work in Estonia as well as all over England. Elveden was later acquired by Lord Iveagh who enlarged the already huge building, preserving the Indian style.

The life led behind the intimidating façades of the vast new country residences was more elaborate than that of any earlier country-house owners. The railways brought flocks of guests for shooting and hunting and for week-end parties, which were now usually devoted to politics or literature. (But to one keen observer at least the quality of English talk had sadly declined. 'There had never been an idea in the house,' says Henry James of Mellows, 'and there was wonderfully little reading.')

232 The mistress of Cusworth Hall, Yorkshire, and her staff, photographed in 1911 as they prepared to serve tea to troops stationed in the neighbourhood. The *châtelaine* stands in the foreground with her lady's maid, steward and housekeeper, while behind the tables are ranged gamekeepers, housemaids, footmen, gardeners, butlers, a kitchen maid and a handyman.

Many new rooms were added to those thought necessary in the Georgian country house – the smoking-room, the billiard-room, the gun-room and the business-room, all of which testified to the emphasis on male ascendancy in Victorian society and to the desire of the men for a special male preserve, the music-room, the ballroom, a revival of the medieval great hall and last, but very important, the conservatory which generally opened from the drawing-room to display the potted Bourbon palms and the collections of tropical and rare plants which were all the rage since Paxton, the Duke of Devonshire's gardener (and architect of the Crystal Palace) had introduced them at Chatsworth.

230

The organization of a large Victorian country house was extremely complicated. It could hardly function, even modestly, with less than eight indoor staff, excluding the retinue of governesses, tutors, nannies and nursery-maids. The Duke of Westminster employed fifty indoor servants at Eaton Hall and the Duke of Bedford at Woburn many more: his staff, indoor and out, with the artificers working on his estate, numbered altogether about six hundred. It was natural in the divided society of the time that the distinction between master and servant should be more rigidly drawn than ever before. The servants' quarters with their back stairs, stairs for the female and stairs for the male staff, and their own dining-hall, were planned so that no member of the family or guest should see or meet a servant without design, and no kitchen smell should penetrate the domain of the 'gentry'. In the words of the late Victorian designer W. R. Lethaby (in *Philip Webb and his Works*), 'it was the affectation of the time that work was done by magic; it was vulgar to recognize its existence or even to see anybody doing it'. This attitude was carried so far at Welbeck Abbey in Nottinghamshire – where the 5th Duke of Portland, an eccentric recluse,

232

added amazing underground extensions – that a servant caught with a broom at the wrong time of day in the master's quarters was instantly dismissed. Then, just as there tended to be rooms for every different pastime of the family, so there was a separate room for each of the tasks on which the servants were engaged. The warren of rooms in the domestic region of an untouched Victorian country house such as Witley Court in Worcestershire, built about 1860 and deserted since a fire in 1937, makes an impression of nightmare. This division of occupation marked by the still-room, the store-room, the knife-room, the shoe-room, the lamp-room, the brushing-room, the china-closet, the pantry, the scullery, the washhouse, the mangling-room, the drying-room, the ironing-room and the folding-room is an image of the departmentalization and the specialization which were already beginning to disorganize instead of organize and to dehumanize society.

The ambiguous position of the landowner in Victorian society was paralleled by the situation of the architect. Confused by the sinister background of industry, no longer able to rely on the protection and friendship of the nobility, his divorce from the craftsman fully accomplished, he had become professional and could produce proof of his ability (a necessity in that commercial age which demanded value for money above all) in the shape of a diploma issued from 1855 onwards by the (later Royal) Institute of British Architects, founded in 1834. But some of the leading designers and architects rightly condemned a system by which the practice of an art should depend on the passing of an examination. They eventually formulated their doubts in a collection of essays entitled *Architecture: a Profession or an Art*, published in 1892. The contributors included G. F. Bodley, R. Norman Shaw, W. B. Richmond and William Morris. They pointed out that the multiplication of the number of men calling themselves architects since the introduction of the qualifying examination was sufficient proof that the system had little to do with art. Between 1855 and 1900 the number of qualified architects who were members of the RIBA alone rose from 82 to 1500. It is ironical that just when he was turning into a professional businessman, the architect should be referred to as an 'artist'. The painter Frederick Goodall's house, Grim's Dyke, built for him by Norman Shaw, was described in the *Building News* in 1872 as 'an artistic house by an artist for an artist', a phase which would have been unthinkable in the periods when the architect was truly regarded as an artist.

The architect's position was rendered more uneasy by the advent of the engineer. All writers on Victorian architecture stress the brilliant technological achievements of the latter and their importance in relation to the developments of our own century. But what we have witnessed is the confusion of the functions of the engineer and the architect, the monopolization of the architect's domain by the engineer, and the imposition of a utilitarian view of building in every sphere, even in the one where it is least acceptable, the domestic. The architect's reaction when this situation was first adumbrated was on the whole to turn his back on the engineer's glass and iron and concentrate on the brick and stone of his traditional past. There were exceptions: the conservatories of large country houses, following the recommendation of Loudon in *Remarks on the Construction of Hothouses* (1817) and the fantastic example of Paxton's Crystal Palace for the Great Exhibition of 1851, were usually built of glass and cast iron, while F. P. Cockerell (grandson of the Cockerell who built Sezincote) chose concrete with stone dressings for Down Hall, Essex (1871–3), though it is significant that he needed the co-operation of the engineer, Charles Drake.

233 Waddesdon Manor, built by the French architect Destailleur in 1874–89; its appearance in the Buckinghamshire landscape is made yet more alien and surprising by the architect's use of golden Bath stone from Somerset.

The monster houses built for the newcomers to the country can hardly be said to show a stylistic sequence: changes were rapid and erratic, the masqueraders favouring now the Gothic, now the Hindoo, the Flemish, Moorish or Venetian manner, now veering towards the Greek, now, as at Château Impney near Droitwich and at Waddesdon Manor, Baron Rothschild's palace, making a sudden essay in the French château mode, and finally aping the Queen Anne style so thoroughly detested by the Gothic Revivalists. Fashions overlapped and conflicted with each other; and there are instances of individuality, such as William Burges's two astonishing castles in Glamorganshire, which cannot be fitted into any scheme. But whatever the architectural fancy-dress, the impulse behind one and all of these frenzied creations can be defined as romantic and Picturesque.

It was natural that as antiquarian knowledge of the past increased stylistic details should approximate more closely to those of genuine examples. Wyatt's Ashridge showed greater historical understanding of the Gothic and Tudor styles than any of Nash's inventions. Belvoir Castle, a spectacularly Picturesque composition on a hill-top site in Leicestershire, with round and square towers, polygonal turrets and battlements, embraces the Norman and the Perpendicular in an asymmetrical sprawl. It was begun by James Wyatt and finished after his death by his sons Benjamin Dean Wyatt and Matthew Cotes Wyatt. The interior, completed by about 1830, exhibits a fine medley of styles, presaging almost all the modes to be adopted later and stating each theme with a good deal of the later hyperbole. A lierne vault and graceful Early English arches yield cathedral-like vistas in the staircase hall and the ballroom leading from it, and the lofty chapel celebrates the Perpendicular style. The Elizabeth Saloon in the great projecting central round tower of the Castle, all crimson and gilt, imitates the Rococo of the French eighteenth century, but turns its brittle sparkling rhythm into a dizzy, eddying movement

223

235

234

xx

created by huge tangential ceiling roundels and semicircles repeated in the carpet design and echoed in the shape of the swelling bay. The most striking object in the room, again suggestive of future developments in its intense realism, is the gleaming statue of the Duchess of Rutland advancing towards us with every semblance of life except for the whiteness. It was carved by M. C. Wyatt, who also painted the ceilings in this room and was the gifted author of one of the most incredibly skilful pieces of sculpture in the country, the monument to Princess Charlotte in St George's Chapel, Windsor; and there is another example of his remarkable dexterity at Belvoir Castle in the ponderously Renaissance dining-room. It is an affrontingly ugly side table where inlaid marble is made to simulate an intricately patterned table-cloth. In its insect-like ingenuity it rivals its counterparts in Baroque Italy, such work as Pifetti's *trompe-l'oeil* inlays in the Royal Palace at Turin, and it springs from the same scenic impulse.

Soon after Belvoir was built an heroic attempt was made to banish the eclecticism of the Picturesque and establish a single style, the Gothic, based on sound structural knowledge. A. W. N. Pugin's informed passion for medieval architecture and Ruskin's eloquent pleading for the same style almost succeded in accomplishing this aim. They were supported by all those who were concerned at the destruction of craftsmanship by commercialism and Pugin's role was much like that of Colen Campbell with Ruskin playing the part of Lord Burlington. The substitution of the Gothic for the classical mode should have made their task easier, for whereas there is something wholly improbable about the application of an alien temple style to English domestic architecture, the language Pugin and Ruskin sought to revive was that of their own past and their own country. Pugin's manifesto, the Gothic counterpart of Campbell's introduction to *Vitruvius Britannicus*, was issued in 1836 in the form of a brilliantly witty pamphlet: *Contrasts; or, A Parallel Between the*

234, 235 Belvoir Castle, Leicestershire, the realization of the romantic dream of a castle picturesquely perched on a wooded hill. Above left: the vista from the head of the grand staircase into the ballroom.

Noble Edifices of the Fourteenth and Fifteenth Centuries, and Similar Buildings of the Present Day; shewing the Present Decay of Taste: Accompanied by an Appropriate Text. In it Pugin compared the fake and flimsy character of Late Georgian architecture with the vitality, solidity and seriousness of Gothic. His argument made a much wider impact than Campbell's first volume. Pious readers in particular warmed towards the author's association of classical forms with paganism and of the Gothic with Christianity and willingly accepted his assumption that the *only* conceivable style for a Christian people was Gothic. Pugin, himself a convert to Roman Catholicism, went so far as to say that 'the degraded state of the arts in this country is purely owing to the absence of Catholic feeling.' His confusion of beauty and morality has been derided often enough, but if it is not altogether true that good men design good buildings, Pugin's instinct which connected the decline in taste and the proliferation of the Picturesque with an attitude to life was not far wrong, for architecture reflects the accepted values of the society for which it is built. What Pugin does not seem to have realized is that the Georgian style was absolutely in key with the aesthetic inclinations and the philosophical and scientific background of the age, whereas no single style, least of all the Gothic as it had been practised in the Middle Ages, could harmonize with the muddled attitudes of the Victorians, with their agonizing conflicts between science and faith, between art and industry and between profit-seeking and social reform.

When he came to deal with the practical aspects of medieval building construction in his *True Principles of Pointed or Christian Architecture* Pugin showed an admirable grasp of the subject. His father, who was an assistant to John Nash, had made pioneer studies of Gothic edifices and Pugin continued his work, travelling widely and making detailed drawings of Gothic monuments. He thus began his career as an antiquarian scholar and made himself so familiar with medieval architecture that he designed in the Gothic manner as readily as if he knew of no other style and was unconscious of any break in the medieval tradition. Houses built in that tradition were, according to Pugin,

suited by their scale and arrangement for the purposes of habitation: the turreted gatehouse and porter's lodgings, the entrance porch, the high-crested roof and louvred hall, with its capacious chimney, the great chambers, the vast kitchens and offices, all forming distinct and beautiful features, not masked or concealed under one monotonous front but by their variety and form increasing the effect of the building.

His two great principles for design were 'First, that there should be no features about a building which are not necessary for convenience, construction or propriety; second, that all ornament should consist of enrichment of the essential construction of the building.'

This sounds unlike Picturesque architecture in its avoidance of irregularity for its own sake. It does not imply that the rooms in a house must be made to conform, whatever the results in inconvenience and oddities of proportion, with a romantic castle design, but urges that the external form of the house is to be dictated by spatial requirements. But paradoxically the association of this logical conception of architecture with the indigenous Gothic style made it impossible of realization. For the Gothic was already inextricably linked with the Picturesque habit of mind. In the small houses that Pugin built, his own home at Ramsgate and the Master's House, Marlow, the exteriors do indeed correspond to the plans behind them, but their steep gables, drip moulds, oriels and casements give them exactly the look of the pattern book house in the Picturesque taste. And what of Pugin's country houses?

xx Opposite: the Elizabeth Saloon at Belvoir Castle, named for Elizabeth, 5th Duchess of Rutland, who commissioned its decoration by Matthew Cotes Wyatt before her death in 1825 (see pp. 220–21).

236   Anyone who goes to Scarisbrick Hall in Lancashire expecting to be impressed by the logic of the great mansion will be thunderstuck as much by the abundance of features not 'necessary for convenience, construction or propriety' as by the staggering size and magnificent incredibility of the image. He will see a high-roofed great hall with an ornate, finialled lantern marking the position of the medieval louver and with a projecting porch at one end, fancy battlements above a frieze of grotesques and two-tiered bays. Round the porch runs the inscription, 'This hall was built by me, Charles Scarisbrick, MDCCCXLII, Laus Deo'. A cross-wing shoots out at the west end, adorned with prominent finials and a large gable figure. To the east, on the far side of the traditional cross-passage, lie the offices, butler's room, butler's pantry and store-room and beyond them again, in bewildering irregularity, rise first an octagonal angle tower with a bevy of great fluttering angels ready to take flight from its parapet, then a bedizened, lofty-gabled block with windows crowned by ogee arches and outsize finials, and then the most unexpected feature of all, a spired tower in Northern French Gothic style soaring up to such a reeling height that it utterly dwarfs the rest of the huge building and is a landmark for miles. Pugin did not intend the tower to ascend quite so outrageously. His beautiful pencil sketch for Scarisbrick shows a more modest feature topped by a lantern instead of a spire. The present monstrous structure was the work of his son Edward Welby Pugin for the sister of Pugin's client, who inherited the property when Charles Scarisbrick died in 1860. To the east of this tower again lie the octagonal kitchen in the style of that at Glastonbury Abbey and, further back, the servants' hall with a gigantic and elaborate fireplace, all designed by A. W. N. Pugin. Nobody would suspect that this richly

236 The entrance front of Scarisbrick Hall, Lancashire. A. W. N. Pugin's house, of about 1840, is dominated by the tower added by his son twenty years later.

XXI Opposite, above: the Great Parlour of Wightwick Manor, Staffordshire, by Edward Ould, perfectly expresses the taste of the 1890s with its blue and white china, frieze of roses above the fireplace in the inglenook, and its fabrics designed by William Morris (see p. 237).

XXII Opposite, below: the Briar Rose Room at Buscot Park, Berkshire, a Neo-classical room panelled in the 1870s with Burne-Jones's paintings of the legend of the Sleeping Beauty, Briar Rose (see p. 233).

237 The overmantel in the Red Drawing-room at Scarisbrick Hall. The painting on the left shows Charles Scarisbrick walking with his mistress and their children.

caparisoned east end of the house was given over to the domestic offices and business-room. The whole ensemble is in fact thoroughly Picturesque. Despite all Pugin's efforts the style persisted. It merely took on another aspect under the discipline of antiquarianism.

The man for whom Scarisbrick was built was as unusual as his architect. Charles Scarisbrick came of an ancient Catholic family who had lived on the site since the thirteenth century. He had made a vast fortune by buying up the land on which Southport was to be developed. He lived a life of isolation in his gargantuan palace and was a source of strange speculations in the neighbourhood, some of which came to the ears of Nathaniel Hawthorne who was living in Southport in 1856–7. 'He is a very eccentric man,' he wrote in *The Scarlet Letter*, 'and spends all his time at the secluded hall which stands in the midst of mosses and marshes, and sees nobody, not even his steward.' Some said he kept a gambling house in Paris, others maintained that he was the prey to some dreadful fear. The truth was that this dark, melancholy man who lived alone kept a mistress and several illegitimate children in Germany. Their portraits appear with his own in panels painted by Pugin over the fireplace in 237 the Red Drawing-room. Wearing medieval dress, they are walking and taking their ease in the grounds of Scarisbrick Hall.

Charles Scarisbrick was an obsessive collector and distinguished himself by patronizing one of the most fascinating contemporary painters, John Martin (he owned twenty-four of Martin's doom-laden canvases). Among his other interests were bronzes, gems, ivories, medieval manuscripts, arms and armour and above all wood-carvings. These included door panels, choir-stalls, church screens, altarpieces, friezes, bookcases and overmantels dating from the Middle Ages to the eighteenth century, and Pugin was asked to incorporate many of them into his designs for the interior of the Hall. Thus, despite himself, the result was a patchwork in the most luxuriant Picturesque taste. The fireplaces in the Red Drawing-room and the Oak

238 Room are typical of the assemblages in mixed styles which determine the whole character of these unforgettable interiors. That of the Oak Room has a hearth flanked by pew ends below a Gothic arcaded frieze surmounted by a stupendous overmantel with a bold, open wavy Baroque pediment adorned with angels and crammed with minutely carved figures in fretted recesses rising above Gothic niches. In the Red Drawing-room Gothic niches and decorated shafts merge with tapering urns, flickering convoluted fretwork, figures brandishing inscribed scrolls, the painted panels mentioned above and Minton tiles bearing Charles Scarisbrick's initials and sharp diagonals. The two chimney-pieces are strange yet convincing combinations of Gothic and Baroque, illustrating the one fundamental resemblance between the two: their aspiring character.

238 The Oak Room at Scarisbrick Hall, created from genuine Gothic and Renaissance wood-carvings collected by Charles Scarisbrick.

The rooms decorated by Pugin at Scarisbrick are certainly as extraordinary as the Chinese Room at Claydon, even though the original furniture has gone. Every surface pullulates with ornament, the general effect of which recalls in its surpassing richness and complexity the screen and overmantel in the hall at Burton Agnes, except that here it is not confined to certain areas but abounds everywhere; and the buoyant white plaster of the Yorkshire mansion has been replaced by wood so that the atmosphere is one of darkly varnished gloom. The astonishing Oak Room is one giant collage of Gothic and Renaissance wood-carvings brought into precarious harmony by Pugin's skilful arrangement and his own design for the starred and beamed ceiling. The Kings' Room, because of the regular rhythm of tall, thin shafts branching into cove-fans overhead, is less chaotic to the eye and here rich gilding and the soft hues of a frieze of canopied paintings of Tudor and Stuart kings and queens and a sumptuously ribbed ceiling impart a festive glow to the sombre woodwork. One visually exciting detail of the exotically carved doors of the huge Tudor arch leading into the Red Drawing-room shows a complete departure from any tradition in its mad realism: certain figures seem to be imprisoned within the

239 Somerleyton Hall, Suffolk, built in 1844–51 to designs by the sculptor John Thomas.

panels, their faces looking into the room, while the backs of their heads emerge in the adjoining apartment. There could hardly be an ornament less necessary for construction or for propriety, to say nothing of convenience.

Pugin built another theatrical Gothic pile, Alton Towers in Staffordshire for Lord Shrewsbury, a three-dimensional exercise in Gothic forms. Here the outside is eloquent of the interior, but it is an unmistakably Picturesque structure in its irregularity and its relation to its setting. The difference between Alton Towers and an early Picturesque castle such as Downton is like that between the fictitious Gothic *donjons* of Mrs Radcliffe and those of Sir Walter Scott. Scott transforms Mrs Radcliffe's spectral Gothic into edifices rising from the soil of actual places, just as Pugin metamorphoses Payne Knight's mock Gothic into firmly based scholarly Gothic. But both Scott and Pugin remain Picturesque and romantic despite their antiquarian knowledge.

Before Scarisbrick was completed Barry had built the inflated, heartlessly correct Genoese palace of Cliveden on the banks of the Thames, its scenic character emphasized by the architect's use of genuine Renaissance balustrading from the Palazzo Borghese; and Somerleyton Hall in Suffolk was begun for Sir Morton Peto by John Thomas, a sculptor by choice who turned to architecture as a more likely source of income. Peto was one of the busiest and most wealthy building contractors of the day, a typically Victorian self-made man who had started life as a bricklayer. His East Anglian retreat, now creeper-smothered and mellowed, has the atmosphere of Charlotte Yonge's Holywell with which it is contemporary. As an image it astonishes by the diversity of the elements which the architect has managed to assemble under one roof. The general shape is Jacobean, with two advancing wings and a towered and orielled central porch, but the row of round-arched dormers, like huge battlements, behind the parapet and the tall round-headed pediments filled with Thomas's sculpture which jut up in so unsophisticated a way from the wing parapets are pure fancy. At one end of the house rises a square Italianate tower of a surprising and unpleasing pedantry by comparison with the rest of the building, with a cluster of irregular projections at its foot; and on the other side a most curious

239

colonnade screens the stable block. This colonnade is surmounted by a pagoda-like cupola and adorned with ornamental pilasters of no classical order and with incongruous spandrel figures, again by Thomas. The asymmetrically grouped stable block is marked by a tower with urn-topped angle pavilions and a domed and traceried cupola. There is an air of vagueness about Somerleyton which would have pleased Payne Knight. On the north are the remains of the huge conservatory for which the house was famous, demolished in 1912. It was pictured in *The Illustrated London News* in 1857: the engraving shows that it had an arching roof, aisles and a central dome beneath which splashed a fountain sculpted by John Thomas. The gardens with their maze, aviary, fountain, stone vases, sculpture and brilliant flower-beds, their terraces and shrubberies, still evoke the mixture of styles and the concentration on plantsmanship, the massing of colour against holly and laurel, which characterized the Victorian version of the Picturesque layout.

Sir Morton Peto's firm went bankrupt in 1866 and Somerleyton became the Suffolk home of an even bigger plutocrat, Sir Frank Crossley of Crossley Carpets, Halifax. His name is commemorated all over his native town, not only by the Crossley Mills but by all the conspicuous Crossley charities, the chapel, almshouses and the orphanage, but in East Anglia where he had no connections he has been forgotten.

240, 241 Somerleyton was preceded by a few years by that unbelievable glorification of the Elizabethan house, Harlaxton Manor in Lincolnshire, built by Anthony Salvin and decorated by William Burn, the gifted pupil of Sir Robert Smirke, to house the collections of the strange Gregory de Ligne Gregory, the source of whose immense wealth is uncertain though his lineage was ancient and his family had been connected with Harlaxton since the Middle Ages. The house is a blown-up Burghley of golden stone, an aspiring, retreating and advancing drama of curves, angular thrusts, upsurging stepped pepperpot domes, oriels, strapwork and a central square tower set back behind the elaborate frontispiece and surmounted by an octagonal parapeted upper stage and a cupola which accentuates the Baroque flavour of the building and prepares the eye for Burn's preposterous fully Baroque interiors.

240 Harlaxton Manor, Lincolnshire, begun by Anthony Salvin in 1831. The giant house is preceded by a curved entrance screen, with massive gate-lodges which seem to merge with the gables and pinnacles beyond.

229

241 Looking up in William Burn's unforgettable staircase hall at Harlaxton, through a half-real, half-fake tower to a distant counterfeit sky.

In the staircase hall, the most remarkable space of the house, the art of illusion has 241 been carried to extremes seldom exceeded even in southern Italy. It soars up to a balcony supported by giant scroll-brackets and by muscular Atlas figures. From the brackets, attached to them by real cords, hang plaster curtains looped with plaster swags from which depend huge, lightly swaying plaster tassels. Trumpeting cherubs struggle to free themselves from the curtain folds. Higher still another balcony resting on colossal shells held by trumpet-blowing, twin-tailed merboys, encloses an arcade, the arches of which consist of mighty scrolls, from beneath which turbulent counterfeit drapery billows over the great chasm of the hall. Above this arcade six gargantuan pendants swarm with putti and carry two Father Time figures brandishing real scythes, one hung with a flag showing a plan of Harlaxton, the other suspending the relief portrait of a woman. They are all poised against an airy illusionist sky of the clearest blue.

The conjunction at Harlaxton of the Elizabethan and Baroque styles underlines the affinities of the two and the relation of both to certain aspects of Victorian society. But the relation was not strongly enough felt to excite emulation. Harlaxton had no followers: it was just a terrifyingly solid piece of scenery, and only a few years later Salvin himself was working in a totally different manner. He was building a romantic castle on a rugged Cheshire hill to rival the silhouette of a genuine fortress, Beeston Castle, which confronted it from the next crest. Peckforton Castle is a fine composition, and that it is Picturesque rather than convenient the plan makes

abundantly clear, for the kitchen is sixty yards distant from the dining-room. The
architect's charming preparatory drawings and watercolours of the castle also show
how much he stressed the pictorial elements of the asymmetrically disposed groups.
The subject of these drawings might well be taken for a true medieval relic, but alas
the repellent, mechanical stonework of the reality at once reveals its period. In the
interior the fortress atmosphere is conjured up with grim strength. The stony,
vaulted hall, staircase, dining-room, and especially the wine-cellar at the base of the
main tower, with its enormous central column, are architecturally impressive but
much more forbidding than the rooms of any medieval castle. It is hardly surprising
that Peckforton has not been lived in for the past quarter of a century. And just as
the architectural masquerade is overdone, so the man for whom Peckforton was built
overplayed his role of feudal landlord. Lord Tollemache was the father of twelve,
passionately evangelical, a Bible-reader and stern Sabbatarian and generous to his
dependants on a prodigal scale. Every one of the labourers on his estate was given a
substantial new cottage and three acres, and he built about sixty new farmhouses,
each the centre of a farm of two hundred acres.

Even Sir George Gilbert Scott spoke of Peckforton as a 'pageant', as 'unreal' and
as 'the height of masquerading'. Yet he did not perceive that the serious, brutally
ugly country houses he was himself in the course of building could be described in
exactly the same way. Kelham, for instance, a hard red-brick monstrosity in Nottinghamshire, built for John Henry Manners-Sutton, cunningly and learnedly fuses
details from the cathedrals of England and France with others from the palaces of
Venice in a whole as daunting and as much of a pageant as Peckforton. It is one of
the most crushingly assertive of Victorian country houses, grim as the Victorian
Sabbath, colder and more unrelenting even than the menacing Gothic pile of Alfred
Waterhouse's Eaton Hall. The richly decorated interior with its painted vaults,
gilded capitals and mouldings oppresses more than any other of its time. The

242 Salvin's drawing of
the outer wall and great
tower of Peckforton
Castle, Cheshire, dated
1849.

243 William Morris's
Red House at
Bexleyheath, Kent,
designed by Philip
Webb in 1859. Its
revolutionary features
include windows in the
servants' quarters which
gave them unrestricted
views of the garden.

mechanical, unyielding carving of the conspicuous capitals in the music- and drawing-rooms showing foliage, flowers, corn, birds and the more formalized motifs of Venetian Gothic, bruises the eye; and its historicism seems ludicrous in a house which was gas-lit and central-heated.

Kelham was begun in 1858. In the next year William Morris commissioned his friend Philip Webb to build him a house. In almost every respect the famous Red House at Bexleyheath presents a contrast to the buildings so far described in this chapter. It differs from them above all in its simplicity and lack of pretension. Webb built a small country house in the manner which the architect he most admired, William Butterfield, used for cottages and vicarages. It seems to mark a moment of sanity in the feverish escape from industrialism in pedantry and ostentation which we have been witnessing. The effect of the L-shaped grouping with steep roofs at different levels and with bull's eye and segmental-headed windows, pointed arches, tall chimneys and a staircase projection with a pyramidal, flèche-crowned top, is certainly picturesque, but it is an honest expression of Morris's passionate desire not so much to escape from the machine as to oppose it and the ugly commercialism it engendered by good design and artistic integrity.

Morris's house was designed by a friend (Webb) and friends collaborated in its decoration and furnishing. From these activities sprang the firm of Morris, Marshall, Faulkner and Co. for the design of textiles, wallpapers, stained glass, metalwork, murals, tapestries and furniture. But its products were bought only by the wealthy discriminating minority and Morris realized that social reform must come before aesthetic revival. With a nobility which is profoundly moving this great artist cried 'Let Art go; it will rise again whatever else lies there', and plunged into the Socialist League for which he worked ceaselessly until his death. Yet the factories, the tenements and the multiple shops could not be wished away and the vision of a lightly populated world of craftsmen's guilds and white towns could not be translated into reality. Morris had said of the Red House that it was 'very medieval in spirit' and 'in the style of the thirteenth century'. With all his insight into human motives and his awareness of the evils of regimentation and enslavement bound up with the misuse of the machine, he was enchanted by the same dream of old romance as the magnates of industry. He differed from them in wanting all to share the dream.

It is the vanity and poignancy of this escape-dream which creates the curious
XXII atmosphere of the Briar Rose Room at Buscot Park. The fairy-tale of the Sleeping
Beauty suited Burne-Jones's languid genius and through it he conveys his gentle
despairing nostalgia for a legendary past remote from the discord of ambivalent,
philistine, technological and urban society, in images of memorable conviction and
plasticity. The owner of the house, Alexander Henderson, acquired the picture
sequence in 1871 and Burne-Jones himself designed the setting of the panels while he
was staying in the neighbourhood with William Morris.

Because of Morris's enthusiasm for the virtues of a mythical Middle Ages it was
impossible for either him or his followers to break away from the Victorian
architectural masquerade. William Burges, probably the most gifted, individual
and vital of those who sympathized with Morris, turned to an intensified and
extremely personal medievalism, as divorced from religious associations as it was
from reality.

Burges's architectural preferences were formed by early travels in Normandy,
Belgium, Germany and Italy and he always expressed himself in Continental
Gothic, generally of the thirteenth century. But he used his profound scholarly
knowledge of the period to escape from industrialism into a timeless medieval
world entirely of his own imagining. At home he wore medieval dress; and the
lengths to which his play-acting could go are revealed by the fact that although he
was a confirmed bachelor, he included medieval day and night nurseries in the house
he built for himself in Melbury Road, Kensington, at the age of 53. But his robust,
assertive visions were very different from the pensive yearnings of Burne-Jones.
In his work the country house masquerade goes forward with a new and burning
energy and with an extravagance and disregard of rational limits which has something in common with the music of Wagner and with the fairy castles built under
the composer's influence by Ludwig II in the Bavarian mountains. There is the
same unlikely use of massiveness, grossness even, to create a dream impression, the
same strange concentration on fabulously ornamented bedchambers – like that of
Lady Bute at Castell Coch near Cardiff in Wales, with its painted, finialled and glass-
knobbed bed, and its washstand in the form of a castle gatehouse, as though to
emphasize the architectural conception of a place of dream.

Of course the two astounding castles that Burges re-created after 1865 for the
Marquess of Bute are his most significant contributions to Victorian domestic art.
But they stand on Welsh soil and thus lie outside the geographical confines of these
limited pages. The character of his unique fantasy is however apparent, if not fully
developed, in two other houses, one in Devonshire, the other in Buckinghamshire.

244 Knightshayes, near Tiverton in Devon, was commissioned by Mr J. Heathcoat
Amory, a Liberal Member of Parliament and a rich manufacturer whose money
came from lace-making both locally and in Leicestershire. The simple, basically
traditional hall-house design, seen from a distance, does not at first appear to offer a
startlingly new experience. But the near view is unforgettable. This is the furthest
possible extension of that old combination of central block and cross-wings in
terms of solidity, weight, stoniness and strength. It is an overwhelmingly powerful
piece of make-believe, wholly suited to the role assumed by the prosperous businessman who lived in it. The sense of masquerade is encouraged by a scale which dwarfs
the human figure and would have been heightened still more if Burges's original
plan for enclosing the platform on which the house is sited with great walls and
bastions had been carried out. The drama, vigour and tension of the whole

conception is lessened by their absence, and further softened by the planting of the platform carried out by Sir John and Lady Heathcoat Amory as part of their great romantic garden combining formality with exotic woodland.

The details of the building, though as forceful as the bulk and weight of its simple shapes, lighten them by sheer exuberance of imagination. It is not only the actual ornament, the exaggeratedly bold plate tracery of the towering bays, the sudden crenellated castle elements, the animated sculpture of the central gable or the sprouting finials which imparts this feeling of exuberance, but the subtle deviation from symmetry in the main façade, achieved by slight differences in the numbers of window lights and slight variations in spacing. The device has no rational function, it is merely an expression of high spirits. The interior of Knightshayes, including a great hall for the reception of tenants, was to have been completely overspread with Burges's crowded, story-telling decoration, with bulging sculpture, knights in armour, mythical creatures and symbols, naturalistic painting, tiles, glittering mirror glass and metal; but much of it was never carried out and scarcely a trace of it now remains.

The only place outside Wales where something of the extraordinary atmosphere Burges was able to create, something of his urgent, utterly convincing and vastly entertaining vision can still be experienced, is Gayhurst in Buckinghamshire. Three of his amazing dynamic chimney-pieces can be seen there, crocketted, canopied and with a riot of chimerical figures and shapes crawling about their strange, inelegant proportions which, while they are certainly not medieval, are violently anti-classical. On two of the fireplaces motifs from *Paradise Lost* and *Paradise Regained* gave Burges an opportunity to indulge his love of grotesque reptilian creatures, winged beings, plants, birds and streaming hair; the third states its powerful themes to the poetic accompaniment of minutely-observed, naturalistic paintings of every conceivable variety of English flower, entirely covering the wall panels. The full development of this union of tenderness and delicacy with fierce energy is one of the marvels of Cardiff Castle.

Another characteristic product of Burges's overspilling imagination enlivens the upper floor at Gayhurst, where a muscular male caryatid stoops above a massive door to bear the weight of a curiously placed twisting stair. He makes the same shattering impact of superhuman energy as the figures which start forth so dramatically from the columns of the Summer Smoking Room at Cardiff.

Gayhurst is a late sixteenth-century house which was twice altered before Burges added his emphatic contribution for Lord Carrington, son of Robert Smith, the banker, for whom Wyatt had built Wycombe Abbey. Externally Burges's work consists of no more than a service wing, but the whole atmosphere of the place has been charged with new excitement by the singular group. The contrast between the Victorian architect's compact, sculptural, circular, rectangular and polygonal forms and the original building is in itself arresting but the really exhilarating, enjoyable aspect of the image is the way in which heavy, earthy solidity and a tremendous grasp of spatial arrangement consort with a gay, buoyant indifference to utilitarian concerns. Airy weathervanes and spiky cast-iron trimmings mock the pressing weight of the masonry; four lavatories take the shape of a circular, buttressed structure upon the tall conical roof of which gabled dormers cluster about a battlemented ventilating shaft straddled by a sturdy winged demon; and the kitchen, alluding to the medieval monastic example at Fontevrault, soars up to an open pyramidal roof raised on flying buttresses, while inside the architect's con-

cern was less with the essential purpose of the building than with the provision of a quaint oriel from which the cook could keep an eye on her underlings.

243   The Red House with its tiled and hipped roofs has a strong flavour of Kentish local tradition: it started a new phase of the Picturesque in which vernacular styles were either closely imitated or synthesized, and this at the very time when rapid transport and the use of mass-produced materials was rendering those styles obsolete. Philip Webb continued to build simply by comparison with his contemporaries but his quiet pastiches of manor-house and farmhouse styles, of which Clouds in Wiltshire (now much altered) was his most ambitious, laid the foundations for the later suburban and garden-city dwellings which were the end-products of the Picturesque movement. George Devey, who carefully copied the local village style for cottages he built at Penshurst for Lord de L'Isle and Dudley, carried the Picturesque to new limits when at Betteshanger, also in Kent, he created a bogus effect of different dates and styles in a rambling 'old English' mansion. William Eden Nesfield chose the Elizabethan mode for Cloverley Hall, the house he built in Shropshire for the Liverpool banker J. P. Heywood, and decorated it with prominent chimney-stacks, texts and a Morris-inspired frieze of sunflowers and lilies made in lead by Albert Moore with a touch here and there of the Oriental ornament that was beginning to be fashionable in all 'artistic' houses. Norman Shaw, in whose work Picturesque eclecticism reaches its climax, followed Devey's Betteshanger idea at Adcote in Shropshire, suggesting a house built at different periods. It counterfeits a medieval hall with Elizabethan alterations and additions. The hall is a fine room, fitted with a screen and minstrels' gallery and a dais end lit by a huge transomed bay window, and huge stone arches like the one that distinguishes the hall at

21 Ightham Mote (see p. 29) support the timber roof. It is symptomatic of the insidious effects of the Picturesque attitude that despite the contempt of earlier Victorian architects for sham materials the wall panelling in the Adcote hall should be carried out in embossed paper, the 'lincrusta' of suburbia, instead of wood.

244 Knightshayes, Devon, a huge house of dark red sandstone set off by yellow ashlar, built by William Burges in 1869–71.

235

245 Cragside, Northumberland, seen from the valley. A small Tudoresque house, still visible in the centre, forms the kernel around which Richard Norman Shaw's spectacular house expanded from 1870 onwards.

Shaw's Cragside, in Northumberland, is a monster, full-blooded forerunner of 245 the anaemic jumble of vernacular and period styles which make up the suburban scene. The typical Victorian energy and fertility of invention are vividly illustrated by the fact that Shaw planned the whole of this palace while his fellow guests at a country-house party were out for a day's shooting. Cragside is a most theatrically sited Picturesque composition combining half-timber, clusters of tall, diagonally set, twisted and moulded chimneys, panels of sunflowers, gargoyles and battlements in a tree-girt, rocky eyrie which expands the idea of the old-world English house to princely size without any regard for a particular regional tradition. Cragside was the retreat of Lord Armstrong, who had made a great fortune from his engineering works at Elswick on the Tyne specializing in hydraulic cranes and lifts and in the manufacture of the Armstrong gun, a type of weapon invented by himself to fire a shell instead of a ball. When he died in 1900 he was the owner of the biggest armaments factory in the world.

Wightwick Manor in Staffordshire, built by Edward Ould for a paint- and varnish-manufacturer, Theodore Mander, who read Ruskin and was also a cricket enthusiast, is a mellower, less aggressive version of the Old English style and its richly patterned half-timber successfully reproduces the ornate vernacular of the district. But the design also includes a brick, battlemented tower and a range of details deriving from every period between the late medieval and the Jacobean. The interior XXI with its beams and inglenooks is architecturally mainly of seventeenth-century inspiration, with exceptionally good imitations of the plaster ceilings and friezes of that date by the talented L. A. Shuffrey, while the rich decoration includes William Morris wallpapers, stained glass by Charles Eames Kempe, inlaid furniture, Oriental carpets and pots and intricate tiles. Wightwick is one of the most affecting as it is one of the latest of Picturesque country houses.

By the time Wightwick was finished in 1893 it had become clear that the landed proprietor no longer dominated and never again would dominate the social fabric. The agricultural depression of the last part of the century had irrevocably completed the evolution from a rural to an industrial state which had begun before Pugin was born. The idea of an aristocracy, which had once meant land and wealth, had shrunk to mean wealth alone, and now the end of the plutocracy too was at hand. 'We did not cut off their heads, we only cut off their incomes', a female Labour Minister gleefully remarked. The few country houses built after Wightwick were survivors of a way of life that had no future.

The principal architect of such houses, Sir Edwin Lutyens, embraced the full range of Picturesque interests with brilliant eclecticism and his scholarly knowledge of regional building construction and local materials was unrivalled in his day. His restorations and additions at Great Dixter show that in this respect he surpassed such predecessors as Devey and Shaw. But with all his gifts his houses strike us as 246 low-spirited and lifeless. The well-known Tigbourne Court, Surrey, begun in

247 Lutyens' Castle Drogo in Devonshire, a cold design extravagantly representing a doomed way of life.

1899 for Sir Edgar Horne, is a clever interpretation of the Elizabethan style carried out in local Burgate stone, galleted throughout like the fabric of neighbouring cottages (flints are wedged into the mortar between stones), and articulated by thin bands of tiles. The main gabled block of the house, which hints at the Elizabethan synthesis in its inclusion of a classical loggia, has two low wings ending in tall, severe, diagonally set chimney-stacks with screen walls curving away on either side of them. Castle Drogo in south Devon, which must be the last baronial stronghold to be built in this country – it dates from 1910 – is a vast, cold exercise in the manner of Raglan executed in local granite with Norman columns within and a vaulted chapel in the basement. But it is only necessary to compare this fortress with Peckforton or Castell Coch and Tigbourne with Somerleyton or Adcote to become aware of the loss of force and conviction. Lutyens and his works were anachronisms, for the pageant of over-produced castles and palaces and manor houses was done. It had no place in a world which had given up the attempt to abandon or even to disguise its exclusive concern with the economic growth of a classless society. Many of the subjects of this nostalgic survey are now museums, others have been deserted and have sunk into ruin, others are schools or have become homes for the aged and mentally afflicted; in those which are still privately owned the impoverished inhabitants will usually be found crouching in a few rooms in one wing. An art and a way of life have come to their appointed end.

247

242,
246,
239

Numbers in italic type refer to illustrations; roman numerals indicate colour plates

National Trust properties are marked with an asterisk (*)